D0024915

MILITARY MARXIST REGIMES IN AFRICA

MILITARY MARXIST REGIMES IN AFRICA

Edited by
JOHN MARKAKIS
and
MICHAEL WALLER

FRANK CASS

First published 1986 in Great Britain by
FRANK CASS AND COMPANY LIMITED
Gainsborough House, 11 Gainsborough Road,
London E11 1RS, England

and in the United States of America by
FRANK CASS AND COMPANY LIMITED
c/o Biblio Distribution Centre
81 Adams Drive, P.O. Box 327, Totowa, NJ 07511

British Library Cataloguing in Publication Data

Military marxist regimes in Africa.
1. Military government—Africa 2. Africa
—Armed forces—Political activity
3. Africa—Politics and government—
1960-
I. Markakis, John II. Waller, Michael
III. The Journal of communist studies
332'.5'096 JQ1875

ISBN 0-7146-3295-3

This group of studies first appeared in a Special Issue on
Military Marxist Regimes in Africa of *The Journal of
Communist Studies* Vol. 1, Nos. 3 & 4 published by Frank
Cass & Co. Ltd.

Printed in Great Britain by Antony Rowe Ltd., Chippenham
Typeset by Williams Graphics, Abergele, North Wales, U.K.

Contents

The help of Catherine Moreland
in translations from the French
is gratefully acknowledged.

List of Abbreviations

AEF	*Afrique Equatoriale Française*
AKFM	Congress Party for the Independence of Madagascar
ANC	African National Congress
AREMA	Vanguard of the Madagascan Socialist Revolution
CDR	Committee for the Defence of the Revolution
CEAO	*Communauté économique d'Afrique occidentale*
CFA	*Communauté financière africaine*
COPWE	Commission for Organizing the Party of the Working People of Ethiopia
CSB	*Confédération syndicale voltaïque* (Trade Union Federation of the Volta)
CSP	Council of the Safety of the People (*Conseil de salut du peuple*) (Burkina)
DOP	*Discours d'orientation politique* (Political Orientation Speech) (Burkina)
DRM	Democratic Republic of Madagascar
ECOWAS	Economic Community of West African States
EPRP	Ethiopian People's Revolutionary Party
HCR	High Council of the Revolution (*Conseil suprême de la Révolution*) (Madagascar)
IMF	International Monetary Fund
LIPAD	*Ligue patriote pour le développement* (Patriotic League for Development) (Burkina)
MEISON	All-Ethiopian Socialist Movement
MPLA	Movimento Popular de Libertacao de Angola (Popular Movement for the Liberation of Angola)
MRCNP	Military Restoration Committee for National Progress (*Comité militaire de redressement pour le progrès national*) (Burkina)
NCO	Non-commissioned officer
NCR	National Council of the Revolution (*Conseil national de la révolution*) (Burkina)
OCAM	*Organisation commune de la communauté africaine et malgache* (Organization of the African and Malagasy Community)
OCV	*Organisation communiste voltaïque* (Communist Organization of the Volta)
PAI	*Parti africain pour l'indépendence* (African Independence Party) (Burkina)
PCRV	*Parti communiste révolutionnaire voltaïque* (Revolutionary Communist Party of the Volta)
PCT	*Parti congolais du travail* (Congolese Workers' Party)

PDV-RDA   *Parti démocratique voltaïque-Rassemblement démocratique africain* (Democratic Party of Volta-Democratic African Rally)

PMAC   Provisional Military Administrative Council (Ethiopia)

POMOA   Provisional Office for Mass Organization Affairs (Ethiopia)

PPD   *Programme populaire de développement* (People's Programme for Development) (Burkina)

PSD   *Parti social-démocrate* (Social-Democratic Party)

PWPE   Party of the Working People of Ethiopia

RCC   Revolutionary Command Council (Sudan)

SCP   Sudanese Communist Party

SDR   Special Drawing Rights

SME   Small and Medium Enterprises

SRC   Supreme Revolutionary Council (Somalia)

SRSP   Somali Revolutionary Socialist Party

SSU   Sudanese Socialist Union

SWAPO   South-West Africa People's Organization

UDI   Unilateral Declaration of Independence

UGEV   *Union générale des étudiants voltaïques* (General Union of Voltese Students)

ULC   *Union des luttes communistes* (Union of Communist Struggle) (Burkina)

Editorial

This volume and Special Issue of *The Journal of Communist Studies* offers a survey of radical military regimes in Africa, a spreading political fashion on that continent. Not all such regimes adopt a Marxist discourse and align themselves diplomatically with other Marxist regimes. We shall be concerned with those that do because of the Journal's focus of interest. We are aware that we are dealing with a category that overlaps with others; the current regimes in Ethiopia and Burkina resemble those in Libya and Ghana in more respects that either resembles the Soviet Union or Vietnam. Moreover, the extent to which the regimes treated here are to be regarded as Marxist, or as forming part of a communist movement, is not a simple matter to determine, and the grounds for any judgment are certain to be controversial. Also, there have been cases where a commitment to Marxist principles and an alignment with the Soviet Union have not been very long-lasting.

The articles in this volume provide material to inform assessments of these radical African regimes. The limited task of this editorial is, first, to introduce the category of regimes that will be treated, indicating some of their key characteristics; second, to review the arguments and facts on which any judgements about those regimes' Marxism should be based; and, third, to examine briefly what light is cast on the history of communism by the emergence of these regimes and by the claim that they lay to the mantle of Marx.

The interests of Africanists and of analysts of communism meet in this novel phenomenon, just as they met in the distinct and more easily digested category of Marxist guerrilla movements in Africa that have fought their way to power in Mozambique, Angola and elsewhere. But although their interests meet, their conclusions have not yet come together in a broadly accepted framework. Since it is not our aim in this editorial to suggest any final conclusions on a phenomenon whose outlines are still not fully clear, but rather to suggest where points of analytical interest lie, we present the Editorial in two parts, as a counterpoint between two approaches: that of the Africanist and that of the student of communism.

The first section is by John Markakis, our guest editor for this issue and an Africanist; the second is by Michael Waller, whose interest has been in the linkages within the communist movement. The counterpoint of the editorial is taken up again in a concluding analytical article from an Africanist, Samuel Decalo.

The authors of the articles presented here adopt varied approaches to the regimes that they cover, and this is reflected in their terminologies. It seemed neither simple nor wise to edit out these terminological differences in an exercise of this kind. They have been left in as a reflection of the present state of the discussion on an African phenomenon that is still in the process of formation.

I

John Markakis

Resort to military rule has occurred widely in Africa as a conventional prop for shaky post-colonial regimes, and civilian rule is now a rarity in that continent. Conventional military interventions change nothing in essence, and provide at best short-term relief from political malaise. What is new in the cases presented here is an attempt by soldier rulers to shore up the foundations of the post-colonial state by constructing a new political consensus based on Marxism. It was the prominent role assigned to this ideology that prompted the editors of the *The Journal of Communist Studies* to ask several specialists for articles on these regimes.

Limitations of space have not allowed our authors to delve into the situation that gave rise to radical military rule. However, a glimpse of the context is essential to understanding the nature of these regimes and their relationship to Marxism. Although details of the situation are different in each instance, the principal common feature is perennial political instability, whose causes are the same in these cases, as they are indeed for nearly all African states. These patchwork creations of colonialism attained independence under regimes whose main power-base was the state, a relatively modern and integrated structure governing largely traditional and highly heterogeneous societies.

The colonial state had promoted the formation of a modern economy that quickly overshadowed the traditional subsistence economies of Africa. The pattern of the colonial economy was highly uneven, with capital investment and technological innovation concentrated in a few profitable sectors and privileged regions, and highly iniquitous as well, with some ethnic groups and social classes benefiting, while others gained little and some lost a great deal during this period. This pattern did not change after independence, and social tensions deriving from material and social disparity became exacerbated. Often these were expressed in ethnic and regional terms and gave rise to political movements that sometimes developed autonomist or separatist tendencies. Otherwise, they were expressed in class terms and gave rise to militant labour movements and radical political parties of the left.

Having played a seminal role in the formation of the modern economy under colonialism, the state assumed an even more prominent role in it after independence, through increased public investment, extensive nationalization and tight regulatory control. As a result, the state became the controlling agent in the processes of production and distribution of material and social resources. Access to it proved essential to human welfare and, inevitably, the state became the focal point of social conflict as underprivileged regions, ethnic groups and social classes fought for a greater share of power monopolized by the ruling elite. Post-colonial regimes were confronted with manifold opposition stemming from alienated social classes that challenged their control of the state, and from dissident ethnic and regional groups that challenged the existence of the state itself. As a result, political instability became the hallmark of the post-colonial state.

Effective control of the opposition was hindered initially by an array of constitutional, legal and political restraints of Western design that burdened the state at the dawn of independence. These impediments had to be removed and state power had to be centralized and used without restraint against the opposition. The process of centralization began with the rejection of demands for decentralized state structures and regional autonomy even before independence was attained. Where such demands had to be conceded in order for the country to become independent, they were quickly scrapped afterwards. Subsequently, the opposition was stripped of political and legal protection through the imposition of the one-party system, a universal experience in Africa. The process of centralization was accompanied by a spectacular expansion of the state apparatus, particularly the military and security branches, the cost of which could be met only by securing foreign patronage. This made it possible for the state apparatus to grow in the midst of economic stagnation. Even so, the civilian post-colonial regimes were unable to contain the opposition, and eventually gave way to military rule of the conventional type, thereby reaching the apogee of centralization and authoritarianism, a fate common to most African states.

The cases presented in this volume are not conventional military interventions designed to uphold the status quo, but radical departures that displaced the ruling elite and attempted to restructure the political system in order to prevent a restoration. The radical soldiers seize power for themselves and exercise it directly, hence the term 'praetorianism' is a misnomer in their case. The radical military regimes espoused Marxism as their political creed and took action to prove they meant it. Marxism was fused with nationalism in an attempt to produce a political consensus in support of the state whose preservation is the principal goal of these regimes, as it was for their predecessors. To this end they use conventional means, such as the promotion of state nationalism, the expansion of the state apparatus, particularly the military and security branches, and the forceful suppression of the opposition. The economic role of the state is further strengthened by bringing more sectors of the economy under state ownership and management, a policy depicted in terms of Marxist principles. The latter are also used extensively to promote mass participation in state-controlled organizations to justify the elimination of independent associations and to portray a future society devoted to the welfare of the masses and under their control.

The conversion to Marxism of professional soldiers on their way to power is not a wholly principled affair, nor is it an entirely base one either. Rather it is a mixture of idealism, naiveté and self-serving considerations. The usurpation of power requires legitimation through a credible alternative to the overthrown regimes, if it is not to prove a transient affair. It so happens that, after a century of experience with colonialism and capitalism, the only credible alternative in Africa is socialism. In situations of accute material deprivation, political oppression and social conflict, its appeal rests on the promise of rapid development, social justice and popular sovereignty.

There is no doubt that the radical soldiers were attracted by this promise, as were large sections of the population, and the early days of radical military rule were exhilarating and creative. The soldier rulers share the illusion that socialism can be attained speedily and by decree, and they see themselves carrying out a 'revolution from above' using the state as the principal means. In the words of Siad Barre of Somalia, 'Socialism for us is simply defined: it is a system in which the state takes primary responsibility for the political, social and economic development of the nation'. In one sense, this is the apotheosis of the state, the extreme end of the process of centralization that has continued since independence, and this seems to be the aspect of socialism that soldier rulers find most attractive.

Radical military regimes came to power in situations of acute structural crises of the state and the invocation of socialism in this context served a primary need by coming to the defence of the state. Its function is to disarm the opposition ideologically. Socialism seeks to cut across ethnic and regional divisions in order to weld classes into a new political consensus underpinning the state. Turning the focus on class contradictions not only reduces the significance of ethnic conflict but ultimately denies that it has any significance at all. Such conflict is presumed to fade away naturally in a classless socialist society and the state, now a people's republic, becomes the common weal.

The same rationale is used to deny legitimacy to the class-based opposition which undermined the civilian regimes and continues to seek a share of power under radical military rule. Theoretically, a socialist system has no need for autonomous organizations that defend class and corporate interests, and this provides the justification for dismantling political parties of the left, trade unions, professional associations and the like, and replacing them with monolithic organizations attached to the state. The emasculation of the trade union movement stems from economic as well as political considerations. The former have to do with the regime's concern with the cost of production, a large part of which is accounted for by labour costs. Ownership of the means of production burdens the state with the classic entrepreneurial concerns, such as labour costs, productivity and discipline. In order to control them, the labour movement must be stripped of autonomy and turned into an adjunct of the state.

The radical regimes' paramount concern with the preservation of the centralized state has prevented them from coming to terms with ethnic and regional demands for autonomy. In this respect, they failed to match the achievement of Lenin, whose example they claim to follow, and to that extent the espousal of Marxism has not, in my view, turned these African states into communist regimes, a task for which conventional armies are hardly suitable. The insistence on centralization, quite natural in professional soldiers, has also led them to reject civilian participation in government after an initial period of flirting with radical political groups. Ultimately this is bound to lead to the failure of mass mobilization and the weakening of popular support, both of which reach an impressive level in the first phase of radical military rule. These failures embroil these regimes in the same kind of conflicts and against the same opponents that confronted their predecessors, and force them to rely increasingly on force to retain power. Beset, in addition, with grave economic difficulties, their chances of moving towards the goal of socialism are very limited.

Is socialism then simply the handmaiden of beleaguered post-colonial states in Africa? The choice of socialism was dictated by desperate popular need and aroused great expectations. This is a telling verdict on the failure of conventional economic strategies and the regimes that applied them in Africa. The fact that socialism appears as the only credible alternative is an indication of the status attained by this ideology in the Third World. Yet socialism is unlikely to be realized under the type of regime surveyed in this issue. Nevertheless, radical military rule has changed the scope and terms of political debate, and socialism remains an option for the future.

II

Michael Waller

The slackness of the communist movement's bonds and the wide variation in organizational practice that it secretes make precarious any attempt to set precise boundaries to the movement or to locate an organizational 'model'. With broader and less demanding categories such as socialism and development at our disposal why should we puzzle over what, beyond a heartland in Eurasia, is to count as communist or Marxist-Leninist and what not? Why should a group of radical military regimes in Africa be described as anything other than precisely that — radical military regimes?

Faced with this question historians of communism have the comfort at least of knowing that they have been here before. If the departures from Soviet orthodoxy of the Yugoslavs and the Chinese were not too difficult to digest, the emergence of a Cuban regime calling itself Marxist-Leninist but with no ruling party jolted existing ideas quite considerably. Castro put that right in 1965 with the creation of today's Communist Party of Cuba; but further problems were to arise over Angola, Mozambique, South Yemen and the Sandinistas. It has come to be accepted now that things have changed radically since the days when ex-Comintern parties such as the Yugoslav or the Chinese set out consciously, on coming to power, to transfer Soviet political and economic forms of organization to their own countries. Organizational imitation of a Soviet 'model' is now but one element, often a minor one, in a network of linkages that are more complex and more tenuous than in the past, and must be sought not only in the realm of organization but also in those of diplomacy and the legitimation and mutual support of ruling national elites. Also, in so far as organizational imitation does exist, the Soviet Union itself is no longer the single 'model'; the Committees for the Defence of the Revolution that will be encountered in these pages, for instance, are a good example of the genus 'mass organization' that was bred in the Soviet Union; but the species is a Cuban one, transplanted, in the present case, into African soil. The same is true of the rhetoric. When Thomas Sankara ends a speech with the words 'Fatherland or death; we shall overcome!' he is voicing a nationalist sentiment of the kind that has been strong in the Soviet Union since Stalin's rise to power, but the phrase itself is Cuban, and the direct identification is with Cuba.

The radical military regimes of Africa are distinguished, of course, by having been established not by a party but by an army. To that extent an important link with communism as we have known it to date does not exist. But, on the other hand, since in most cases the military leadership now claims to rule through a Leninist 'vanguard' party, the possibility has to be entertained that military rule will be the antechamber to party rule. The evidence contained in these pages is not very promising in that respect. The question is, however, how eccentric this situation really is, given the recent course of communist history and, particularly, the example of Cuba. For what came to power in Cuba in 1959 was a military force − not a standing army, but a military force none the less − that did not embrace the ex-Comintern Popular Socialist Party until it had broken the power of that party and purged its leadership, and had subordinated to the state the trade unions in which the PSP influence was strong. Until 1965, when a ruling Communist Party of Cuba was proclaimed, and indeed whilst the party was being settled into place, the state was run, to a great extent, by the army, the *Fuerzas Armadas Revolucionarias*.

Moreover, the question of whether it is a party or an army that is at the apex of power in the state may count for less than the nature of the state power that the party or the army wields. For what is important is not so much the policies that a regime has adopted, as the means chosen to carry them through, and the resulting political, economic and social order. It is here that the core of the Soviet 'model' or 'reference' is located, and it is this that the Ethiopian, Beninois and Congolese regimes appear to have, at least to a significant extent, in common with the Soviet Union, China and Vietnam. What has emerged is a certain kind of state formation, a distinctive collectivism. *It is the state and not the party or the army* that deserves our *prior* attention. This particular form of the state creates the political space for a 'leading role of the party' but it is not, despite first appearances, too fussy about what X fills that space. In the Soviet Union it was the party, in China in the early months of the regime (and again during the Cultural Revolution) it was the army, in Cuba in the early years it was a composite Movement of the 26 July, the main element of which can be seen as military but is better seen as the personal following of Fidel Castro. In a rather exceptional case − although exceptions are the rule in the history of the communist movement − the military can send the party on leave in Poland in December 1981 while a little spring-cleaning is done. And now, in Africa, it is a standing army, or rather leaders emerging from a standing army, who set out to overturn existing social relationships and to establish, to the extent possible, a strong collectivist state involving a dialogue between themselves and the popular masses.

In sum, the helpful question to ask in the case of a regime that espouses Marxist-Leninist principles is not so much 'is this regime Marxist-Leninist?', since this question invites chop-logic at worst, and at best a reference back to first principles that is only partly appropriate. Much more helpful for understanding communism and the history of the century is to ask, first, why do the elites of these new states use this rhetoric? And second, what is the nature of the society that they are constructing? The more emphasis that is placed on the second question, the less important is it whether it is an army or a party that is creating this new social, political and economic system.

That said, it remains possible to argue that only the establishment of a mass-based party will ultimately ensure the stability and the continuation of the regime. That was clearly the thinking behind Soviet pressures on Castro, and then on Mengistu, to create such a party. This argument is incontrovertible, since stable and enduring Marxist party-states abound, whilst Marxist army-states have had only an ephemeral existence and have tended to resolve themselves into, or revert to, party-states. This precisely is the interest of the Marxist military regimes of Africa; their situation remains unresolved, and until it resolves itself, final conclusions are impossible.

Before going on to examine other factors of similarity between the Marxist military regimes of Africa and earlier Marxist regimes, it is important to be clear about the central phenomenon that confronts us. What communism to a great extent has been about, from the birth of the Soviet Union to that of Burkina, is revolution in countries that have suffered from being weak, and often both poor and weak, in relation to the West. Not all such revolutions: the Mexican revolution happened, as it were, before Lenin came along; the Muslim world provides a parallel channel for what Azcárate has described as 'the great revolutionary commotion' that has occurred during this century; and the Eastern European regimes are exceptional, in this as in many other ways. But at the heart of Marxism-Leninism as it has developed since the Russian revolution lies a particular *predicament*: that of the elites of poor nations whose power and whose projects depend upon economic development and upon the survival of the political and social unit in which their power is exercised and to which their projects relate – the new nation. Or rather, the new *state*, for in addressing that developmental predicament they have evolved certain particular political, economic and social forms. The leading role of the party is one of them; but far more fundamental, as John Markakis points out above, has been the creation of a very strong state of a rather particular kind.

This shared developmental predicament and the particular state formation that has emerged in response to it are the major factor of analytical contact between these African military regimes and more familiar Marxist regimes elsewhere. They are not, however, the most evident link between them. There are other and more visible factors. First, the ideology, or rather the discourse in which the ideology is couched, since the variety of contexts in which the rhetoric of Marxism-Leninism is used are many and the perceptions and practices that result endless; second, the relation of a given party or regime with the Soviet Union; third, policies in general and strategies for development in particular; and finally, a lingering vestige of historical continuity from a now defunct Comintern.

First, then, the ideological link. The adoption by certain radical military regimes of a Marxist-Leninist discourse has drawn a great deal of attention – partly because a regime's discourse is its most public aspect, and partly because of the apparent discrepancy between words and practice. There is, first, the familiar dissonance concerning proletariats and internationalism in a world of peasants and nationalism; but there is now a new one between what goes on in these radical military regimes in Africa and what has gone on under the label of Marxism-Leninism elsewhere before in similarly agrarian contexts.

The first of these discrepancies is unquestionably the greater – we remain in an agrarian universe of strengthened states. But they both emphasize one and same fact, that ideology in the communist movement may be to some extent about blueprints, but that it is much more about the creation of an identity for new states and about the legitimation of their governing elites, and about securing the social cohesion required for a programme of development.

Communism in the Soviet Union, then in China and elsewhere, established an option for regimes that have come to power in a break with the past – through revolution, through independence from colonialism, or through coups following independence. The world provides newly emerging regimes with certain 'rafts' that offer support in a turbulent and uncertain sea. An identification with Marxism-Leninism has become one of these rafts – not the only one, but one that has distinct merits since nationalism itself, though it has so often provided the rallying cry for the revolution itself, is not enough to give the emerging elite an identity in the wider world or with a viable picture of the future. Although so often the driving force of the revolutions of the twentieth century, nationalism has less of a mobilizing appeal once the revolutionary regime is in place and contradictions are opening up among the forces that urge change. Marxism-Leninism does three things for an emerging national elite: it legitimates that elite's rule; it makes it possible to mobilize society behind an austere programme of development; and it enables the elite to assure the people, the world, and no doubt themselves too, that what they are doing in their corner of the world is linked to the destiny of humanity.

Finally, what precisely is this ideology to which these regimes are said to subscribe? We publish in this issue one programmatic statement put out by an African radical military regime – Sankara's Political Orientation Speech of 2 October 1983. It will be seen to be Marxist in talking of exploitation and the class struggle and in embarking on a class analysis of Voltese society. But the bulk of the rhetoric that is not expressly concerned with nationalism pure and simple (and arguably including that) is Marxist-*Leninist*. It is the language of the communist movement since the Russian revolution. Class terms are given small initial letters in the official text; the People has a capital letter. The revolutionaries move among the people like fish in water. And, as already noted, its final slogan consecrates the Cuban contribution to the history of Marxism-Leninism.

Second, as concerns the relationship of a given party or regime with the Soviet Union, what seems to be merely a diplomatic matter is really a great deal more. It is first a matter of material aid, including military aid, on which depend, as John Markakis points out above, the regime's independence, and also its ability to put through developmental economic programmes and a restructuring of society.

In this latter respect the very substantial contribution that the German Democratic Republic has made to the security systems of Third World states that have chosen a socialist orientation is to be noted. It is a matter, also, of the training of the regime's cadres, again including military training. These are very substantial material inducements to emerging nations to identify themselves diplomatically with a socialist camp that they have reason to expect will understand their developmental situation.

As for links in the realm of policies, the history of communism reveals that adopting a Marxist-Leninist discourse does not mean instituting proletarian rule in any but the most abstract sense. The policies that have regularly and characteristically been adopted by revolutionary elites espousing Marxist-Leninist principles have been land reform, more or less dynamic literacy and educational programmes, and state-led economic development. These things are what, in terms of policies, practical communism has largely been about. The problem of first principles, of the demands that Marx and Engels listed at the end of the Communist Manifesto in 1848, not to mention their expectations for the future, is now thoroughly familiar and it remains, of course, a major analytical problem. But it has been treated in works too numerous to mention, and it has been displaced by a second problem, identified some time ago by John Kautsky. If a category of communism is to be built on policies of land reform, literacy campaigns and state-led economic development, then the boundaries between communism and the politics of development in general are tenuous in the extreme. Where the policies adopted by the African radical military regimes have reproduced those adopted earlier by communist parties in power, they are policies that many non-communist Third World leaderships have adopted too.

On the other hand these policies of land reform, educational development and state intervention in the economy, whilst the last has apparently not gone very far in some cases, have none the less been adopted by these regimes. They are, in fact, the mark of their radicalism. What adds the extra element that might reasonably be seen as bringing these African regimes close to a more specifically communist way of tackling the developmental predicament goes beyond the mere content of policies and takes us into the realm of organization – including, particularly, the organization of the state. Here it does begin to make sense, in a restricted area, to talk of a Soviet organizational model, or at least of a model that all the ruling Marxist-Leninist parties have taken a hand in creating. This brings the discussion back to its starting point: the nature of state power in these societies.

Direct imitation or replication of Soviet organizational structures and processes, although it no longer has pride of place in the links between a Soviet heartland of communism and an increasingly variegated periphery, none the less lives on. It could hardly be otherwise. From a shared predicament stems a shared range of possible options for emerging from it. However, it is most important to distinguish political from economic organization. Instances will be found in these pages of varying degrees of state intervention in the economy, and of attempts to set up co-operative and collective forms of agriculture. But the very patchy success of these attempts and the small scale of some of the economies involved make it difficult to talk of adherence to a Soviet 'model', any more than such an adherence is to be found in China. It is rather in the realm of *political* organization that replication is to be sought. As far as the economy is concerned, it is not the degree or manner of collectivization or of state intervention and planning that counts, it is the political will to undertake them, and the way in which the state equips itself for its economic and social tasks. It is here and, above all, in the mechanisms of orthodox democratic centralism, consecrating as it does single-party rule of a collectivist and deep-reaching kind, that a tradition can be seen to be at work.

Before concluding on the possible links between the Marxist military regimes of Africa and Marxist regimes that have preceded them, there is one factor that might be regarded as providing a link, but has to be treated with caution: historical continuity from the Comintern past. The problem is not that Sub-Saharan Africa lacked communist parties during the Comintern's lifetime. This is indeed the case in a formal sense; but communist ideas and organizational principles were transmitted to the colonies by the parties of the metropolitan countries. In the francophone countries the influence of the French Communist Party and of the trade union organization that it dominated – the *Confédération générale du travail* – was substantial. In those cases where African military regimes have adopted a radical stance, they have turned initially to the syndicalist and student left for support, just as Castro had forged a link with the ex-Comintern Popular Socialist Party and the trade union movement, in which the PSP was strong, during the revolutionary period. To that extent an historical link does exist between a defunct Comintern and the new leadership in certain of these countries.

Equally important, however, was the way in which that leadership was to turn on these organizations of the left. The LIPAD in Burkina was neutralized in much the same way as the PSP and the trade unions had been neutralized in Cuba. Such lingering influence as the Comintern exerted in francophone Africa may have played an initial role in the establishment of these regimes, but it was soon to be subordinated to the dynamic implantation of the new regime.

Such then are the linkages between the Marxist military regimes of Africa and communism as we have so far known it. It is possible to go further, however, and to suggest ways in which this important new turning point casts light back on the history of communism, putting earlier events and turning points in a new perspective by corroborating some underlying trends.

First, the great detour of communism into the poorer nations, which followed the Russian revolution, is further confirmed. In such novel and inauspicious circumstances, this confirmation appears as caricature. This African caricature of Bolshevism is military in provenance. It was suggested above that the fact that the revolution was made and consolidated by army officers and not by a vanguard party is less significant than is often thought. But how, then, does this affect the *myth* of the party? That myth was created, if by any individual, by Lenin. If armies can do the party's work, if what is important is that work itself and not so much the agent, then it is not unreasonable to ask how much of Lenin's insistence on the party as the organizational form appropriate to the revolutionary struggle, as against rival Western European notions of syndicalism, workers' councils and the mass strike, derives from the predicament of revolutionary Russia – not one of the world's poorest nations, but holding its own militarily by sheer manpower and economically through foreign capital and by exports of grain guaranteed by relative popular destitution.

Second, the predicament of these African regimes and their response to it, coming after and reinforcing in so many ways the predicament of Castro's regime in Cuba on the morrow of revolutionary success, casts light back on the whole main sequence of Marxist-Leninist revolutions since 1917. Given that there has been a continuing association of communism with development it is not only possible, but probable, that the clues to a proper reading of Soviet history lie in the experiences of subsequent Marxist regimes. Paradoxically, the more apparently exotic these regimes, the more graphic the presentation of the clues.

Soviet economic organization, and especially the planning system, serves as an example. For the Webbs and for many since then, what has been happening in the Soviet Union has represented a practical application of Marx's recommendations for a socialized economy, with society being run, in a sense, as a single factory. Even the collectivization of agriculture, despite the way in which it was carried out in the Soviet Union, seems to correspond to that idea, and to owe its origin to it. Judgements start, in other words, with a view of the radical policies that pertain to the socialist (in this case the Marxist socialist) idea, and assume that that is the primary derivation of the Soviet economic structure.

Yet it is possible to start the assessment in quite another way, and in a sense from the other end, with a governing elite that is the product of revolution in a country culturally and economically underdeveloped and subject to foreign penetration. That governing elite inherits from the process of revolutionary turbulence a position of dominance. It would be quite rational, simply in order to secure the nation's future and its own position in power, for that elite to gather into the hands of a strong and centralized authority all the goods and the productive processes of society. Soviet history is not normally presented in these terms, and notions derived from a Western Marx still tend to provide the privileged frame of reference for assessments of that history. But as more and more regimes arise that establish, for one reason or another, a strong collectivist state authority that wears down rival authority of a local, ethnic or corporate kind, the more Soviet collectivism, the nature of the Soviet state, and the role of the party in society all appear as products of a particular predicament. Moreover, the way in which this central authority is drawn into a vacuum that it has itself created by its radical stance — through 'intervention' in the economy, for example, as the national bourgeoisie and foreign investors sell out, abandon or sabotage their businesses: all this reinforces centralism, authoritarianism and a stress on the collective good. This has been pointed out, perhaps in slightly different terms, many times. But it is repeated here because these pages offer some important corroborating evidence.

This is not to say, of course, that Soviet communism is not a valid example of socialism in practice. Quite the reverse; it has provided the very definition of one of the strongest currents of that broad stream. However, Soviet socialism has developed on its own base and in a particular way, predominantly in response to a certain predicament, and it is in comparable circumstances that it has been reproduced elsewhere. Wherever it has taken root it is nationalist, it is populist in its discourse, and it is collectivist in the social form that it has created. The mechanisms of that collectivism – encapsulated in the orthodox interpretation of democratic centralism – are weaker in some regimes than in others, but they tend to strengthen once a Marxist-Leninist orientation has been proclaimed. It is ultimately more useful to focus on the radical military regimes of Africa as the upshot of the mainstream of revolution in the twentieth century, and in this sense comparable with Soviet communism, than on the detail of what Marx said.

The chief characteristics of the regimes treated here are analysed below by Samuel Decalo. They include, first, the fact that in them military personnel, normally of junior rank, have adopted or presided over a radical turn in social, diplomatic and to some extent economic policy. Second, an alignment with the Second World and the use of a Marxist-Leninist discourse has secured these regimes material aid within an international system of alliances. It has also been an important support of the regime's legitimation, enabling the regime to mobilize the people behind a programme of development, and has had at least some, and at times a quite considerable, effect on political and economic organization and policies. Third, this radical turn has normally been accompanied by an initial link between radical soldiers and urban-based left-wing forces, although these initial supports have been characteristically set aside as the radical regime consolidated itself, and they have been replaced by new forms of organization linking the regime to the masses that give the masses an element of involvement and the regime a channel for popular mobilization. Fourth, significant attempts have been made to change social relationships through land reform and changes in the pattern of ownership; these reforms have achieved little success in terms either of production or of popular self-management, but they have clearly increased the penetrative power of the state.

It is on this increased power of the state that this editorial has focused. In the first part it was recorded and its importance emphasized. In the second part the question was raised whether the way in which this strong, centralized state power is articulated in the radical military regimes of Africa does not resemble to a significant extent the pattern of political, economic and social organization that has been historically linked with communism.

Let the reader judge; but three considerations must influence any judgement. The first is that time alone will show whether these regimes, or any one of them, will develop along the lines of their radical turn, or whether they will gradually lose a significant part of the characteristics that at present distinguish them from other African military regimes. The second is that at the heart of the form of organization associated with the communist tradition since Lenin's day has lain a ruling party that fully encadres society through its membership and its regional apparatus; is this the way in which our regimes are evolving? The final question is whether the tradition itself may not be evolving: as long as the party's traditional job is being done in an acceptably comparable way by an acceptably comparable political force, even soldiers may pass muster.

In the Russian revolution the peasant sickle was added to the proletarian hammer, and communism acquired, over Lenin's dead body, its populist tone. But even with Lenin alive the soviets were soviets of workers', peasants' and soldiers' deputies. In the 1970s, the Chinese issued a postage stamp with a hammer, a sickle and a rifle all in a line. Is the Communist world, with Cuba showing the way, moving to an extension of the tradition, whereby an army either creates the conditions for party rule, or itself performs a strictly comparable role? Is vanguardism extendable, so that from the party as vanguard of the workers in their struggle to build communist society we move to an army as vanguard of the party?

Radical Military Regimes in the Horn of Africa

John Markakis

Radical military regimes seized power in the Sudan and Somalia in 1969 and Ethiopia in 1974. These were not conventional military interventions designed to steady shaky post-colonial establishments, but radical departures whose advent displaced the ruling elite and, in Ethiopia, brought to an end an antique social order. Moreover, the soldiers espoused socialism and took action to show they meant it. Initially, they were able to attract support from political groups of the left, which provided ideological and policy guidance, as well as political and administrative talent from the intelligentsia. The alliance with the left was designed to rally support among the groups that had opposed the toppled regimes, and also to lend credibility to the military regime's proposed solutions to the crises confronting these states. The crises, which had undermined their civilian predecessors, were the result of multiple cleavages in the structure of society along ethnic, regional and class lines, which were reflected in the fragmentation of the body politic. The uneven and iniquitous pattern of socio-economic development tended to exacerbate social and political tensions stemming from such cleavages, and the post-colonial regimes were confronted with manifold opposition from alienated social classes that challenged their control of the state, and from dissident ethnic and regional groups which challenged the existence of the state itself.

In the Sudan, the Anya-nya rebellion in the south threatened the integrity of the state, while class and sectarian struggles in the north undermined the ruling parties which had been forced to turn to the military in 1958–64 for support. In Ethiopia, the Eritreans in the north, the Somali in the east, and lesser groups in the south, were fighting to shake off Ethiopian rule, while landless peasants, workers and the intelligentsia launched an attack on the imperial regime that paved the way for the military intervention. In nine years of independence, the Somali political system was splintered into clan-based factions, around 70 of which contested the elections of 1969. Civilian rule also suffered due to its failure to liberate the Somali-inhabited territories in Ethiopia, Kenya and Djibouti.

The defunct regimes had sought to protect the state and themselves by resorting to centralization of state authority, propagation of state nationalism, expansion of the military and security apparatus and suppression of the opposition. All these were to be carried to extremes by the radical military regimes. However, they also sought to tackle class contradictions by bringing more sectors of the economy under state ownership and management. While this expanded the economic role of the state and swelled the bureaucratic apparatus, it had little positive effect on development or on eliminating class and regional disparities, the root cause of political dissension. Indeed, beset by a world-wide recession, civil strife, and recurrent drought, the economies of all three states deteriorated markedly during the 1970s. Economic degeneration rekindled the political conflict and confronted the military regimes with the same challenges faced by their predecessors. Below we look at each in turn.

Sudan: The May Revolution

The 25th May 1969 Revolution in the Sudan began with a coup d'état carried out in classic fashion by middle-ranking officers, who dismantled the parliamentary regime and arrogated power to a Revolutionary Command Council (RCC) headed by Colonel Mohammed Gaafar Nimeiry.[1] The second military intervention in thirteen years of independent existence was not exactly unforeseen. Indeed, the bankruptcy of the civilian regime had posed the question not 'whether or not the existing set up could ever be saved but what the

---

SUDAN

The fundamental characteristic of the Sudan is the difference between the north and the south, in terms of climate (arid in the north, equatorial in the south), settlement of the population (scattered units in the south, dense concentrations in the north), patterns of production, and culture ('Arab' in the north, 'African' in the south).

Islam spread throughout the north by the nineteenth century, whilst the south stayed free from outside influences. But it was during that century that the history of north and south merged when the Sultan of Egypt, Mohammed Ali, conquered northern Sudan in 1821 and opened a trade route into the heart of the south.

The unity that independence brought between north and south in 1956 dissolved almost at once. Three political forces emerged after independence: (i) the powerful Muslim sects; (ii) the army; and (iii) the Sudanese Communist Party (10,000 members at its peak). From 1956 to 1958 unstable coalition governments came and went, until in 1958 a right-wing coup under General Ibrahim Abboud set out to remedy the inefficiency of the political parties. This regime was unable to control rebellion in the south and fell in 1964. In that year the democratic opposition, including the Communist Party, was brought into the government. But a show-down between the Muslim sects and the left led to the exclusion of the Communists.

In May 1969, the army again took control. Its new leader, Colonel Gaafar Mohammed Nimeiry, belonged to the army's progressive anti-imperialist movement, and acted to bring about radical reforms, in pursuit of which he neutralized the Muslim sects and then turned on his natural allies — the SCP, the trade unions and the radically-inclined intelligentsia. Nimeiry was ousted in a further coup that followed a week of riots and demonstrations in April 1985.

alternative should be'.[2] The soldiers offered a credible alternative by striking an opportune alliance with the radical political coalition headed by the Sudanese Communist Party (SCP), the principal opposition to the defunct regime, and by adopting the ideological perspective of the left. Although small in numbers, the radicals were entrenched in most professional and social organizations and were able to mobilize popular support where it counted, that is, in the towns. The communist party was the main lever in the mobilization of this sector and 'seemed the only political party that was capable of demonstrating popular support to establish the legitimacy of his [Nimeiry's] intervention'.[3]

The alliance with the left was struck on the eve of the coup, and the Communists had no part in its preparation. The first cabinet was predominantly civilian. It was headed by Babiker Awadallah, himself a leading progressive, and included three members of the SCP central committee.[4] Several other well-known figures of the left were included in this cabinet, which was the face the military regime presented to the country, and succeeded in attracting enthusiastic support marked by impressive demonstrations organised by the Communists and their allies in Khartoum.

The junta of ten colonels and majors that comprised the RCC had no distinct ideological bond. Its initial stance was not radical and the justification offered for the coup was commonplace. The soldiers' aspirations were depicted in familiar nationalist terms and the regime's spokesman described it as 'nationalist – whatever else is said about it'.[5] Inevitably, they were depicted as 'inspired by Nassirism' and, in fact, Nassir's regime became the prototype of what may be termed 'garrison socialism' in the Horn. In the Sudan, the political tendency identified with Nassir was known as 'Arab socialism' and is described as having 'socialistic but not Marxist ideological orientation, an emphasis on strengthening relations with Egypt and other left-inclined Arab countries, and a tendency to advocate patterns of political and economic development based on Egyptian experience'.[6] The first prime minister was a leading exponent of this tendency and like-minded people formed a majority of his cabinet. The diffuse 'Arab socialist' tendency was ideologically leavened in the early days of the regime by the alliance with the communists, and helped steer it towards the proclamation of socialism on the first anniversary of the coup.

Precisely what was envisaged in the espousal of socialism was not made clear. In a speech on 16 July 1970, Nimeiry gave a garbled version of 'Sudanese socialism', cautioning against dogmatism and copying foreign models, and declaring 'we want to draw from all schools of socialism that which will benefit our Sudan'. From the Prime Minister came a number of contradictory statements which pledged the government to expand the public sector, not to nationalize domestic or foreign capital, and to strengthen 'national capitalism'. A series of nationalization decrees was announced on 25 May 1970, the regime's first anniversary. They affected mainly foreign enterprises, including banks, and several concerns owned by Sudanese living abroad. In November of the same year, a National Charter was issued dedicating the regime to 'scientific socialism'. Capitalist methods of development were said to have led the economy to a dead end and to a total dependence on foreign influence. The Charter was short on specifics. It envisaged a pluralist economy with several sectors – state, mixed, co-operative and private. Emphasis was placed on industrial development. Agriculture was mentioned only as a foreign exchange earner whose output for export would be raised, while nomadism was described as 'a fetter on social development'.

Sudan's foreign policy was reoriented to match the regime's radical stance. Among its first acts was to recognize East Germany, signalling its defiance of the Western bloc. The connection with the Soviet Union was strengthened with Nimeiry's visit to Moscow in November 1970, when the two parties discovered they had a 'complete identity of views' on current international issues. Sudan secured a significant increase in Soviet military assistance, and the number of advisers from that country and Eastern Europe sent to the Sudan reached about 2,000 by the end of 1970. More important, because of the impact it had domestically, was the regime's commitment to the cause of Arab unity and the struggle against Israel. The latter's intervention in support of the Anya-nya in the south was common knowledge by now, giving the Sudan immediate cause for wishing to close ranks with the Arab states, particularly its immediate neighbours, Egypt and Libya, both ruled by radical military regimes. At the end of 1970, the Sudan entered an alliance with both these states and commenced negotiations for their political union. Like many similar schemes initiated by Egypt, this was not carried much further. Nevertheless, proposed unity with Egypt became a card often played by Nimeiry in the years ahead to trump domestic and foreign opposition.

Domestic opposition was initially manifested by the fundamentalist sectarian groups, the Ansar and the Muslim Brothers, who were understandably disturbed by the soldiers' radical posture and the political prominence attained by communists and other radicals, as well as the strengthening of ties with Egypt, where the Muslim Brothers had been suppressed by Nassir. After the coup, the Ansar leader, Imam Hadi el-Mahdi, barricaded himself on the island of Aba, surrounded by thousands of armed followers as a gesture of defiance. Attempts to mollify him failed and the island was attacked by a large government force at the end of March 1970. The Ansar were crushed with heavy loss of life, and the Imam was killed while trying to cross into Ethiopia; his nephew, Sadiq el-Mahdi, the former Prime Minister, was exiled to Cairo. The challenge from the right was easily contained, but it was far from eliminated.

The clash with the left was not long in coming. Opposition from that quarter was spearheaded by the communist party which opposed the dissolution of political parties demanded by the RCC and the suggestion that their members join a national movement of progressive elements due to be organized by the regime. Bearing the fate of the Egyptian communist party in mind, the experienced SCP leader, Abdul Khaliq Mahjoub, proposed instead a national front of existing progressive organizations. He had the support of a majority in the SCP, and was supported within the RCC by Major Hashim el-Atta and a couple of other officers sympathetic to the party. An influential faction within the SCP, headed by Ahmed Suleiman and Muawiya Ibrahim, took a different line, arguing that the soldiers' lack of experience and ideological immaturity presented an opportunity for the communists to steer the RCC in a radical direction: 'If we are not here to influence them, they will bring in others'.[7] The factional split weakened the SCP, and the RCC sought to widen the gap by demanding that communists serving in government resign their party membership. The SCP had been operating clandestinely all along and refused to cease its activities now.

The RCC proceeded first by purging its own ranks of SCP sympathizers. In November 1970, three of its members were dismissed, including two prominent supporters of the SCP, Babiker el-Nur and Hashim el-Atta; Major Farouk Osman Hamadallah was the third. Thirteen other officers with alleged links to the SCP were dismissed, and a purge of communists in government service was launched. A distinction was drawn between 'nationalist communists' whose first loyalty was to the Revolution, and those who remained faithful to their party. In February 1971, Colonel Nimeiry vowed publicly to crush the communists, and soon afterwards their leaders were arrested.[8] In April, a draconian State Security Law was enacted imposing the death penalty for acts calculated to subvert the state or threaten national unity. At the same time, the SCP's affiliated organizations were dismantled and new social and professional organizations were formed by the regime to replace them. In May, plans to restructure the trade union movement, the SCP's stronghold, were announced. The press was nationalized in August, and it was announced that a new political party patterned on the Arab Socialist Union of Egypt was to be created.

On 30 May 1971, the SCP central committee met and decided to seek the overthrow of the Nimeiry regime. The party's role in the preparation of the abortive coup d'état of 19 July 1971 was freely admitted later by Abdul Khaliq Mahjoub under questioning by Nimeiry himself. The attempt was made by its sympathizers in the army, and the leaders were the three officers dismissed earlier from the RCC. They succeeded at first in seizing control of the capital, placed Nimeiry under arrest and proclaimed a 'revolution of correction' against individual dictatorship. But they failed to rally significant military or civilian support and when other units came to Nimeiry's assistance the attempt collapsed. Before the end, the rebels carried out a mindless massacre of more than three dozen officers held by them.

There were severe reprisals afterwards. The coup leaders and many of their supporters were executed, and the army's ranks were purged of suspected radicals and communist sympathizers. The regime also settled accounts with the SCP by hanging its secretary-general Abdul Khaliq Mahjoub, the trade union leader Shaafi Ahmed el-Sheikh, and Joseph Garang, its most prominent southerner. A pogrom of communists was launched by Nimeiry, who urged the Sudanese to hunt 'every renegade communist who belongs to the Communist Party'. Many were jailed, and many more lost their jobs in the widespread purge of the state service that followed. The result was a severe setback for the left in the Sudan.[9] More significantly, the attempt marked a change of direction for the military regime which was to lead it swiftly away from 'revolutionary socialism'.

Having subdued the opposition, the RCC proceeded to create the political structures that were to house the new regime. The designers comprised a group of miscellaneous individuals without an organizational or political base whose influence was entirely dependent on the soldiers' need for ideological and political guidance in the early days of their reign. They were not to retain their posts for long; consequently, they were not able to influence the evolution of the institutions they designed which were to take a path that deviated greatly from the expressed intention. The institutional consolidation of the regime began with the proclamation of an interim constitution in August 1971 which renamed the state the Sudan Democratic Republic and described it as a socialist state founded on the alliance of the 'people's active forces', that is, farmers, workes, soldiers, nationalist intelligentsia and national capitalists. It sketched out a form of government based on the presidential system and in October 1971, Gaafar Nimeiry assumed the office of president and dissolved the RCC. In the meantime, the regime had been fashioning a network of associations, including town and village development committees, professional organiz-ations, youth and women's groups, which was to form the building blocks of the Sudanese Socialist Union (SSU), founded in January 1972.

The SSU described itself as a 'revolutionary socialist vanguard', whose task was to mobilize the 'active forces' of the nation to fulfil the aims of the 25 May Revolution. For that purpose, it was assigned supreme political authority over all organs and activities of the state, and its structure was designed to parallel the state administration at all levels. Fifty per cent of its membership was to represent workers and peasants, and democratic centralism was to govern its internal organization. Actual emphasis was on centralism, with the president of the SSU, who was also the president of the Republic, enjoying wide powers, including the right to name all top SSU officials and half the members of its central committee. Rather than rely on the 'active forces' to animate its political movement, the regime mobilized the bureaucracy, particularly local government officials, to form branches and guide their activities. By 1974, when the SSU held its first national congress, it claimed some four million members, and had become a massive parastatal agency whose task was to provide a façade of popular representation for the military dictatorship as well as an additional lever of political control. It was run by professionals who were, most frequently, simultaneously serving the state in other capacities. As a result, many Sudanese had no clear conception of the distinctive nature and role of the SSU.[10] The role of the 'active forces' was limited and, contrary to its stated principles, the SSU relied significantly on the support of local notables known for their links with the banned political parties.

The process of institutionalization was completed with the promulgation of a permanent constitution – Sudan's first – in May 1973. It proclaimed the Sudan a unitary, democratic, socialist republic, the common weal of the 'active forces'. It consecrated a form of government in which an all-powerful president not only had absolute executive powers, but also could veto legis-lation passed by an elective People's Assembly and, when required, could rule single-handed by proclaiming a state of emergency. The post was tailor-made for the regime's strongman, who had by now established an undisputed personal dominance and was able to dispense with all but one of the original members of the Revolutionary Command Council. The constitution preserved undiluted the key elements of northern Sudanese nationalism. Islamic law and custom were to be the main source of legislation, and Arabic remained the official language. Nevertheless, in order to facilitate the rapprochement with the rebellious south, Christianity was granted official recognition and customary law was sanctioned for non-Muslims.

The May Revolution's outstanding achievement was the settlement of the conflict in the south on the basis of a political compromise that preserved the unity of the state while granting regional autonomy to that region. The compromise was forced on the state by the impossibility of suppression and the rising cost of the war. From their rag-tag origins, the Anya-nya had become a serious foe united under the leadership of Joseph Lagu, with secure bases in Ethiopia, material assistance from Israel and propaganda support abroad orchestrated by influential religious bodies. A stepped-up effort by the newly installed military regime with Soviet technical equipment at the end of the decade had little impact. In the aftermath of the Communist-backed 1971 coup, relations with the USSR soured and Soviet aid ceased in mid-1971. The Sudanese forces were left without a supplier from abroad, a precarious situation for an African army. To their credit, its leaders recognized the futility of established policy and proposed a realistic alternative. The proposal was realistic because it addressed itself to the major contradictions that gave rise to the conflict and proposed ways of resolving them. More specifically, it addressed the main grievances of the key social group, that is, the southern intelligentsia, to whom it offered unencumbered political control of their region; in other words, a share of the state.

The south did not attain equal status with the north in a federal system, but a large measure of self-government within a unitary state. Whether or not, as M. O. Beshir wrote, 'the national aspirations of both parties were satisfied' remained to be seen.[11] Nevertheless, the accord provided a workable arrangement within which the outstanding demands of the social groups that led the dissident nationalist movement could be satisfied. The three southern provinces comprised a regional unit with its own legislative and executive authorities. The regional assembly was directly elected, and its jurisdiction was confined to local affairs. A High Executive Council was headed by a president appointed by the state president on the recommendation of the regional assembly. This arrangement allowed the central government a direct role in the governmental affairs of the southern region, a role Nimeiry was to play forcefully in the years ahead. The regional government was granted authority to raise revenue from economic activities originating in its own area but, since such activities were scarce, the south was to get grants from the central government, upon which inevitably it became dependent. A special development plan for the south was also to be financed from central government funds and foreign aid.

It was agreed that southerners would be represented in the armed forces in accordance with their share of the total population, and the regional government was given joint authority over the army in the southern region. A beginning was made by incorporating about 6,000 Anya-nya fighters (2,000 from each province) in separate units in the Sudanese army, and about 200 of them were commissioned officers. About as many who claimed membership in the guerrilla army were absorbed in the police and prison services and other departments of the regional administration. The autonomy of the regional civil establishment guaranteed a monopoly of state posts to the southern intelligentsia, thus removing a major grievance. They were also guaranteed a share of civil posts under the central government, where the tradition of having three ministers from the south was preserved. The language problem was de-fused, rather than resolved, by proclaiming English the 'principal language' in the south, while Arabic remained the official language of the country. Freedom of religion and regional control of education offered assurances of protection against enforced Arabization. Thus, the Addis Ababa Agreement appeared to satisfy the major grievances of the southern dissidents and it was accepted by most of them.

Economic inadequacy proved the regime's Achilles heel. By the end of the decade, the Sudanese economy was in a parlous state. Its trade deficit had multiplied tenfold, and the country was importing goods costing three times as much as the value of its exports. The foreign debt amounted to 6,300 million Sudanese dollars, and servicing it absorbed 70 per cent of export earnings, or one-quarter of the state's annual budget. The economy had been placed under supervision by the International Monetary Fund, which kept it afloat by providing loans of 300 million dollars annually from 1979 to 1982. More aid was provided by the United States, which made the Sudan its prime beneficiary in Africa, and other Western powers, especially West Germany. With inflation running at 50 per cent per annum, the IMF imposed four currency devaluations between 1972 and 1982. In the beginning of the 1980s, the IMF also dictated the ending of subsidies on basic consumption goods, together with restrictions on personal credit and government expenditure. The result was mounting opposition which revealed the extent of the regime's political isolation after a dozen years in power. In its futile search for political support, the regime moved all the way across the political spectrum, ending up in an alliance with the Muslim Brothers and pandering to their demands for a theocracy. This only served to inspire the civilian opposition to greater efforts, which succeeded in toppling Nimeiry in April 1985.

Somali Republic: The October Revolution

The 21 October 1969 revolution in Somalia was launched with a military coup d'état whose leader was no upstart, but the commander of the armed forces, Major General Mohammed Siad Barre. The twenty-five-man Supreme Revolutionary Council (SRC) that took over power included officers above the rank of captain and represented most major clans and regions of the country. The coup was an army affair, but six high-ranking police officials were invited to join the SRC afterwards.

At the outset, the military regime made no extraordinary claims. Its justification for intervention was a familiar one. 'It was no longer possible', claimed Siad Barre in his first speech, 'to ignore the evil things like corruption,

SOMALIA

Somalia has 3,200 km of coastline on the Horn of Africa. Its population of 6.3 million (1983 estimate) are mostly Sunni Muslims. The various Somali clans share a common cultural, linguistic and religious background, and the official language is Somali.

The Democratic Republic of Somalia that became independent in July 1960 united the territories of the previously existing British protectorate and the Italian Trust, but sizeable Somali populations remained outside the new state, notably in the Ogaden and in Kenya. Somalis in both areas have since taken up arms and serious clashes involving Ethiopia and the Somali Democratic Republic occurred in 1964, and flared up again in the late 1970s.

The civilian administration that followed independence proved unable to curb increasing corruption and inefficiency, and on 21 October 1969 it was replaced in a bloodless coup led by Major-General Mohammed Siad Barre. He and his ministers adopted the designation 'Jaalle' or 'Comrade' and propounded a socialist philosophy with an emphasis on self-help. Government was centralized under a Supreme Revolutionary Council. The period 1970–78 saw a turning towards the Soviet Union and the Eastern European countries.

bribery, nepotism, theft of public funds, injustice and disrespect for our religion and the laws of the country. Intervention by the army was inevitable.' The regime's political creed, formulated in a brief First Charter, was unremarkable. Clannishness was singled out as the soldiers' particular *bête noire*; even mention of a person's clan affiliation was proscribed. The ritual drive against corruption, calling the guilty to an 'accounting without shame', was launched; former high office-holders were investigated and a number were detained, including the deposed Prime Minister, Ibrahim Egal.[12] Army officers were posted to ministries and state agencies to monitor the behaviour of civil servants. The usual invocation of nationalism was coupled with a strong emphasis on equality and social justice, and the SRC promised in the First Charter 'to embark upon the task of creating a nationalism that will not detrimentally differentiate the rich from the poor and the educated from the illiterate, the urban from the nomad, the high from the low'.

The First Charter signalled a halt in the pro-Western drift of Somali foreign policy initiated by the government of Ibrahim Egal. It proclaimed support for positive neutrality and national liberation movements throughout the world, and condemned imperialism and neo-colonialism. Three months after coming to power, the SRC expelled the American Peace Corps contingent, and soon afterwards established diplomatic relations with East Germany and North Korea, as a result of which the United States cut off its economic aid to Somalia in May 1970.[13] Relations with the United States soured as a result of the first abortive attempt to overthrow the RCC in 1970, which, it was suspected, had CIA backing.[14] Relations with the Soviet Union on the other hand were strengthened and the number of Soviet advisers in Somalia rose to about a thousand soon after the coup. Eastern Europeans and Cubans also arrived to assist the new regime.

The SRC sought to rally support among the budding Somali intelligentsia, and appointed a number of young educated men to a cabinet that was initially composed largely of civilians. Many had studied abroad, mostly in Italy and the Soviet Union, where they had become acquainted with Marxism.[15] Although of limited currency in Somali society, socialism was not an unfamiliar concept even in this isolated corner of Africa. Somalia's closest foreign relationship was with Egypt, and Nassir's appeal here was no less than elsewhere in the region. It was strongest among the educated Somalis, including several army officers who had studied in Egypt. Others had trained in the Soviet Union. Among them was Colonel Mohammed Ali Samatar, who emerged as Siad Barre's right hand man and the regime's Marxist ideologue. Socialism also had a small organized following in the form of two minor political groupings. One of them was the Somali Democratic Union, led by Hadj Mohammed Hussein, the one-time president of the Somali Youth League and founder of the Greater Somalia League. His party sponsored Somali youth for studies in Eastern Europe and the Soviet Union, and some of these served the new regime in key posts. The other group, which called itself the Work and Socialism Party, was founded in the early 1960s by Abdul Aziz Hersi, a lawyer educated in Egypt and Italy. Some of its leading members were appointed to high posts by the military regime.

These individuals and minuscule groups were the conduit for the radical notions that reached the inner councils of the SRC in the early years of the revolution. As in the Sudan, the new rulers of Somalia had to produce a credible alternative to the regime they had overthrown. 'The natural choice', says Lewis, 'was some form of socialism'.[16] The appeal of socialism lay in the perception of it as the system most likely to promote rapid development in backward societies, a perception shared widely by the intelligentsia, military men included. In Somalia, adds Lewis, they regarded socialism as 'first and foremost an ideology of development'.[17] Socialism was expected to overcome the manifold constraints that inhibit development in the Third World, although how this is done was not clear.

A start was made in May 1970 with the nationalization of banking, insurance, petrol distribution, electricity production, and the country's sole sugar refinery. All these enterprises were foreign-owned – a fact cited in justification of the takeover. In his speech announcing the nationalization, Siad Barre made no mention of socialism. Thus, the announcement a few months later, on the first anniversary of the revolution, that his regime was committed to 'scientific socialism' came as a surprise. The chairman of the SRC was emphatic that Somalia was opting for 'scientific socialism', and specifically rejected alloys – such as Arab, African or Islamic socialism – that had been proclaimed elsewhere. He did not elucidate the meaning of the chosen dogma, nor did the Second Charter of the Revolution that was issued shortly afterwards. Perhaps the clearest and most revealing definition of it was offered by Siad Barre himself in an interview, when he said: 'For us socialism is simply defined: it is a system in which the state takes primary responsibility for the political, social and economic development of the nation'.[18]

To the intellectuals collaborating with the SRC fell the task of translating the complicated concepts of socialism for mass consumption in the language of − nomad society. Even the word for revolution had to be invented. The term for 'socialism' had appeared earlier in the title of the Work and Socialism Party: it was *handiwadaag*, meaning 'sharing of wealth'.

The task of propagating the official ideology was entrusted initially to the Ministry of Information and National Guidance, headed by Captain Ismail Ali Aboker, who became the regime's propaganda chief and a leading member of the SRC. Foreign-language newspapers were closed down and the rest nationalized, giving this Ministry a monopoly of the media of communication. Plays, songs and poems were widely used to convey the message of the revolution to the illiterate masses. The SRC launched a campaign of mass mobilization that was to reach impressive proportions and to carry the regime through the first half of the 1970s on a high tide of popular excitement and expectations. It began as a simple public relations exercise, when a letter-box was placed in front of the National Theatre to receive communications from the public. The Public Relations Office (PRO) was established to process them, and it grew octopus-like into a multifaceted organization whose tentacles reached every corner of Somali society. It sprouted numerous departments, spawned mass organizations for youth, women and workers, and founded a militia force named the 'Victory Pioneers'. The first head of the PRO was a Soviet-trained officer, Major Jama Ali Jama, and under him the organization mushroomed into a vast parastatal establishment with branches in every region of the country, organized in parallel with the state administration. Its regional and local committees were recruited from all sections of society, but it was the youthful and educated element that became its moving spirit. Launched into successive mobilization campaigns in the first half of the decade, they came to rival the staid state bureaucracy that some activists aspired to supplant. In 1972 the PRO, which had come 'to possess an embryonic political party structure', was renamed the Political Office and incorporated in the President's Office, thus putting it under Siad Barre's personal control. Similarly, the militia was transferred to the ministry of defence, and one of Siad Barre's sons-in-law was put in charge of it.

There were successive campaigns against tribalism, corruption and laziness, and for cleanliness, scientific socialism and sex equality. An injunction against tribalism was issued, and a mock burial for this and other assorted social afflictions was carried out by the chairman of the SRC in January 1970. Self-help schemes and crash programmes, ranging from sand-dune stabilization to tree planting, were undertaken. A lasting achievement was the choice of a script for the national language, an issue civilian regimes had been unable to resolve. Here the military regime acted with speed and determination to cut through the Gordian knot of conflicting arguments and interests. On the third anniversary of the revolution, Siad Barre informed the nation that the Latin script, with some modifications, had been adopted. It was then decreed that the script should be taught to the masses through a national literacy campaign, and all pupils from the last two elementary grades and above, their teachers, and many civil servants were dispatched to the countryside to teach nomads and peasants their national language. The campaign lasted for eight months and was accounted a resounding success. It coincided with the onset of the famine caused by the drought of 1972–74, and turned into a relief operation for the stricken pastoralists. Drought affected the north and central regions where famine took an estimated 20,000 lives and killed one-third of the livestock. A quarter of a million people took refuge in camps, and about 100,000 of them became part of a novel project for the resettlement of nomads in fishing and cultivation schemes in the south.

More nationalization measures were announced in January 1972 affecting foreign trade, as the state took over the import of cereals, fuel, medicine and films, and (some time later) the export of bananas, hides and skins. Foreign schools were taken over in the same year. Aliens had earlier been banned from employment in posts that could be filled by natives. All these were popular actions, as was the freezing of prices, the reduction of rents, and Somalia's entry into the Arab League in 1974. Other measures, such as salary reductions of up to 40 per cent in the civil service, were less welcome, but they were justified on grounds of equity and did not provoke any reaction.

The soldiers showed from the outset that they were not inclined to tolerate opposition of any kind. A law on the security of the state, known as the twenty-six articles, was proclaimed in September 1970, which decreed the death penalty for 'anyone harming the unity, peace, and sovereignty of the state'. Military 'security courts' were established and many persons were condemned for, *inter alia*, tribalism, corruption, and rumour-mongering. Another abortive attempt against the ruling faction was announced in May 1971, and two members of the SRC and a third officer were executed. In January 1975, the regime executed ten religious notables who publicly criticized Siad Barre's interpretation of the Koran, when he introduced the Family Law that established sex equality and banned polygamy.

By this time, the process of institutionalization of the October Revolution was well under way.[19] The Somali Revolutionary Socialist Party (SRSP) came into being in June 1976 through the metamorphosis of the Political Office. The founding congress included about 3,000 Political Office representatives and members of the military and security branches, who had been nominated by the regional governors. To their astonishment, a number of prominent Political Office cadres found themselves excluded. Some of them, particularly those trained in Eastern Europe, had their own notions about the structure of the party and the role it ought to play. Their presence in the congress was deemed undesirable, in view of the fact that these matters had been settled beforehand. A committee appointed by Siad Barre prepared the constitution of the SRSP and chose candidates for the various offices; these were subsequently approved by the congress. The chosen leaders were the regime's top men. The political bureau was composed of the SRC chairman, its three vice-chairmen and the chief of security. The central committee of 74 included 20 generals, 12 colonels and a solitary woman. The machinations involved in this exercise proved an eye-opener for many young radicals who had embraced the October Revolution in the belief that it offered a genuine alternative to the debilitating corruption of the parliamentary regime. They discerned the regime's design to use the socialist party as a political front for military rule and, behind it, the consolidation of Siad Barre's personal power. They were the first to know disillusionment and to break with the regime.

The process of institutionalization was completed with the enactment of a constitution in 1979. This document assigned to the SRSP 'supreme authority of political and socio-economic leadership' in the renamed Somali Democratic Republic. It also sought to legitimize the personal ascendancy of the regime's strongman by designing a form of government in which the president had well-nigh unlimited powers, including the right to appoint one or more vice-presidents, as well as a prime minister, 'if he shall deem it appropriate'.[20]

In the field of socialist economic development, the military regime's main contribution was the nationalization of foreign trade and finance sectors that were mainly in foreign hands and whose takeover involved no political risk. The livestock trade, where strong domestic interests were involved, was not touched. Nationalization did not extend to production, even where, as in the case of bananas, it was foreign-owned.[21] Somalia's plans for economic development in the 1970s were confounded by drought (1972–74) and war (1977–78). The actual plans for 1971–73 and 1974–78 were simply lists of projects, the cost and duration of which were grossly understated, and whose rate of implementation was impossible to assess. A third plan for 1979–81 was designed to complete them.

Not surprisingly, the events that were to mark the reign of the radical military regime were dictated by the categorical imperative of Somali nationalism, that is, the pursuit of national unification. A major effort was made to build up the Somali army and paramilitary branches with the aid of the Soviet Union, Iraq, Cuba and North Korea. The Soviet Union had an obvious strategic interest in a country that borders the Red Sea and the Indian Ocean in the vicinity of the Arabian Gulf. In return for its aid, it secured access to the port of Berbera, where it proceeded to construct a major naval base, its first firm foothold in Africa. With Soviet aid, the Somali forces expanded rapidly. Their size was estimated between 30,000 and 40,000 in 1976. The cost of arms imports during 1971 to 1975 equalled 43 per cent of the total non-military budget. Between 1971 and 1975, the Soviet Union provided Somalia with $32 million in economic aid and $132 million in military assistance. In mid-1977 the Somali forces were launched on an ill-fated invasion of the Ogaden and Bale provinces of Ethiopia. After an initial success, they were expelled by a revived Ethiopian army supplied and advised by the Soviet Union and assisted by Cuban combat units. In a remarkable switch, Moscow dropped Somalia in order to embrace the radical military regime in Ethiopia, a country far more important in the region, and a regime that seemed far more determined to embark on a socialist path.

After this setback, the Siad Barre regime sought the patronage of the United States, offering in return the Soviet-built base at Berbera. Although keenly interested, the Americans were abashed by the extravagant demands made by the Somalis, and remained wary of encouraging another assault on Ethiopia.

Agreements for limited military aid were signed in 1980, but the United States was wary also of committing itself to a regime with little popular support and an uncertain future. The October Revolution's turn to the West reinforced the opposition by alienating the last of the radical activists who had rallied to the call of socialism. Many fled abroad, while others ended in prison. There they were joined by numerous top officials who were purged at the beginning of the 1980s. By this time, nearly all the civilians who had served the regime in the revolution's halcyon days, as well as most of the military officers, were in prison or exile. Addis Ababa was now able to turn the tables on its enemy by training and arming Somali dissident groups, which began to infiltrate and carry out raids within Somalia in 1980, forcing the regime to declare a state of emergency in October of that year. The Military Security Court became a dreaded inquisition chamber, against whose verdict there was no appeal. Somalia turned into a garrison state where power lay exclusively with the army whose numbers now exceeded 65,000, plus 31,000 in paramilitary units, and was most visibly exercised by the security branch whose dreaded operatives functioned with complete immunity. The dream of the October Revolution had become a nightmare.

Ethiopia: The 1974 Revolution

The deposition of Haile Selassie on 12 September 1974 brought to an end the first phase of the revolution in Ethiopia, a phase marked by spontaneity, mass participation, great expectations and the absence of bloodshed. The soldiers who came to power constituted themselves as a Provisional Military Administrative Council (PMAC). This was the *alter ego* of the Dergue, the committee that had guided the armed forces towards the seizure of power in the previous months. The Dergue comprised 108 members chosen *ad hoc* to represent various branches and units of the military, police and the Territorial Army.[22] They ranged in rank from private soldier to major, with non-commissioned officers forming the single largest group, and a contingent of 45 officers – a markedly different composition from that of the Sudanese and Somali juntas. A heterogeneous group, they met for the first time in June 1974. Apart from displaying a generally mutinous disposition and a desire to hobble the ruling clique of aristocrats and imperial retainers, many members of the Dergue had no clear conception of what ought to replace that ruling clique. For many, the deposition of Haile Selassie was going far enough and they approved a decree that preserved the monarchy and offered the throne to his son.

The soldiers made no ideological claims at the outset. Initially, the Dergue contented itself with the bland slogan of nationalism, *'Ethiopia tikdem'* (Ethiopia first), that became its motto. The themes expressed by it were commonplace amelioratives, not revolutionary sentiments. The first man they chose as Prime Minister before the emperor's deposition was Mikael Imru, a scion of the royal nobility, though considered liberal. The man they chose to chair the PMAC after the deposition was a retired army general, Aman Andom, of wholesome reputation but conventional political inclinations.

ETHIOPIA

Class and ethnic divisions undermined the imperial regime of Haile Selassie and brought about its collapse in 1974. But long before the opposition of the new social classes became felt at the centre, Ethiopian rule was challenged in two areas on the periphery of the state. The Somali-inhabited Ogaden region in the south-west was claimed by the Ethiopians during the late nineteenth century expansion. Resistance to Ethiopian rule increased after 1960 when the Somalis over the border gained their independence. In mid-1977 Somalia invaded the Ogaden.

The problem in Eritrea was even more obdurate. Despite their defeat at the battle of Adowa in 1886, the Italians were allowed to retain the northernmost region in the colony that they named Eritrea. Italian rule having dismantled the feudal structure, and the British administration (1941–50) having permitted political activity, the Eritreans developed a strong political awareness that focused on the issue of independence.

In 1952, Eritrea was given self-government within a federal union with Ethiopia, and developed an open political life that contrasted with the feudal reign across the border. It lost its autonomy in 1962, being reduced to the status of a province. A year later the Eritrean Liberation Front was founded and a deadly struggle began.

By the early 1970s numerous challenges had eroded the authority of the *ancien regime* in Ethiopia. Throughout the spring and summer of 1974 the intelligentsia, students and workers waged a campaign of strikes and demonstrations in the towns, whilst peasants rose against the landlords in many parts of the south. Simultaneous mutinies in the armed forces shattered the regime's main pillar of support.

Ethiopia has a population of 42 million. The majority of the population are either Christian or Muslim. The national language is Amharic, English being the second official language.

Yet, on 20 December 1974, the PMAC issued a ten-point programme which proclaimed a 'specifically Ethiopian socialism' and equated it with self-reliance, equality, the dignity of labour, the supremacy of the common good and the indivisibility of Ethiopian unity. This was hardly Marxism-Leninism, but it was a start. More important, it was in line with the radical mood of social groups opposed to the Haile Selassie regime.

The opponents of the imperial regime had highlighted some of the major problems facing Ethiopia and generalized solutions to them had been mooted. Pre-eminent among these was the legacy of feudalism and land expropriation in the south and the urgent need for land reform. Although the precise form of it was not defined, land reform enjoyed wide support among the intelligentsia, the working class, and the lower ranks of the military – social groups that had no vested interest in rural landed property and which recognized that the conjunction of class and ethnic divisions in the south was a major obstacle to national unity.

The social and economic backwardness of the country and the lagging pace of development were other major issues, and the imperial regime was held responsible for perpetuating this state of affairs. Its dependence on foreign capital and management was denounced for mortgaging the country's assets and its future. The exploitation of Ethiopian workers and the atrophy of the labour movement were likewise laid at the door of the regime and its foreign partners. A self-reliant economy under national control was advocated and, typically, it was vaguely perceived in a socialist guise, although nothing specific was proposed. Even the trade unions did not propose nationalization in the early days of the revolution. Nevertheless, such a step had a lot to recommend it. Given the paucity of domestic capital, it carried little political risk and had many a precedent in Africa. Also, it had the advantage of putting capital under the control of an expanded bureaucracy manned by the intelligentsia.

Thus, a climate of opinion emerged during the twilight of the imperial regime favouring radical action couched in socialist terms, without defining specific measures. Nor did the few months of turmoil that preceded the military takeover produce a political organization capable of claiming power. Given the absence of political organization, the burden of formulating popular demands fell on existing organizations of the intelligentsia, the trade unions and student groups. The Confederation of Ethiopian Labour Unions, the Teachers' Association, the University Teachers' Forum and university and secondary student associations performed this role. These groups had to be won over or neutralized if military rule was to gain acceptance.

The measures imposed by the Dergue were formulated by a relatively small group of men, mainly officers, who initially composed what was called its Planning Committee, and later headed the various sub-committees of the PMAC. Sharing the general viewpoint of the radical intelligentsia and keenly conscious of the need to carry the support of the civilian opposition, these men drew inspiration from the radical exegesis and sought out specific policy guidance from radical circles. Young radicals were appointed to high posts in the state service and were asked to produce proposals for basic change. Ethiopian ambassadors from several countries were recalled and questioned about developments in those states. The ambassador to Somalia impressed them with the achievements of the October Revolution there, and a number of Somali initiatives were adopted in Ethiopia.[23] Not all the measures enacted in the name of the Dergue were approved by the entire membership, or even communicated to it ahead of time. However, the most important were discussed in plenary sessions, in an atmosphere charged with tension and a sense of insecurity about the staying power of the military regime. A key group in the early days were the non-commissioned officers who had launched the military rebellion. They were inclined to back the views of officers whom they knew and trusted, and they could carry the simple soldiers with them. Consequently, although they did not initiate policy, their support was essential for its approval.

Before the new regime was two months old, it had broken with the civilian radicals and had its first internal crisis. Fearing a stagnant military dictatorship of the type familiar in Africa, the radicals precipitated the break by clamouring for a popular government and seeking to rally the urban population against the soldiers. They gained support in the trade unions, and a week after the seizure the power, the Confederation of Labour Unions called a general strike to demand a people's government. The strike failed, and the Dergue was alerted to the danger posed by an autonomous labour movement. The university students who mounted the most determined opposition were also marked early on as enemies of the regime. The demand for popular participation in government had some supporters in the Dergue itself. Indeed, most of its members considered their rule an interlude until a civilian government was formed, and such a promise had been made publicly. A civilian advisory council was formed in a lame attempt to accommodate this demand. As opposition to its rule multiplied and stiffened, the regime's hardliners convinced the rest that the alternative to military rule was chaos and the disintegration of the state. After the blood-letting began, there was no longer any possibility of yielding power.

The worsening situation in Eritrea triggered the first outburst of violence. The Dergue had inherited the problem, and such was its potential for divisiveness that it was not discussed by the full body for fear it would cause violent dissension. General Aman, who was of Eritrean origin himself, took on the task of finding a solution. Rather than approach the Eritrean nationalist fronts, he sought to outflank them. Twice he toured the province, addressing the public and conferring with Eritrean notables. His message was that the overthrow of the imperial regime had liberated all the peoples of Ethiopia, so there was no justification any longer for demanding secession and continuing the war, and he promised reforms in local government without specifying their substance. Public response in Eritrea was not encouraging, and the guerrillas continued to press on the towns. At that time, a so-called 'small Dergue', a provincial replica of the parent body, controlled the armed forces in Eritrea. Fearful of a guerrilla onslaught on the towns, it was demanding reinforcement with men and arms. The latter were in short supply because the United States was holding up deliveries of weapons promised to the imperial regime. General Aman assumed responsibility for expediting this matter as well but the Americans, having no connection with the Dergue, procrastinated.

Aman's failure to resolve either of the two pressing problems weakened his position. His influence derived solely from this past reputation and he was not a member of the Dergue.[24] When he refused to approve the dispatching of reinforcements to Eritrea in his capacity as Minister of Defence, he effectively challenged the Dergue's authority and raised fears of a counter-coup. He was killed on 23 November in his home when he resisted an attempt to arrest him. The same night, 59 other prisoners were executed, including many former high government officials, aristocrats and senior military officers. Immediately afterwards, reinforcements were sent to Eritrea, and the new regime became entangled in a rapidly escalating conflict that was to dominate its reign for the next ten years.

In January 1975, a series of nationalization measures was announced, followed in February by a 'Declaration on Economic Policy of Socialist Ethiopia'. In addition to financial institutions and insurance companies, 72 manufacturing concerns were taken over by the state. Most were owned and managed by foreigners. Nationalization resulted in the replacement of foreign nationals by Ethiopians, thereby greatly improving the employment prospects of the intelligentsia. Within two years, 200 nationalized units were under native management and by the end of 1977, 30,000 posts had been added to the public sector. The declared policy on socialism envisaged the familiar three-tiered economy, with coexisting state, mixed and private sectors. Foreign capital was to be allowed in certain sectors that could not be developed without it.

In March 1975, a radical land reform was proclaimed. It nationalized all rural land, thereby abolishing private landed property, and forbade the transfer or renting of land in any form, thus preventing its alienation and accumulation. A maximum of ten hectares for individual shares was set, but land was to be divided equally among those who tilled it. It was an historic achievement, bringing the feudal era to an end. The mass of tenants in the south were freed of landlord exactions, and since the Church was not excluded, some benefit was gained also in the north. The proclamation established peasant associations to carry out the reform and to exercise local authority. In July of the same year, urban land was nationalized along with extra housing, and house ownership was limited to one unit per family. Rents were reduced by up to 50 per cent. Urban dwellers' associations were formed to administer housing and local affairs. No compensation was offered to owners of land or housing.

This was the creative phase of the revolution, and these were far-reaching reforms. In each instance, the soldiers opted for the most radical of the options put before them, and the result was a veritable social revolution. It shattered the economic base of the *ancien régime*, eliminating any possibility of restoration, and precluded a bourgeois succession by preventing private capital accumulation. Henceforth, the regime's claim to socialism commanded attention, especially among sympathizers abroad who were convinced that Ethiopia had embarked on the 'non-capitalist path to development'. The Dergue was credited with having carried out a 'revolution from above', using the state as its main instrument.[25] On a less abstruse plane, credit was given to the officer who ultimately emerged as the regime's strongman, Colonel Mengistu Haile Mariam, who was reportedly endowed with revolutionary convictions and foresight.[26]

Such interpretations highlight the role of institutions and individuals, which no doubt is of some importance. On the other hand, they discount the impact of social forces, which is of the greatest importance. Ethiopia in 1974 was in the throes of revolutionary ferment involving contending national groups and social classes which caused the collapse of the old social order. The soldiers were affected by this ferment in the same way as others were, since the social conflict that undermined the *ancien régime* was faithfully reflected within the military establishment. The mutinous soldiers were as susceptible to the appeal for radical change as were other sections of the populace. Inchoate and ill-defined, change was conceived possible only in the guise of socialism, and no other model was considered. In adopting it as its own, the Dergue was undoubtedly following the inclinations of the majority of its members who sprang from the social classes that stood to gain from it. It was also following the popular current that could not easily be stemmed. The success of the radical military regime in its initial and creative phase was due precisely to its ability to join and lead the revolutionary current. The notion of a social revolution imposed from above, if such were possible, is inapplicable here, for it presumes resistance and going against the current. In Ethiopia, the decay of the imperial regime was so advanced that no meaningful opposition was forthcoming from the former ruling classes. Indeed, the main opposition the Dergue faced came from the radical left, and this served to push it towards a more radical path.

This opposition was manifested even before the Dergue had taken power formally. Every step it took since it was formed was incisively analysed and criticized by *Democracia*, the underground organ of the radical left, which became the most avidly read publication in Ethiopia's history. It was published by a group of militants, most of them former university students, who were in the process of forming the Ethiopian People's Revolutionary Party (EPRP), an organization that drew active support mainly from the intelligentsia and students, but proclaimed itself a proletarian vanguard party.[27] The EPRP infiltrated the trade union headquarters, where a couple of its leading members were employed, and won over a group of younger and better-educated trade unionists who were seeking to replace the pre-revolutionary leadership of the labour movement. The EPRP was also active in the Teachers' Association, the University Teachers' Forum and student organizations, all of which were strongly opposed to military rule. Lacking organized political support of its own, the Dergue took this opposition very seriously. Partly in order to relieve the pressure, it sponsored a rural development campaign on the Somali model and sent students and teachers to the countryside from early 1975 to mid-1976.

This challenge forced the Dergue to seek allies in the radical camp. It found them initially in the All-Ethiopia Socialist Movement, known by its Amharic acronym as MEISON. A group of the same provenance as the EPRP, it chose to collaborate with the military rulers, as one faction of the Sudanese Communist Party did, and with the same hope, forlorn as it turned out, of becoming its political mentors. MEISON and some other minuscule radical cliques provided valuable ideological guidance to the soldiers in the initial phase of their rule. They drafted the Programme for the National Democratic Revolution issued in 1976. This envisaged a popular democratic republic, under the leadership of the proletariat acting in alliance with the peasantry and supported by the petty bourgeoisie, and promised the formation of a workers' party.[28] MEISON qualified its position by making its support conditional: it felt free to oppose policies it deemed were not progressive. Such unremitting pressure from the left made it politically crucial for the Dergue not to be outflanked on that side, and this was no small factor in its own radicalization.

MEISON and other collaborating radical factions initiated the process of institutionalization for the regime. As a first step, a Provisional Office for Mass Organization Affairs (POMOA) was established early in 1976 to mobilize mass support, conduct political education, and lay the foundations for the workers' party. POMOA established the familiar massive apparatus parallel to the state administration and set out to recruit cadres for the regime. All existing social and professional associations were dissolved, and new ones were founded under the aegis of POMOA. The trade union federation was banned and replaced by a new trade union organization. POMOA also took charge of the urban dwellers' associations and turned them into vigilante bodies used in the bloody purge of the opposition that was to follow in early 1977.

By that time, the Dergue had undergone two more violent purges of its own that claimed the lives of several leading members, including the second PMAC chairman, General Teferi Bante. A hardline faction, which favoured military solutions to most problems, emerged dominant. Its leader was Colonel Mengistu Haile Mariam, who now became the undisputed leader of the Dergue and chairman of the PMAC.[29] The EPRP had marked his rise to prominence earlier with an attempt to assassinate him, an act that signalled the start of an urban guerrilla campaign by the radicals to overthrow the military regime. In March 1977, Mengistu retaliated by declaring war on the EPRP and launched what was officially labelled a campaign of 'red terror' against the youthful radicals. MEISON members and POMOA cadres led the armed squads of the urban dwellers' associations in a joint effort with the army to exterminate the opposition.

At the height of the red terror in mid-1977 came the Somali invasion in the Ogaden. The Dergue's fortunes were at their lowest ebb at that point. The Somalis cut off the railway line to Djibouti. An Afar uprising threatened the road to Assab where the oil refinery is located and the Eritreans were besieging Massawa, Ethiopia's third port of entry. Another dissident nationalist movement had appeared in Tigrai, and its guerrillas were harassing traffic on the main road artery to Eritrea. Encouraged by all this, the remnants of the imperial regime made a co-ordinated attempt at counter-revolution. They organized the Ethiopian Democratic Union (EDU) in London, secured bases in the eastern Sudan, and commenced operations in western Ethiopia, where they captured two border towns in March 1977. It was at this time also that the link with the United States was finally broken, when Washington announced the suspension of aid to Ethiopia, citing civil rights violations as the reason. The military regime survived, thanks to the prompt action of the Soviet Union, which came to its aid with massive military provisions that began to arrive in Ethiopia a couple of months after the Somali invasion.

Hundreds of Soviet advisers followed, as well as thousands of Cuban troops and a tank unit from South Yemen. Libya offered financial assistance and several Eastern European states sent specialist aid to the beleaguered regime in Addis Ababa.

Capitalizing on the patriotic fervour excited by the invasion, the Dergue launched a nationalist crusade with the slogan 'Motherland or Death'. The war overshadowed all other issues, and put all opposition movements at a disadvantage. From now on, state nationalism could be invoked without inhibition to mobilize support against the regime's domestic and foreign enemies. The red terror succeeded in destroying the urban base of the EPRP. MEISON did not outlast its rival. Seeing itself as a vanguard proletarian party, MEISON nourished hopes of attaining political leadership and easing the military out of power. To that end, it strove to establish a base in the parastatal organizations spawned by the revolution whose powers and functions it sought to augment at the expense of the state bureaucracy. It overreached itself when it sought control of the militia, a potential counterweight to the army itself, arguing that it ought to be placed under revolutionary control. In August 1977, MEISON was violently suppressed, many of its members falling victims to the red terror they had helped to unleash.

The suppression of the radical opposition in 1977 marked the end of the creative phase of the military regime. From then on its energy and the available resources were consumed by the twin tasks of (a) the consolidation of the state and (b) the institutionalization of the regime. The first requirement was the expulsion of the Somalis from the Ogaden and Bale, a task speedily accomplished with the help of Soviet advisers and Cuban troops in the spring of 1978. This did not bring peace because Somali guerrillas remained active in these provinces, while in the north the Eritreans and Tigrai nationalist movements proved irrepressible. To maintain an adequate supply of manpower the Dergue imposed universal military conscription in 1983. The Soviet Union continued to supply the weaponry, the cost of which dwarfed what the United States had provided for Haile Selassie's army. Although the Soviet Union offered soft credit terms − a ten-year period of repayment at two per cent interest − the cost of maintaining the largest military force in Africa far exceeded the country's resources, and Ethiopia was saddled with a mounting debt. The effect of militarization on such a scale was widely felt. It had a serious impact on overall resource allocation; it pre-empted a major share of imports and of foreign exchange; it removed people and resources from productive activity, and it retarded development in other fields: the regime's agricultural policy, for instance, was influenced by the heavy food requirements of the military.

The assumption on the part of the radical factions that they would provide the nucleus of the much-discussed proletarian party obstructed for some time the process of institutionalization. After their elimination, the regime proceeded in 1979 to set up a Commission for Organizing the Party of the Working People of Ethiopia (COPWE). Workers, peasants, intellectuals and soldiers were identified as prospective party members. In June 1980, COPWE held its first congress and elected its leadership. This turned out to be identical with the leadership of the regime, a mixture of high military and bureaucratic officialdom, leavened with a few surviving specimens of radicalism. The central committee of 93 full and 30 candidate members included 79 members of the armed forces. The political bureau was made up of the Dergue's top leaders, without any civilians, and eight of the central committee's nine sub-committees were chaired by soldiers. COPWE became another parastatal edifice controlled by the state. In its second congress, Mengistu complained about the composition of its membership, a full two-thirds of which consisted of soldiers, bureaucrats and intellectuals.

Five years later COPWE spawned the Party of the Working People of Ethiopia (PWPE), whose founding congress coincided with the celebrations of the revolution's tenth anniversary, in September 1984. The PWPE was simply a conversion of COPWE. All the participants in the founding congress were cadres of the latter and, according to figures presented there, more than 40 per cent had education above the secondary level, 31 per cent were workers and peasants, and six per cent were female. The structure of the party closely followed the Soviet model. A crucial difference lay in the composition of its leading organs. The political bureau of 11 full and six candidate members included 12 officers, the core members of the regime. The central committee's ranks included all the members of the PMAC's standing and central committees, and a contingent of at least 80 military men among its 134 regular and 64 candidate members.

Given the manifold struggle for survival which claimed the regime's energies and the state's resources during the first decade, it was to be expected that economic development would receive low priority. In fact, no real economic planning occurred during this period, and for ten years the economy of socialist Ethiopia operated without central planning or control. Nationalization brought the whole of the modern industrial plant under state ownership and management. This caused far greater disruption in production than the land reform did in agriculture: manufacturing production in 1975/76 was six per cent below that in 1972/73.

The military regime also opted for the Soviet model of collectivization as the most promising long-term solution to the problem of food production. The 1975 land reform envisaged the formation of production and consumer co-operatives as the foundation of socialist agriculture. To encourage their growth, in 1978 the tax paid by members of producer co-operatives was set at half the rate paid by others. In 1979, an elaborate scheme was designed, according to which producer co-operatives would advance through four stages to reach full collectivization. By the mid-1980s, although the bulk of the peasantry belonged to associations, and a large number had joined consumer co-operatives − mainly in order to obtain consumer goods − fewer than one per cent had joined producer co-operatives, even though the state supported them with equipment, fertilizer and credit, and assigned cadres to oversee their operation.

The main effort to promote agricultural production focused on the expansion of the state farm sector, managed by the Ministry of State Farms and using wage labour. This sector grew out of commercial plantations taken over in 1975, to which more land was gradually added. By the beginning of the 1980s, state farms occupied about 800,000 acres, that is, about four per cent of all cultivated land. The bulk of state investment went to this tiny sector of production, which consumed 82 per cent of all fertilizer, over 73 per cent of improved seed, 80 per cent of agricultural credit, and nearly all other inputs provided by the state in the early 1980s.

The land reform restored control of the land to the peasant, thereby changing the relations of production, but did not affect the size of holdings for most peasants, nor did it change the method of production. Since land distributed by the reform was already under cultivation, production increases had to come from additional inputs. The low priority assigned to the peasant sector by the regime did little to improve production. Neither did the policy of compulsory purchasing at fixed prices encourage peasant productivity, and the upheaval of war and persistent drought put great additional strain on the fragile base of Ethiopian agriculture. An even greater threat, unrecognized until then, was revealed in 1984 by the first attempted census in Ethiopian history. This was an exceptionally high rate of population growth, nearly 2.9 per cent per annum. Preliminary results showed a total population of some 42 million. This was shocking news which put Ethiopia at the bottom of the scale of most economic indicators for Africa, and signified a frightening deficit in food production. The Central Planning Supreme Council estimated that the average consumption of food grain had fallen below the internationally recognized daily famine ration of 400 grammes per person. In other words, Ethiopian peasants were starving in fair weather, before drought unleashed another horrendous famine in 1983.

Conclusion

Radical military regimes came to power in the Horn in situations of acute structural crises for the states, which the regimes they toppled had been unable to resolve. The collapse of the *ancien régime* in Ethiopia raised issues of fundamental social importance, which neither the Sudan nor Somalia had to face, and the radical resolution of some of these issues made the Ethiopian experience a truly revolutionary event that marked the passing of an era in that country. The Ethiopian regime, however, although not the same as the Sudanese and Somali juntas, was not different essentially. Its defining trait, as of the other two, is state nationalism and its main task the preservation of the state. To that end, all three carried centralization, a process that began earlier, to new extremes. Moreover, they militarized the institutions of government and reigned over garrison states. The invocation of socialism served a complex function which is discussed in our editorial. A major aspect of it was to defend the state by disarming its opponents ideologically.

NOTES

John Markakis is Professor of African Studies in the University of Crete.
This article is part of a major study by the author on national and class conflicts in the Horn of Africa, to be published shortly.

1. Nimeiry was born in 1903 in Omdurman, the son of a man from Dongola who had been a soldier in the colonial army. He served in the southern Sudan from 1959 to 1963. An accomplished conspirator, he was dismissed from the army in 1957, and was again arrested for political activities in 1967.
2. Muddadir Abdel Rahim, 'Arabism, Africanism and Self-Identification in the Sudan', in Dustan M. Wai (ed.), *The Southern Sudan: The Problem of National Integration* (London: Cass, 1973), p. 23.
3. Bona Malwal, *People and Power in the Sudan: The Struggle for National Stability* (London: Ithaca, 1981), p. 123.
4. Babiker was a former Chief Justice who resigned his post in 1967 over the expulsion of the communist deputies from the Assembly.
5. Colin Legum, *Africa Contemporary Record* (1969–1970; B58).
6. T. C. Niblock, 'The Role of the SSU in Sudan's System of Government', paper submitted to the Centre of African Studies, University of Edinburgh, November 1980, p. 14.
7. Legum, op. cit. (1969–70; B52).
8. Mahjoub was exiled to Egypt in March 1970; he returned a few months later and was placed under house arrest.
9. The SCP elected a new General Secretary, Ibrahim Nogud, and continued its activities underground.
10. Niblock, op. cit., p. 14.
11. Mohammed Omer Beshir, *Revolution and Nationalism in the Sudan* (London: Rex Collings, 1981), p. 110.
12. Nearly all were released in 1973, except Egal, who was sentenced to 30 years' imprisonment for corruption.
13. A special relationship with North Korea was cemented with two visits there by Siad Barre. Among other forms of assistance, the North Koreans, who resented Ethiopia's participation in the Korean War, trained Somali guerrillas of the movements warring against Ethiopia.
14. Its leader was said to be the former police commander, General Jama Ali Korshel, who had been named vice-president of the SRC.
15. In 1968 there were nearly 500 Somali students in the USSR, 272 in Italy, and 152 in Egypt: see L. Pestalozza, *Chronique de la révolution somalienne* (Paris, 1973), p. 274n.
16. I. M. Lewis, 'Kim Il Sung in Somalia', in W. A. Shack and P. S. Cohen (eds.), *Politics in Leadership* (London: Oxford University Press, 1979), p. 14.
17. Ibid., p. 16.
18. A. Castagno, in *Africa Report*, 16 Sept. 1971, p. 24.
19. In October 1975, a People's Assembly on Social and Economic Problems brought together about 1,500 people chosen by the regional governors, most of whom were military men. They were invited to speak their minds in front of Siad Barre, and among other complaints voiced was the absence of political institutions for popular participation in government.
20. Elections to the People's Assembly were held in 1979, and the SRSP's single list of candidates was declared to have won 99.91 per cent of the votes.
21. One-half of banana production was in Italian hands.
22. The Dergue appointed 12 administrative officers to assist it. This gave the widely shared impression that its members numbered 120. Information on this and other aspects of the Dergue's organization and operations were provided by Mikael Gebrenegus, a former Eritrean police officer and a member of the Dergue in 1974. There were four Eritreans in the Dergue: three officers, all of whom defected and joined the EPLF, and one non-commissioned officer, who was killed in an incident in Asmara.
23. These ranged from superficial ones, such as the Orwellian all-seeing eye of the Somali Victory Pioneers that was superimposed on the map of Ethiopia, to major projects like the rural development campaign.

24. Aman also opposed an approach to the Soviet Union for military aid.
25. Such a thesis is put forward by F. Halliday and M. Molyneux, *The Ethiopian Revolution* (London: Verso, 1981).
26. This is the view of R. Lefort, *Ethiopie: la révolution hérétique* (Paris, 1981).
27. On the basis of its class position, not its class base.
28. The national democratic revolution, a formula of Maoist Chinese vintage, admits the participation of all progressive classes.
29. Little definite is known of his background, although rumours about it abound. His father is said to have been a soldier and later a lowly retainer in a noble household; allegedly, neither of his parents are Abyssinians. Mengistu dropped out of secondary school to join the army, and later went through officer training at the Holeta Academy on a course designed for promising non-commissioned officers. In 1974 he served as an ordnance officer with the Third Division in Harrar and was chosen to represent it in the Dergue.

Socio-economic Constraints on Radical Action in the People's Republic of Congo

Samuel Decalo

Even in a continent striking for the diversity of its political systems, leadership styles, development paths, ideological amalgams and civil-military hybrids, the People's Republic of Congo stands out sharply. It is the first sub-Saharan state to declare itself formally for Marxism (in 1963), and doyen of the continent's people's republics (formed in 1969), and strident radical rhetoric has spewed out of the capital, Brazzaville, and its *Voix de la Révolution* since the three days of student and trade unionist demonstrations ('les trois glorieuses' − subsequently enshrined as the 'Revolution') toppled the reactionary and venal regime of the defrocked Abbé Fulbert Youlou.[1] Since those heady days vehement diatribes have been hurled both at Congo's myriad internal class-enemies (variously categorized as bandits, situationists, infantile leftists, CIA lackeys, fetishists, opportunists, deviationists, incorrigible anti-Marxists, Hitlerites, juvenile delinquents, tribal reactionaries, Trotskyites, anarchists, etc.), and at the expatriate (French) and global (capitalist-imperialist) exploiters of the toiling Congolese masses.

Nowhere in Africa has international risk capital been more roundly and consistently vilified at home, and at the same time so assiduously courted abroad. Nowhere have the country's fundamental socio-economic problems and their optimal solution been more clearly defined, with subsequent corrective policies so utterly ineffective. Certainly in no other Marxist regime in the continent is the level of dialectical sophistication and ideological rhetoric so high as in the Congo, and the self-criticism of its leaders so sincere, without either of these having the slightest effect on matters relating to the real world. Indeed, few African states have projected such an image of militancy and power, while exhibiting utter impotence to effectuate virtually anything in any domain.

For, even in a continent where fact and fiction are sometimes blurred, and intentions and attainments confused, the disjunction between rhetoric and reality has been especially sharp in the Congo. State policies have been mutually contradictory, ideologically inconsistent, and often clearly incapable of implementation. The chasm between the officially enunciated goals of society and the empirically visible aspirations of the people has been immense. Under all four presidents since the revolution − the moderate schoolteacher Alphonse Massemba-Debat, the charismatic pistol-toting Marien Ngouabi, who developed the anachronistic concept of 'revolutionary tribalism',[2] the non-Marxist(!) Joachim Yhomby-Opango, whose hedonistic excesses shocked even jaded Brazzaville,[3] and the debonaire Cardin-suited (over a bullet-proof vest) 'hardliner' Denis Sassou Nguesso − Congo has followed a radical path of

CONGO

Congo has an area of 342,000 square kilometres and a population of 1.92 million (1984). Congo has been producing oil since 1968; oil now accounts for 90 per cent of net revenue, and 70 per cent of the budget. French is the official language, Brazzaville having been the capital of French Equatorial Africa from 1910.

The Congo became an overseas territory of France in 1946, and the formation of the country's first political parties followed. In 1956, the Abbé Fulbert Youlou, a Roman Catholic priest, was instrumental in founding a new movement, the *Union Démocratique de la Défense des Intérêts Africains*, as the local branch of the *Rassemblement Démocratique Africain*. In September 1958 the country voted in favour of remaining a self-governing member of the French community. However, the Congo became independent on 15 August 1960, Youlou being elected President.

In April 1963 legislation was passed making the country a one-party state, but on 13 August trade unions, supported by student unions, began a general strike, forcing Youlou to resign two days later. Alphonse Massemba-Debat formed a provisional government the next day. The disintegration of the civilian regime led Captain Marien Ngouabi to assume power. On 5 August 1968 the army announced the formation of a *Conseil National de la Révolution*. Massemba-Debat resigned the presidency on 4 September after a disagreement with the army and Ngouabi was named the acting president.

On 21 October 1969 Ngouabi announced the formation of the *Parti Congolais du Travail* as the country's sole political party. A new constitution introduced in January 1970 confirmed Ngouabi as president, renamed the country the People's Republic of the Congo and committed it to scientific socialism based on Marxist principles. The circumstances following Ngouabi's assassination in 1977 and the politics of the regimes that followed him are the subject of this article by Samuel Decalo that follows these editorial background notes.

development as ideologically orthodox on paper as it has been conservative and pragmatic in practice.[4]

Although Africa's classic praetorian system, and to all appearances the continent's most politicized and ideologically polarized country – with attempted putsches, conspiracies and periodic demonstrations regularly punctuating the country's otherwise placid way of life[5] – observers 'doubt [whether] the revolution really got out of the radio booth' because 'the Congolese couldn't care less about politics'.[6] Among Africa's most urbanized and socio-economically developed states, and with one of the continent's most youthful and educated populations, Congo remains a country in which fetishism, complex death rites, and messianic and syncretic cults continue to play a role, as attested, until recently at least, by the Matsouanist political hold over the Lari areas in the advanced south.[7]

Congo possesses Africa's most visible, vocal and virulent ruling Marxist-Leninist party, the Congolese Workers' Party (*Parti congolais du travail* – PCT); yet its membership has been so small (some 2,000, plunging as low at 164 following purges!) that observers have questioned even the *likelihood* of a truly revolutionary or radical option in the country, given such a minute pool of leadership cadres and the active participation of such a tiny militant segment of society.[8] A country at the forefront of the anti-apartheid and anti-UDI movement, cattle-deficient Congo was freely penetrated by Rhodesian fresh meat ('Botswana beef') and South African products, via unmarked midnight cargo flights or scheduled passenger airliners granted landing privileges rare in the continent. Stern, larger-than-life posters of Comrade Ngouabi remind the *citoyens* of the 'Stalinist' virtues of patriotism, vigilance, hard work ('Seven hours *of* work, not *at* work'), honesty, self-sacrifice and revolutionary dedication. They strike a jarring note, plastered on billboads adjacent to supermarkets stocked with luxury imports, and lively cafés where the easy-going Brazzaville civil service meets to conduct its lucrative 'private affairs' during office hours.[9] 'A schizophrenic society', according to the view across the river in Kinshasa;[10] or, as Young more politely expressed it, Marxism in Africa's first people's republic 'is at once ubiquitous and evanescent'.[11]

What appears to be a bizarre, hectic, 'undecipherable, kaleidoscopic procession of events'[12] in post-revolutionary Brazzaville may seen to defy classification or explanation.[13] Yet Congolese political life is hardly so complex – indeed, quite the reverse, unless one remains riveted to the ideological dimension of its periodic Byzantine volte-faces, invariably justified as required by the ongoing struggle against imperialism and capitalism and their local allies. Yet beneath Brazzaville's seemingly titanic tug-of-war over socialist rectitude – strikingly reminiscent of its counterparts in Stalin's Soviet Union, Mao's China and Bishop's Grenada (and so compared in the rhetoric of the leaders)[14] – there lie much more mundane bedrock issues of contention and strife.

The inconsistencies of the zigzag course of the Congolese revolution, the causes and origins of military rule itself, and the constraints upon radical socio-economic action in Brazzaville, all have less to do with the ideological dimension than with the administrative weakness of a state that cannot impose its authority throughout society, and also with fundamental divisions and conflicts stemming from the country's particularly sharp ethnic and regional polarization, inter-generational antipathies and a straightforward competition for control of patronage and jobs. Indeed, much of the political strife in the Congo may well be conceptualized as a simple power struggle 'between the ins and the outs, each interpreting the ideology to suit its own needs'.[15] Viewed from this more simplistic but nevertheless dynamic perspective, the Congolese enigma falls into sharper focus, allowing a more realistic assessment of the role of ideology in the Congo and the true constraints on radical military rule in the country.

The complex ideological tumult so characteristic of the Congo is thus in essence a very straightforward political conflict between ambitious elites within a praetorian environment: *some* within the elite may be ideologically motivated, but the concrete issues are power and patronage. The conflict is couched exclusively in Marxist jargon, but this need not delude the initiated since it is the required *lingua franca* of all serious formal discourse in the people's republic; indeed, merely 'to survive [politically] at such a time you had to know the revolutionary jargon, at the very least'.[16] Although those involved in the political tug-of-war mobilize their cohorts, much of society remains at the periphery of the power conflict, uninvolved spectators; their prime preoccupations are non-political, certainly not ideological, and better served by political quietism. Those in the subsistence economy sector may even be outside the tumult altogether if they are 'largely unaware of the political leaders in the towns', and only moderately affected by the peculiarities of the 'Marxist' nature of the state, over which the conflict ostensibly takes place.[17]

The Revolutionary Matrix

The three days of social tumult that ushered in the radical option in the Congo were neither a classical coup d'état nor a revolution, though they opened the door to a future permanent role for the military in politics, elevated Marxism to the status of a legitimate developmental alternative, and sparked the further radicalization of society, especially the youth. The overthrow of the crassly neo-colonial regime of Youlou, and the subsequent defiant adoption of Marxism at a time when such proclamations were hardly commonplace, was more of 'an instance of political rage produced by political impotence', to use Jowitt's apt phrase.[18] Apart from the more parochial issues at stake – connected with the regime's myopic inability to address, let alone satisfy, society's fundamental needs – the upheaval tapped deeply-felt hostilities in response to the Congo's experience of harsh colonial oppression, and frustrations with the non-existent fruits of independence that clashed cruelly with national aspirations and strivings.

The cautious and pragmatic socialist administration that replaced Youlou's was rapidly engulfed in powerful conflicting pressures set loose by the external reaction to the revolution – a 'revolution' that had actually changed little except style, rhetoric, heroes and villains – and by the anticipatory arch-revolutionary postures assumed by youth and unemployed labour in the urban centres. In attempting to reconcile the demands of these diametrically opposite vectors, the cleavage between what was pledged at home and assured abroad, and that between ideological pronouncements (symbolic outputs) and concrete policy, could not but begin to widen. Moreover, the regime was progressively forced to 'radicalize' its stance at home by the appointment to the cabinet of ultra-radical fire-eaters – although external exigencies made even the most Maoist among these proceed with the same deferential attitude towards France and the world's capital markets as had pre-revolutionary ministers.[19] Massemba-Debat, the ever down-to-earth pragmatist (at a time when Congolese youth felt history was bending under the weight of their assault), frequently bemoaned the lack of realism of his numerous critics on the left. He was particularly bitter about the strident demands expressed in an increasingly threatening manner by the role-expansionist paramilitary youth formations that sprang up (or were formed by aspirants to power) to 'protect' the revolution.[20]

On 4 August 1968 the unstable Massemba-Debat civilian interregnum collapsed, weighed down by perennial factional infighting and plotting and by the near-anarchy in the streets that threatened the corporate integrity of the armed forces: these had already indicated refusal to be subject to civilian authority. The sharp radicalization of the Congolese revolution that accompanied Ngouabi's coup d'état took the form of a declaration of a people's republic and the establishment of a Marxist-Leninist party, together with all the outward trappings of a communist state. Yet in origin these were probably little more than 'an attempt at political differentiation'[21] and popular legitimation, in the manner deemed most appropriate in a Brazzaville youth culture seething with revolutionary ardour, by a usurper (Ngouabi) popular in the army but conscious of his suspect northern (Kouyou) ethnic credentials in a country dominated by southerners (Bakongo).

Ngouabi's rise to power had nothing whatsoever to do with a desire to further Marxism, socialism or the Congolese revolution, although some civilian and military elements supported his takeover, seeing in him a vehicle for their own advancement (having been excluded from Massemba-Debat's cabinet) or for the more rapid radicalization of society. Ngouabi was dragged reluctantly into the centre of the political stage for personal reasons (there had been two attempts to purge him, including one for his refusal to allow political indoctrination in the army), and out of a corporate sense of outrage at the unruly paramilitary's arrogation of the role of defender of the revolution; his Marxism was quite evidently a self-taught *ex post facto* evolution.[22] The declaration of a people's republic was the only wild card left within a highly volatile Brazzaville on the brink of total anarchy. It immediately outflanked on the left a host of fiery aspirants to power, each mobilizing youth gangs by radical rhetoric and the espousal of millennial dreams, in an effort to build stepping-stones to power. In due time Ngouabi mastered the jargon of the revolution and learned to change course when necessary with the prevailing currents. Constantly balancing conflicting ideological pressures, liquidating any of them when they appeared over-threatening, he projected the image of an orthodox Marxist founding father, while in reality holding a very moderate centrist position. Marxist-Leninist rhetoric regarding the supremacy of the party over other structures notwithstanding, power in Congo has stemmed from the barrel of the gun since 1968. Although Sassou Nguesso's penchant for Paris-designed suits is in stark contrast with Ngouabi's military fatigues (at times adorned with pistol and loaded grenades), both gave no quarter to civilian politicians. In every one of Congo's purges (and there have been several, including two massive ones), it has always been the *military* head of state who has purged the Central Committee, Politburo and party of those deemed unreliable from his personal vantage point.

Indeed, Ngouabi, the father of Congolese-African Marxism, the subject of a massive personality cult since his still mystery-shrouded assassination in 1977 at the hands of his immediate political heirs,[23] insisted on personal loyalty above socialist rectitude *or even commitment.* His main props of power, in descending order of importance, were: (a) his 'personal' command, the First (Brazzaville) Paracommando Regiment (composed primarily of his ethnic kinsmen), that had twice rescued him from Massemba-Debat's clutches; (b) a number of fundamentally apolitical key military officers, both northerners and southerners (although in the latter case overwhelmingly of 'peripheral' origin),[24] their personal loyalty cemented by self-interest and Ngouabi's charisma; (c) leftist civilian politicians hoping by weight of numbers and manipulations of Marxist dialectical orthodoxy to prise power from the smaller and less intellectually-minded military component of Congo's Marxist-Leninist party – only to discover the personal nature of power in Congo, and Ngouabi's deviationism on the issue of party supremacy over the army; and (d) youth in general, supportive of all revolutionary rhetoric; (nevertheless, after the JMNR was physically crushed youth became more immersed in bread-and-butter issues).

The 'political rage' of the Congolese lumpenproletariat that triggered the Brazzaville experiment in scientific socialism was the product of a set of socio-economic circumstances virtually unique to equatorial Africa, and to the Congo more particularly. For, at the root of Congo's early radicalization, its bitter internecine strife and intense volatility, lie the sharp ethnic polarization of the country, the particularly brutal exploitation of the colonial era and the aspirations of its highly urbanized population that simply cannot be fulfilled by the relatively weak state. The present net effect of these socio-economic processes is to impose powerful constraints upon *any* policy of inducing socio-economic change in the Congo, and this outweighs constraints deriving from political divisions and those stemming from the hostile international environment.[25]

These 'internal constraints' on change produce tensions in the relatively sophisticated and proud Congolese society. Exacerbated by the frustrations of youth at its all-too-obvious impotence in consummating the 1963 revolution, and fanned by revolutionary strivings and the psychological need for a meaningful global role, these tensions encouraged the emergence, and fuelled the progressive growth, of a divergence between rhetoric and reality in Brazzaville. For, as Erny has pointed out, Congolese youth had developed 'a culture of the word, in which spoken words seemed all-powerful.... The management of words ... was regarded as the key to the social drama in which they were all involved'.[26] This capacity for self-delusion is not dissimilar to that noted by other scholars in other cultures and other regions.[27] In post-revolutionary Congo such a culture has resulted in greater concern with words and intentions than deeds and actions; reification of semantic sophistry; pre-occupation with the more easily 'attainable' (but in itself meaningless and superficial) cosmetic change, and the minutiae of 'revolutionizing' structures. Since the socio-economic order is much more resilient to change, and possibly beyond the capacity of the polity to transform, it presents an unpalatable context that must be camouflaged by structural changes and ideological rhetoric. These paper over inconsistencies and at least signify the adoption of ideologically and historically 'correct' postures, intentions and revolutionary ardour. The consequence, however, is the harsh judgement of Marxist and non-Marxist observers alike that 'the Congolese revolutionaries have primarily made a verbal revolution, a salon revolution'.[28]

Congolese Social Dynamics

Major demographic dislocations accompanied the French conquest, exploitation and subsequent opening of the Moyen Congo. French Equatorial Africa, and Congo in particular, had been the core sphere of operations of the concessionary companies[29] and their brutal excesses that left indelible social and psychological scars. The comparatively large forced labour needs of the Congo-Ocean railway – for the construction of which 25 per cent of the Congo's adult population was harnessed, together with manpower from as far away as the Sara savannah lands of Chad – further pulverized traditional norms, and sparked both the proletarianization of labour and what was to become a massive rural–urban drift. Moreover, the calibre of colonial personnel dispatched to the Congo, as one of the least desirable of France's overseas postings, ensured the continuation, even after the abolition of the concessionary company itself, of the same exploitation, colonial neglect, abuse and misrule, and the piling-up of anti-French resentment.[30] Later, for much the same reasons, the exploitative mentality of the lower-class expatriate petite bourgeoisie, attracted by a life in the dense, humid and malarial tropical forests, further augured ill for the evolution of smooth race relations.

The French intrusion had also disturbed the fluid population dynamics in the Congo basin region, adding new dimensions to the ethnic tug-of-war. The designation of Brazzaville as the federal capital of French Equatorial Africa further exacerbated some of these trends by elevating the public role of the southern and coastal populations. And later, after the break-up of the colonial federation, it gave Brazzaville a cosmopolitan ethos, a physical infrastructure and civil service hardly in tune with the modest needs of a small tropical mini-state. The complex Prospero–Caliban,[31] love–hate, emulation–rejection relationship with the metropolitan power that sprang out of some of these counter-pressures produced the atavistic or syncretic (sometimes both) anti-colonial cults so visible in the Congo basin; and it was later to be the nourishing soil for more modernist ideologies of rejection.

At the same time, the uneven pattern of colonial penetration and interaction with the indigenous ethnic groups in the area resulted in their differential levels of socio-economic development. This tended to reinforce existing cleavages and historic hostilities with roots in pre-colonial conflict and the slave-trading era during which each group had played a different role.[32] The fundamental split was along the north–south socio-cultural axis, artificially (according to the Marxist view)[33] pitching the more advanced, educated, Christianized southern populations (primarily the Bakongo, of which the Lari were the main clan) against the Mbochi and other tiny ethnic groups in the north,[34] and bringing the southerners into conflict among themselves as well. Intensified by the crass ethnic favouritism of the Lari-Bakongo administration of Youlou[35] and aggravated by sharp competition for scarce resources,[36] the ethnic and regional cleavage became the most distinctive feature of modern Congo. Ethnicity, only indirectly intertwined with ideology, is the key to Congolese politics.[37] 'Notwithstanding the attempts over a decade or more of Marxist-minded leadership to replace tribal with other loyalties',[38] ethnic considerations and 'tribal equations, as much as Marxist dialectics, played the role of historical motor of the Congolese Revolution'.[39]

The ethnic cleavage was greatly sharpened by prevailing conditions of economic scarcity. In 1969, seeking to find reason and logic in the chaotic struggle for power that had engulfed Congo, *Le Monde* suggested that the intense civil–military and radical–conservative political struggle was in essence nothing more than a clash over patronage, and specifically over the control of the allocation of jobs in the public sector. That particular issue of *Le Monde*, having hit too close to home, was promptly banned from the streets of Brazzaville.[40] The rather mundane reconceptualization of what had officially been rationalized as a lofty struggle over socialist rectitude would not go away, however. Modified, rephrased and refined over the years, it has periodically resurfaced, as observers have identified ideological divisions camouflaging a simple struggle for patronage.

The demographic facts of Congo throw considerable light on the evolution of this dimension. Resulting from 'one of the most spectacular rural exodus problems in the whole of sub-Saharan Africa', arising out of the historical processes noted above, Congo's population of just under two million (double its 1965 estimate) is 'urbanized to an alarming degree' (80 per cent), with the capital, Brazzaville, and the main port, Pointe Noire, alone accounting for 50 per cent of the total.[41] Astonishingly, there were, according to one source, fewer than 100,000 men of working age in the entire countryside, a fact that necessitated the harvesting of the country's 1984 coffee crop with the assistance of military manpower.[42] Since the rural sector is small and utilizes only three per cent of the land, it cannot produce sufficient staple crops to feed the large masses in the ever-growing urban centres. Hence Congo currently imports over 70 per cent of its foodstuff needs at the staggering cost of 80,000 million francs CFA (nearly double its food bill of 1980), even as it faces an equally monumental fiscal burden stemming from the need to provide the bloated urban population with modern services and with employment. The magnitude of these problems – and the absurdities that they create – is dramatically illustrated by the fact that in 1975 the government's payroll of 1,700 rural agricultural agents (of whom some 30 per cent actually resided in the cities) was *higher than the total gross product of the entire agrarian sector* they were supposed to revitalize![43]

Congo's population, moreover, is extremely youthful and among the continent's best-educated: in this the Congolese example invites comparison with the People's Republic of Benin.[44] Yet, despite the potentially dynamic developmental role that youth could have played, it has been one of the main destabilizing elements in the country, and the main drag on the economy. Roughly 60 per cent of the population is below the age of 16, giving Congo much of its distinctive youth culture and political volatility, while levels of scholarization, reaching 92 per cent, explain its ideological sophistication.

Youth played a central role in the riots and demonstrations that toppled Youlou in 1963; it later formed a quasi-anarchic 'Maoist' left opposition to Massemba-Debat, hastening his demise. Youth was likewise Ngouabi's major sparring partner and political nemesis, both at the outset, when organized as the highly threatening, role-expansionist JMNR formations and, later, when youth rallied behind a multitude of destabilizing causes and demonstrations. Yhomby-Opango assumed power after Ngouabi's assassination in a surprisingly orderly succession following rules of military seniority, and although he proved in general to be quite maladroit, it was the early vocal sniping from youth about his 'false revolutionary attitude' and hedonistic living 'like a capitalist in his luxurious villa ...'[45] that finally eroded his iron grip over the country. The current presidency of Sassou Nguesso, much more managerial in style, has likewise not been immune from confrontations with youth, although it has been greatly stabilized by increased patronage consequent upon the gush of petro-dollars into the country.

Despite the constant opposition of youth to every government that has come to power in Brazzaville, it has nevertheless been the final constituency in the country, courted by all leaders, who have hence tried to cater to its needs, as the group to whom they are ultimately accountable.[46] With the educational network constantly churning out ever larger numbers of utterly unemployable graduates, the rural−urban exodus increasingly concentrating them in urban areas, and confronting a scarcity of jobs in the private sector,[47] all governments have faced inexorable pressures to expand the public payroll and provide at least some jobs for the urban unemployed.[48]

A decade ago, Ngouabi drew attention to the fundamental dilemma in Congolese education that created overwhelming constraints on the Congolese economy, restricting public policy choices and imposing severe limits on the pace of any radicalization that might be possible in the future. Lamenting the fact that 'more than half the school-age population is unqualified and destined for unemployment', Ngouabi warned that 'if the current situation is not radically transformed, the neo-colonial schools will produce in 1985 more than 400,000 new unemployed'.[49] Although unemployment and the competition for jobs remain extremely serious problems in Brazzaville, Ngouabi could not have foreseen the sharp economic boom that visited Congo, and the even sharper upswing in public revenues (from oil royalties) that greatly stabilized subsequent administrations.[50] For 'inevitably it is the state which has to employ the educated youth that are disgorged by the country's education system into the urban employment market'.[51]

Sassou Nguesso's prime preoccupation in office today − only slightly different from that of all previous administrations − remains the 'recurrent trauma'[52] of perpetually juggling public finances to meet pressing and impossible payroll deadlines; seducing private capital into the country by assuring investors that official state rhetoric is irrelevant; satisfying the voracious needs of the urban masses, youth and the armed forces for jobs, services and sinecures; and warding off civil, military, personalist, ethnic, leftist and reactionary assaults on his authority − all while protecting an image of orthodoxy internally and in the communist world, and one of pragmatic

socialism externally in the capitalist world. Ideological preoccupations are not
central to Sassou Nguesso's agenda, except as a means, a tool, for the attainment of the more critical goals mentioned above, just as they have not been
central to the concerns of any previous Congolese leader. One could even argue
that the magnitude and urgency of the constraints stemming from Congo's
particular socio-demographic make-up allow leaders little time for the luxury
of serious preoccupation with ideology.

Economic Constraints on the Revolution

There are a multitude of economic constraints on the radical option in Congo
that have stultified efforts to forge ahead in the direction of a modestly socialist
society.[53] The main constraints stem from the particular socialist order
erected in Brazzaville, and are only secondarily related to the hostile external
environment that inevitably faces every Marxist state. Needless to say, with
the official adoption of 'scientific socialism' foreign investment capital
promptly dried up;[54] only a modest trickle could be attracted to the simmer-
ing social atmosphere of the Congo, despite a liberal investment code and
internationally binding guarantees against nationalization, made by both
Congo and France. On the other hand, foreign capital had not flowed into
the country under Youlou either, despite Congo's substantial natural resources.
It was essentially only after the discovery of exploitable oil-shales that Congo
began to appear slightly more attractive to investors.

Most of Congo's economic difficulties arose from impossible budgetary
pressures on the economy.[55] Stemming from some of the internal *social* im-
balances noted above, these fiscal demands cannot be shunted aside, trimmed
or ignored, as Youlou was to discover in 1963. They impose a severe drain
on both internal and external sources of revenue; they preclude consistent
investment and development (even after oil revenues started gushing in); they
perpetuate Congo's dependency upon outside sources of finance and largesse;
and they ensure that the country has to run fast simply to stand still.

The budgetary allocations to individual sectors directly reflect some of these
social pressures for a slice of the national pie. Massive fiscal allocations are
necessary just to quench some of the needs of Congo's upwardly mobile,
urbanized population. Nearly 55 per cent of the oil-rich budget[56] goes
towards meeting a constantly expanding national payroll, with an emphasis
on including northerners demanding their place in the northern-dominated
sun. Reflecting the two main constituencies in Congo, over 33 per cent of
personnel costs are in the area of *education*, with 21 per cent allocated to the
defence forces; by contrast, the budgetary allocation for health and social
affairs personnel consumed less than 7.3 per cent of the 1979 budget.[57] Apart
from these ever-increasing payroll drains, there is a veritable 'siege' on the
budget from the side of the party ideologues, demanding the expansion of
Congo's public sector *at all costs* (i.e., even if projects are intrinsically unviable or would lead to a budget deficit, or both); and there is phenomenal
wastage of resources resulting from widespread corruption and plunder
of the state sector by quasi-autonomous, fiscally unaccountable public

hierarchies, headed by a Marxist-Leninist party leadership as tainted as the rest of society.

The civil service and parastatal sector are often viewed as prime sources of patronage in the Third World.[58] Indeed, whatever the objective merits of a public sector, economists tend to agree that in practice it rarely performs any significant *economic* functions in Third World countries.[59] In a like manner, whatever valid arguments may be made for an expansion of the skeleton administrative network inherited from colonial days, certainly the end result is often an over-staffed, inefficient, little supervised and overwhelmingly urban hierarchy that does not in reality enhance state control or promote the better administration of state services in the countryside. And the progressive expansion of what are in essence wasteful, non-productive and corrupt sectors of society usually acquires an indelible leitmotif of its own. Despite its imposition of massive drains on scarce resources that have brought African economies to their knees while destabilizing administrations, it has in many cases proved impossible to reduce the size of the civil service and to impose accountability and fiscal restraints on the state sector.[60] Indeed, in no other domain are the weak administrative, regulative and coercive capabilities of African states more poignantly visible than in the spectacle of a government unable to enforce its own freezes on hiring, its own recruitment policies, its budgetary cuts and accountability procedures.

In Third World Marxist systems, especially in Africa, bureaucratic aggrandizement is also perceived as the process of establishing tighter control over a society still beset by class divisions, internal inconsistencies and vestiges of neo-colonialism, and in need of firm leadership and ideological re-education – all part of the eventual transformation into an integrated command economy. The erection and expansion of a public sector is likewise central to the concept of an economic 'engine of the revolution' that will serve as the vital national core of the budding socialist economy and provide the drive, the catalyst and the profits for a further socialization of the means of production. Thus, beyond motivations of economic nationalism, state enterprises and expanding central bureaucracies enjoy a built-in legitimacy that is resilient in the face of challenges based on economic arguments and immune to considerations of cost effectiveness, these being seen as 'capitalist' criteria.

In the case of the Congo, the slow nationalization of the economy and the establishment of new para-state enterprises resulted in a mushrooming public sector. A number of new industrial ventures were set up with the aid of public funds and technical assistance from the communist countries, and a number of French companies were nationalized. But the core of the state sector developed around marketing and purchasing monopolies, the public utilities, financial services (banking, insurance and reinsurance), and small-scale cottage industry. Nevertheless, notwithstanding the large *number* of state companies in existence by 1980, the most important and profitable enterprises and the most sensitive areas of the economy have always remained immune from state interference; nationalization has largely been reserved for the marginal or ailing sectors, or companies about to be abandoned by private capital as no longer profitable.

It was, for example, the beleaguered sugar industry that was taken over (to collapse financially under state mismanagement), rather than the more profitable timber sector, thoroughly dominated by arrogant expatriate interests; the bankrupt Hollé potash mines were nationalized – not the highly lucrative oil-fields. The background to the Hollé nationalizations is instructive. From their inception, the potash mines (among the largest in the world) were plagued with problems, and failed to meet their economic break-even point. With an apparent global glut and depressed producer prices, the Hollé mines were about to be abandoned by their French owners when severe flooding made their expensive rehabilitation and operation even more absurd economically. Despite the huge reconstruction costs and unprofitable operation, the mines were taken over by the state.[61] On the other hand, the oil companies have been virtually unaffected by the existence of a people's republic in power in Brazzaville, even though their royalties genuinely sustain the radical option in Congo – royalties that could be marginally increased to achieve more for Congolese Marxism than any other act of economic nationalism. Petroleum continues to be pumped out of Congo's offshore deposits on conditions more favourable to the European consortiums[62] than similar ventures in liberal, market-economy African states that need not pay a premium to compensate international capital for the risk of investing in a 'Marxist' economy.

The more lucrative segments of the Congolese economy still remain solidly in expatriate French hands: their increased presence and numbers since independence (now 10,000-plus) belie contentions of a partial break-out from neo-colonial bondage, even as they disenchant youth over the prospects of ever attaining meaningful change. Foreign capital is still avidly courted, and seemingly at all costs. These and other inconsistencies in Brazzaville, where over 60 per cent of the economy remains in expatriate commercial and manufacturing hands, have prompted the derisory reference to Congo's developmental approach as 'Marxist-capitalist'.[63]

Revolutionary ardour untempered by rudimentary economic planning or fundamental considerations of profitability; policy inconsistencies stemming from irreconcilable contradictory pressures; and, above all, social unrest over the bleak employment prospects and agitation for 'Socialism Now' – all these factors eventually produced a large, fiscally unaccountable, uncontrollable and bankrupt Congolese socialist sector: a sector 'badly thought out, badly organized, overstaffed, unproductive and budget-devouring', in which 'laziness and theft ... are the rule', to quote Sassou Nguesso's harsh verdict on the product of 14 years of Congolese investment in state enterprises.[64] Again in the words of the Congolese leadership itself, the state sector is characterized by 'lack of vigour and indiscipline', resulting in 'collective impotence'[65] and 'corruption and embezzlement ... reaching disquieting proportions ... allied with the apathy of administrators and imperialism'.[66] Suffused by a conservative ethos, merely 'a simple extension of the civil service',[67] this sector is hardly the core of the economic revolution but a pool of lucrative jobs and sinecures.

The economic cost of setting up such a socialist 'engine of the revolution' was high. The quintupling of the number of public enterprises in the country, and the rapid expansion of the civil service since independence, increased the number of state employees by 650 per cent between 1960 and 1972. Their number further doubled in the next decade, reaching the awesome figure of 62,000 in 1985,[68] in a population of under two million. Public spending inevitably tripled between 1974 and 1980 alone.[69] And since only a fifth of the state enterprises are economically viable at the best of times, rather than pulling their weight they have been a constant financial drag while exerting other negative side-effects as well. Inflationary pressures, higher consumer prices and annual deficits have resulted, for example, from increased mark-ups in public sector manufacturing enterprises in the wake of unscheduled cost over-runs, corruption and inefficiency. Conversely, poor fiscal accountability and other malpractices have resulted in reduced local producer prices paid by state purchasing agencies, thereby encouraging the large-scale smuggling of badly needed indigenous staple crops to neighbouring Cameroon and Gabon.

However, even though the problems of the state sector have been well identified, the regime in Brazzaville has been powerless to exert pressure to correct the situation. Callaghy has noted that 'in general African states are authoritarian, highly personalistic structures that have territorially extensive but relatively limited penetrative, administrative and coercive capabilities'.[70] In Congo the government remains captive to the very monster it created, which requires progressively larger subsidies for the losses it inevitably returns. With the state's fiscal resources tapped to the utmost, and its future manoeuvrability compromised in advance, Congo is constantly engaged in rescuing existing defaulting enterprises, rather than building reserves for the creation of the new enterprises of the future. And in the light of the tight labour market, even were the party ideologues to agree, and were they able to enforce a partial contraction of either the public sector or the civil service, such actions would be extremely destabilizing.[71]

In any case, the party militants have never been willing even to consider such ideological heresies, since these in essence signify a retrograde step from the Marxist vision of control over all the means of production, and a roll-back of labour's hard-fought advances since the days of Youlou's rule. Furthermore (and of political relevance), any such action would contract the pool of patronage and sinecure posts upon which the power base of the Marxist leadership rests. Not surprisingly, then, the sharpest battles in the National Assembly and the Central Committee of the party have been over the future of the public sector, with no regime able to impose its will for a partial contraction, and forced instead to adjust budget allocations to cover ever-increasing deficits.[72]

A few state enterprises have indeed been closed down, but only when their losses became truly impossible to sustain or their foreign sponsors grew unwilling to continue operating subsidies: such was the case with the originally much lauded textile and cement plants built in the late 1960s with funds from the communist countries. In difficulties from their inauguration, since they produced poor-quality, high-cost products for which there was little demand (for example, textiles for Mao-style tunics in a style-conscious Brazzaville), the two plants were hopelessly bankrupt by the early 1970s, and were reluctantly allowed to close down in 1979. Those deficit-producing enterprises that were closed were in a minority, however, and the vast majority of Congo's state sector enterprises continue to amass losses. The state's timber industry is just one of many cogent examples: producing barely eight per cent of the country's lumber, in competition with French private consortia, the state company employed in 1978 the same number of workers as in the 1960s, and at much higher wages, although producing only half as many logs and passing on to the state twice its original deficit.[73] And although the company has its own processing and manufacturing equipment and plant, it has arrangements with the more powerful private French companies in export and marketing (where the real profits lie) that turn it into little more than a pretentious and costly subcontractor of labour.

The outcome of a detailed examination of the state sector in 1979 is highly instructive. Reeling under 'generalized disorder' in the public sector that had brought the national economy to its knees,[74] the regime ordered a reassessment of all state companies. Faced with a crippling external debt of over $1,000 million (repayments on which gouge out 40 per cent of the annual budget), a para-state debt to the state treasury of some 11,000 million francs CFA, and an onerous annual subsidy to state enterprises of 4,000 million francs CFA,[75] the PCT Central Committee examined the viability of the (then) 64 state enterprises (a number subsequently increased). The review emphasized that only 14 of the 64 companies were economically viable, even though many more had been established in intrinsically profitable fields. Of those perennial loss-makers, 36 companies were nevertheless viewed as meritorious and 'worth saving' through further subsidies. Of the 14 deficit companies judged without any redeeming merits, ultimately only *one* was closed down, and even it, although it disappeared structurally, merely had its money-losing activities merged with those of another company.[76]

The 1979 reassessment did, however, bring about the ideologically abhorrent decision to 'recolonize' the public sector in order to eradicate the 'organized bungling'[77] of the past. Previous attempts to impose order and fiscal accountability had made use of military officers in supervisory posts in the public sector – an experiment that transformed the army into a 'sink of corruption'[78] – or a Ministry of State Enterprises whose efforts to control the state sector had merely illustrated the 'collective impotence' of the state apparatus.[79] Many expatriate managerial staff were subsequently invited to assume their old local positions, since the conclusion was inescapable that Congolese technocrats could not withstand either financial temptations or pressures from their workers for better salaries, fringe benefits and reduced work loads. Such powerful pressures on party, state and public enterprises had yielded to Congolese labour (according to ILO calculations) an increase in real minimum wages of 75.5 per cent between 1963 and 1974, an increase second only to Libya's in the entire continent.[80]

Conclusions

The socio-economic constraints on radical military rule in the Congo are thus numerous and varied: the impotence of the Marxist state to establish or control economic priorities and restrain budgetary excesses; residual ethnic tensions that produce strife, division, instability and nepotism; the rather acute demographic profile of the society that seriously aggravates all other pressures; the irrelevance to many of their country's Marxist structures and ideology; the minuteness of the Marxist-Leninist party, and its sharp internal divisions along civil–military, radical–conservative and ethnic and regional lines; the external fiscal constraints on the radical option; and the obvious difficulties faced by small modernizing polities in their efforts to shake off neo-colonial dependency relationships.

In the case of the Congo, however, pride of place among the constraints must ultimately be assigned to its oversized and wasteful public sector and civil service. For their expansion quite manifestly ensures – whatever the effect of other constraints – that the state and its leaders are drained of opportunities for fiscal manoeuvre and robbed of viable options for the future. By sustaining a public sector and an expanding civil service that devours state funds faster than they are generated, governments in Brazzaville preside over what is in essence a never-ending fiscal crisis, a continuing 'financial strangulation which daily threatens the country with bankruptcy'.[81] The degree to which even monumental fiscal bonanzas can be devoured by the needs of the Brazzaville urban bourgeoisie is attested to by the fact that, despite an increase in state revenues of 600 per cent since the acquisition of income from oil, expenditures have more than kept pace with state royalties, and the state remains as close to the brink of financial collapse today as before the royalties began to flow in.

More importantly, however, saddled with such burdens and preoccupations, the government cannot but become mortgaged to the dictates of outside interests, entrepreneurs, international consortiums and pressure groups. Its freedom of choice is limited by its acute fiscal straits; its neo-colonial dependency status is enhanced, rather than diminished, by its own socialist sector. As Young has so aptly summed up the position, in the Congo the 'overdeveloped state itself has proved to be an engine of dependency, not of socialism, much less of development'.[82] Herein may lie the ultimate paradox in a country replete with paradoxes.

NOTES

Samuel Decalo is Professor of African Government in the University of Natal, Durban, South Africa.

1. See Emmanuel Terray, 'Les révolutions congolaise et dahoméenne', *Revue française de science politique*, Oct. 1964; also F. Constantin, 'Fulbert Youlou, 1917–1972', *Revue française d'études politiques africaines*, June 1972; Ronald Matthews, *African Powder Keg* (London: Bodley Head, 1966), Ch. 4; and Philippe Decraene, 'Huit années d'histoire congolaise, ou l'irrésistible ascension des militaires à Brazzaville', *Revue française d'études politiques africaines*, Dec. 1974.

2. *Afrique nouvelle* (Dakar), 10 April 1979.
3. 'He is known to have personal tastes that bear little resemblance to socialist ideals': *West Africa*, 21 Aug. 1978; these reportedly included villas for himself and several mistresses, a private health clinic, a personal zoo of rare animals, and an 80,000-dollar gold vibrating bed. Funds for these were diverted from, *inter alia*, a 400-million CFAF Algerian donation for a water tower: see *West Africa*, 9 April 1979.
4. Arthur H. House, 'Brazzaville: Revolution or Rhetoric?', *Africa Report*, April 1971; Gilbert Comte, 'Le socialisme de la parole', *Le Monde hebdomadiare*, 26 March – 1 April 1970; 'Brazzaville Looks Back 100 Years', *West Africa*, 6 Oct. 1980; 'Brazzaville: Ten Years of Revolution', *West Africa*, 13 Aug. and 20 Aug. 1973 (two parts); and Dominique Desjeux, 'Congo: est-il situationiste?', *Revue française d'études politiques africaines*, June 1980. See also Immanuel Wallerstein, 'Left and Right in Africa', *Journal of Modern African Studies*, May 1971, and 'Left, Right and Centre', *West Africa*, 27 June 1977.
   Of the first three presidents, two were killed and one was purged.
5. 'Revolutionary Rhetoric and Army Cliques in Congo/Brazzaville', in Samuel Decalo, *Coups and Army Rule in Africa: Studies in Military Style* (New Haven, CT: Yale University Press, 1976).
6. David Lamb, 'Congo Finds it Can't Exist on Marxism', *Los Angeles Times*, 20 July 1977.
7. Fulbert Youlou's meteoric rise to power came through his capture of the 'Matsouanist' electoral vote by consciously emulating the latter's style and martyrdom: see the discussion of Matsouanism in Martial Sinda, *Le messianisme congolais* (Paris: Payot, 1972), and Decalo, *Coups and Army Rule ...*, pp. 136–8. For further literature on the prevalence of these cults in the Congo basin, see E. Andersson, *Messianic Popular Movements in the Lower Congo* (New York: W. S. Heinman, 1958); E. Andersson, *Churches at the Grass Roots: A Study in Congo-Brazzaville* (London: Lutterworth, 1968); Etienne Bazola, 'Le Kimbanguisme', *Cahiers des religions africaines* (Kinshasa), July 1968; H. W. Feheran, 'Kimbanguism: Prophetic Christianity in the Congo', *Practical Anthropology*, July–Aug. 1962; John M. Janzen, 'Kongo Religious Renewal: Iconoclastic and Iconorthostic', *Canadian Journal of African Studies*, Spring 1971. See also Georges Balandier, *The Sociology of Black Africa: Social Dynamics in Central Africa* (New York: Praeger, 1970).
8. Hardly the backbone of a revolution: see David Lamb, op. cit.; also 'Congo: plus ça change', *Africa*, No. 78, Feb. 1978; and *West Africa*, 17 Nov. 1975.
9. Jonathan C. Randall, 'Sudden Death, New Hope in Africa', *Washington Post*, 17 July 1977.
10. Interview at the American Embassy in Kinshasa, Zaire, July 1971.
11. Crawford Young, *Ideology and Development in Africa* (New Haven, CT: Yale University Press, 1982), p. 33.
12. Decalo, *Coups and Army Rule ...*, p. 123.
13. *Afrique nouvelle*, 10 April 1979.
14. As, for example, during Propaganda Commissar Ange Diawara's attempted putsch, which was compared to similar struggles elsewhere: 'Who would have thought that Lin Piao would disappear from circulation? Or that Trotsky would betray Lenin's ideas? The socialist path is long, tortuous and full of pitfalls': cited in Colin Legum (ed.), *Africa Contemporary Record, 1972–3* (London: Rex Collings, 1973), p. B534.
15. David and Martha Ottaway, *Afrocommunism* (New York: Africana Publishing company, 1981), p. 107.
16. 'Brazzaville: Ten Years of Revolution', part 2.
17. Colin Legum (ed.), *Africa Contemporary Record, 1969–70* (London: Rex Collings, 1970), p. B419.
18. Kenneth Jowitt, 'Scientific Socialist Regimes in Africa: Political Differentiation, Avoidance, and Awareness', in Carl B. Rosberg and Thomas Callaghy (eds.), *Socialism in Subsaharan Africa* (Berkeley, CA: University of California Institute of International Studies, 1979), p. 148.
19. See Decalo, *Coups and Army Rule ...*, pp. 144–5.
20. For the JMNR, see Pierre Bonnafé, 'Une classe d'âge politique: la JMNR de la République du Congo-Brazzaville', *Cahiers d'études africaines*, Vol. 31, No. 3 (1968). When criticized in 1967 for not proceeding with the socialization of the economy, Massemba-Debat bitterly retorted, 'There is *nothing* to nationalize in the country': see *Afrique nouvelle*, 26 April 1967.
21. Jowitt, in Rosberg and Callaghy, p. 136.

22. Some of his more unorthodox pronouncements were not included in his 'Collected Speeches', however: see Marien Ngouabi, *Vers la construction d'une société socialiste en Afrique* (Paris: Présence africaine, 1975).

23. See, for example, Jonathan Randall, 'Sudden Death, New Hope in Africa', *The Washington Post*, 17 July 1977; and Howard Schissel, 'Congo: Politics, Parties and Presidents', *West Africa*, 8 Aug. 1983, p. 1814. Schissel bases himself, *inter alia*, on the conclusions of *Le Monde*'s very knowledgeable correspondent in Dakar, Pierre Biarnes, as contained in his book *Afrique aux Africains*.

24. For example, Captain Raoul, Ngouabi's long-serving lieutenant, was a well-known conservative, pro-French, bon vivant southerner, raised outside Congo in Cabinda, Angola; Colonel Yhombi-Opango, whose loyalty saved Ngouabi from the dangerous Diawara putsch, was a southerner (Lari), born and raised in the capital of the north, Fort Rousset. For a good source of biographical and other data on the Congo, see Virginia Thompson and Richard Adloff, *Historical Dictionary of the People's Republic of the Congo*, 2nd edn. (Metuchen, NJ: Scarecrow Press, 1984).

25. The *political* constraints, which will not be further outlined here, concern factors such as the civil—military conflict, the particularly fragmented leadership and its bourgeois class origin, the context of praetorianism, and the extremely small size of the party that is continually cut back to the bone by purges. For more detail on these, see Decalo, *Coups and Army Rule* ..., Ch. 4.

26. Paul Erny, 'Parole et travail chez les jeunes d'Afrique Centrale', *Projet*, Sept.–Oct. 1966; see also Erny, 'The White Man as Seen through the Eyes of Congolese (Brazzaville) Children', in Joint Publications Research Service, *Translations on Africa*, No. 475 (1966), translated from the original in *Psychologie des peuples*, July–Sept. 1966.

27. See, for example, R. Harkaby, 'Basic Factors in the Arab Collapse During the Six-Day War', *Orbis*, Vol. 11, No. 3 (1967).

28. Lesjeux, op. cit., p. 27.

29. The classic studies are Cathérine Coquéry-Vidrovitch, *Le Congo au temps des grandes compagnies concessionaires* (Paris: Mouton, 1974), and Samir Amin and Cathérine Coquéry-Vidrovitch, *Histoire économique du Congo, 1800–1968* (Paris: Antropos, 1969). See also Pierre Philippe Rey, *Colonialisme, neo-colonialisme et transition au capitalisme: l'exemple de la 'Comilog' au Congo-Brazzaville* (Paris: Maspéro, 1971), and André Gide, *Voyage au Congo* (Paris: Gallimard, 1927).

30. William B. Cohen, *Rulers of Empire* (Stanford, CA: Hoover Institution Press, 1971).

31. O. Mannoni, *Prospero and Caliban: The Psychology of Colonization* (New York: Praeger, 1956); see also the critique in Albert Memmi, *The Colonized and the Colonizer* (Boston, MA: Beacon Press, 1965), and Franz Fanon, *Black Skins, White Masks* (New York: Grove Press, 1967).

32. See Marcel Soret, *Histoire du Congo Brazzaville* (Paris: Berger-Levrault, 1978); J. M. Wagret, *Histoire et sociologie politique de la République du Congo Brazzaville* (Paris: R. Pichon & Durand-Auzias, 1964); Théophile Obenga, *La cuvette congolaise* (Paris: Présence Africaine, 1976); Hugues Bertrand, *Le Congo* (Paris: Maspéro, 1975); and Woungly-Massaga, *La Révolution au Congo* (Paris: Maspéro, 1974).

33. Joseph Mampouya, *Le tribalisme congolais* (Paris: La Pensée Universelle, 1983).

34. The label 'Mbochi' is often used incorrectly as the generic ethnic term for all the northern groups (including the Kouyou, the actual ethnic group of both Ngouabi and Sassou Nguesso). The true Mbochi comprise fewer than ten per cent of the population (compared with the 45 per cent Bakongo). The north–south ethnic split is sharply visible in the capital itself, where entire quarters are inhabited exclusively by certain groups (for example, the dense 'Mbochi' Lingali-speaking Poto-Poto quarter). In the 1950s and 1960s bitter and very bloody inter-ethnic strife rocked the southern urban centres.

35. Youlou personally was disposed to seeking the national reunification of the Bakonga people, even at the expense of disencumbering himself of the far north (in favour of the Central African Republic).

36. The 'Mbochi', concentrated in the vicinity of Fort Rousset (and not in the practically uninhabited far north), advanced rapidly in socio-economic terms during the last decade of French rule, benefiting from the Lari 'withdrawal' into Matsouanism. Under the 'northern'

administrations of Ngouabi and Sassou Nguesso, the Mbochi entered the administration in large numbers as well, and currently comprise up to 25 per cent of the population of Brazzaville itself.

37. '*Who* the leader of the Congolese revolution is matters as much to us as *what* his specific policies are. Socialism under a *petit nordiste* is simply not socialism to us': interview in Kinshasa, June 1972.

38. Colin Legum (ed.), *Africa Contemporary Record, 1980–81* (London: Rex Collings, 1981), p. B417.

39. Schissel, op. cit., p. 1813.

40. *Le Monde*, 11 Nov. 1969. See also the analysis in J. M. Lee, 'Clan Loyalties and Socialist Doctrine in the People's Republic of Congo', *The World Today*, Jan. 1971, and 'Congo-Brazzaville: East or West', *Africa Confidential*, 21 Jan. 1981.

41. *Africa Research Bulletin*, Economic Series, May 1985, p. 1717. The 1985 census indicated a population of 1.92 million.

42. Ibid.

43. Their number had been increased tenfold between 1963 and 1971: see *West Africa*, 19 May 1976, and Bertrand, op. cit., pp. 188, 256.

44. Samuel Decalo, 'Ideological Rhetoric and Scientific Socialism in Benin and Congo/Brazzaville', in Rosberg and Callaghy (eds.), *Socialism in Subsaharan Africa*.

45. *Jeune Afrique*, 11 March 1972; and *Africa Research Bulletin*, Dec. 1971.

46. *Area Handbook for the People's Republic of the Congo* (Washington, DC: US Government Printing Office, 1971), p. 107.

47. There are about 200 French enterprises, many quite small, operating in Congo; these provide the bulk of the private sector salaried jobs.

48. Entire graduating classes have been 'sent back' for an additional year of studies because of the utter lack of jobs in the country.

49. See Marien Ngouabi, *Vers la construction d'une société socialiste ...*, pp. 74–6. For two fundamental, if by now dated, analyses of unemployment in Brazzaville, see Roland Devauges, *Le chômage à Brazzaville: étude sociologique* (Paris: ORSTOM, 1959); and Michel Croce-Spinelle, *Les enfants du Poto-Poto* (Paris: B. Grasset, 1967).

50. The oil boom (which has by now tapered off, leaving as always major fiscal shortfalls) made Congo one of the fastest-growing economies, and allowed increased governmental largesse and patronage: see Howard Schissel, 'Congo: Debt Problems', *West Africa*, 21 Jan. 1985, p. 101.

51. 'Congo's Economy', *West Africa*, 3 Oct. 1980, p. 2019.

52. Young, op. cit., p. 42.

53. For a recent valuable insight, see Thomas M. Callaghy, 'The Difficulties of Implementing Socialist Strategies of Development in Africa: The First Wave', in Rosberg and Callaghy, *Socialism in Subsaharan Africa*.

54. Public funds from the communist countries (especially China), though modest in quantity, played an important role in the industrialization of Congo before the oil wells came on stream.

55. See Colin Legum (ed.), *Africa Contemporary Record, 1981–2* (London: Rex Collings, 1982), p. 358.

56. At present oil accounts for 90 per cent of exports, and royalties make up 70 per cent of the national budget. As *West Africa* (13 Oct. 1980) pointed out, the utter mismanagement of Congo's economy '[has been] covered up by oil revenue'.

57. *Marchés tropicaux et maritimes*, 16 March 1979.

58. See, *inter alia*, Mary M. Shirley, 'Managing State-Owned Enterprises', *World Bank Staff Working Papers*, No. 583 (Washington, DC: World Bank, 1983).

59. Tony Killick, *The Performance of Public Enterprise* (London: Heinemann, 1981); also *The Role of the Public Sector in the Industrialization of African Developing Countries* (Vienna: UNIDO, 1981).

60. Although a continent-wide phenomenon, the particular travails of Dahomey are instructive: see Samuel Decalo, 'Regionalism, Politics and the Military in Dahomey', *Journal of Developing Areas*, April 1973.

61. At the time, the potash mines had a major symbolic importance in the country – not only had they become one of the largest employers, but also as the first new extractive industry

(in a country replete with mineral deposits) they were seen as the harbinger of Congo's rapid economic transformation: see *Africa Research Bulletin*, Economic Series, June 1978; and *West Africa*, July 1978.

62. A national share capital of 15 per cent, generous amortization terms, and fairly low state royalties.

63. 'Congo: Generalized Disorder', *Africa*, No. 94 (June 1979), and *Africa Research Bulletin*, Jan. 1981.

64. Randall, op. cit. For some examples of mismanagement, see 'Congo: plus ça change', and *Africa Confidential*, 27 Jan. 1977.

65. 'Congo: plus ça change', p. 55.

66. Colin Legum (ed.), *Africa Contemporary Record, 1976–7* (London: Rex Collings, 1977), p. B493. As Legum had earlier put it, 'Weakness of party leadership, lack of liaison between the leadership and the Party and the masses, the irresponsibility of the trade unions, the inflexibility of the State apparatus, the unviability of the State economic sector, the frantic race for material advantages, the excessive number of workers in State enterprises and the incompetence and irresponsibility of cadres ...' are to blame for the chaotic condition of the state sector: Legum, *Africa Contemporary Record, 1975–6*, p. B472.

67. Martin Kakra, 'Waiting for Act Two', *Africa*, No. 99 (Nov. 1979).

68. From 3,300 in 1960 to 21,000 in 1972: Legum, *Africa Contemporary Record, 1976–7*, p. B497; see also Bertrand, op. cit., p. 355, and *West Africa*, 19 April 1976.

69. 'Congo's Economy', p. 2019. For further details on the Congolese economy, see *Marchés tropicaux et méditerranéens*, 3 Oct. 1980, and 'Prospects for Congo', *West Africa*, 23 July 1979.

70. Thomas M. Callaghy, in Rosberg and Callaghy, op. cit., p. 116.

71. Schissel, 'Congo: Debt Problems', p. 101. This inability of the government truly to control its own urgan civil service and state sector is reminiscent of Hyden's comment, in a different context and with respect to another country, that 'as long as large numbers of producers are unaffected by state policies, the power of those who rule is largely illusory': see Goran Hyden, *Beyond Ujamaa in Tanzania: Underdevelopment and an Uncaptured Peasantry* (London: Heinemann, 1980), p. 8.

72. The pressure for 'radicalization' (often simplistically equated with expropriation of the means of production) comes in particular from the Congolese Trade Union Confederation (CSC) and the Union of Congolese Socialist Youth (UJSC) and their allies in the PCT Central Committee.

73. The over-ambitious state OCB at times purchases timber from the French private logging companies, later to resell it, unprocessed and to the same French company, for export: see Young, op. cit., p. 38.

74. 'Congo: Generalized Disorder', p. 37.

75. *West Africa*, 8 July 1985.

76. Legum, *Africa Contemporary Record, 1981–2*, p. B358.

77. Manifesting itself in the granting of various fringe benefits, including thirteenth-month bonus pay cheques in state companies in deficit. In 1978, seven managers of state enterprises were jailed for one month for this practice: see *West Africa*, 2 Jan. 1978.

78. *West Africa*, 15 Aug. 1970 and 2 April 1973.

79. 'Congo: plus ça change'.

80. *World Bank Atlas* (Washington, DC: World Bank, 1978), p. 14, as cited in Young, op. cit., p. 38.

81. Bertrand, op. cit., p. 64.

82. Young, op. cit., p. 42. See also Bertrand's similar conclusion, that 'the hold of the bureaucratic and tribal oligarchy is such that, far from constituting for the political leadership an economic instrument permitting them to overcome foreign economic domination ... it [ties] more than ever the hands of those who would like to transform the country through the State structures': Bertrand, op. cit., p. 64, as cited in Young, op. cit., p. 42.

The Rise and 'Thermidorianization' of Radical Praetorianism in Benin

Michel L. Martin

What Karl Marx dubbed, not without contempt, as 'barracks socialism' — radical militarism in other words — has obviously not been a rarity in the political history of the world. However, only recently has such a political-ideological form become a familiar feature — though still liminal in current government taxonomies — of non-Western nations, particularly in the Middle East and Latin America. In the past few years, this phenomenon has also developed in tropical Africa. There, under the mantle of reformism, but especially of Marxism-Leninism and populism, it contrasts with the kind of socio-political organization that had hitherto abounded under martial governance. Among the states affected by this style of military rule, the People's Republic of Benin is one relevant illustration.

Radical Praetorianism: Perspectives and Hypotheses

Before dealing with the specific case of Benin, two preliminary remarks and a terminological observation are in order. It is to avoid unfamiliar, if technologically correct, neologisms that the commonly encountered terms of 'militarism' and above all 'praetorianism' are used hereafter as alternatives to those of 'military rule' or 'military regime'. But they should be taken in a metaphorical sense and not so much as analogues implying historical similarities with past experiences that they serve to define. A more adequate term might have been — though still requiring qualification — 'militocracy' or 'stratocracy'.

This said, let us turn to the first point. There seems to be a *contradictio in adjecto* in the idea of a revolutionary military regime. Conservative and oligarchic, authoritarian and non-mobilizing, such are the only specifications usually associated with military rule. This view, stemming from a tradition of political reasoning shaped by classical liberal as well as by Marxian axioms and pre-conceptions, is also objectively justified by the institutional and functional essence of the military. What is referred to here is the special relation of the military to the state, its bureaucratic and hierarchical character, its specific ethos and *Weltanschauung*, its segregation from the societal network, and the primacy of corporate and professional concerns among its members. These are some of the major features that, coupled with the conspiratorial and usurpatory origins of its accession to power, devoid of any popular impulse, and the subsequent limited interface with the polity, apparently deny to radical praetorianism any claim to genuine revolutionary virtue and

BENIN

Bordered on the north by Burkina Faso and Niger and squeezed between Nigeria and Togo, the People's Republic of Benin, a former French colony (Dahomey) independent since 1 August 1960, constitutes a territory of 112,622 sq.km. The population amounts to nearly four million inhabitants, with an average demographic growth of 28 per 1000, 90 per cent of whom live in the southern part of the country. Although rural to the extent of four-fifths, the population includes an influential urban educated elite. The level of education in Benin is high and the development of the educational system is an important sector of the state's action. The population is sociologically heterogeneous and the familiar north/south-east/south-west triangle is only one aspect of it; each of these regions is itself pluralized since their internal components (Fon, Goun, Nago, Brazilians in the south, Bariba, Gondo, Somba in the north), though coming from a common ethnic stock, have evolved according to divergent historical processes and along different modes of political, cultural and socio-economic organization.

The economy is predominantly rural. Agriculture represents 40 per cent of the GNP and provides 90 per cent of exports. Although diversifying, it still rests essentially on oleaginous products and cotton. In the last few years, agricultural production has declined. Industry accounts for only ten per cent of the GNP. Today the emphasis is an agro-foodstuffs, textiles, chemistry and the exploitation of phosphate and oil. Trade constitutes more than 30 per cent of the GNP, but traditionally shows a deficit; since 1970, the trade deficit of the commercial balance has increased continually and in 1978 the cover rate of imports by exports was less than ten per cent. Despite important problems, the economy of Benin presents positive assets which suggest that the country is destined to play a far from negligible regional role in the future.

disqualify it from participating in the phenomenon of revolution as conventionally accepted.

In the case of so-called Marxist-Leninist military governments, to which Benin belongs, the ambivalence is even more pronounced. To be authentic, at least from the viewpoint of ideological orthodoxy and doctrinal consistency, such regimes must imply not only a preliminary mass upheaval, but also a subsequent context of military subordination to civilian rule. An admission that the armed forces could assume the vanguard role normally reserved to a communist party is exceptional even in a transient manner, since doctrinally such a situation conforms rather to the category of Bonapartism. Classical Marxist thought infers thus a linkage of antagonism between revolution and the military — one which is historically correct, incidentally, only insofar as no revolution has succeeded without the support of the armed forces and that most of the successful ones took place on a background of military disintegration; Katherine Chorley's classic survey amply demonstrates this.

These emerging forms of radical praetorianism have certainly been different from the kind of military rule that has so far developed on the African continent. That said, they appear at best like modern variants of enlightened despotism in the neo-Bismarckian mode, falling rather within the category of 'revolutions from above'.[1] Actually, given, among other things, the particularity of their political economy, they constitute *sui generis* systems. And as such, they should preferably be assessed, if not necessarily analysed, independently of the framework of reference generally used in this domain of inquiry.

A second note needs now to be made. A survey of the literature on political militarism shows clearly that, when the phenomenon is not altogether dismissed as an unclassifiable aberration, a temporary hiatus in an otherwise coherent − and basically civilian − institutional cycle which alone provides the criteria for defining the nature and the level of political development, the emphasis has been on the variety of regimes generated rather than on the nature of military rule as a whole. This tendency was probably unavoidable. The proliferation and the rapid, often interrupted succession of military regimes required some kind of sorting out which meshed with the research habit in comparative analysis of putting a premium on typologies. As a result, a certain inclination to treat military regimes as discrete and static political phenomena amenable to rigid categorizations settled in. Thus, depending upon the chosen frame of reference, conservative, reformist, or radical, veto or moderator, guardian or praetorian, types of regime, and any combination of them and of others, were opposed to each other.

The impression is then conveyed that these systems have had no real dynamic of their own, and that, in a case of multiple coups d'etat and successive governments, each of these is a separate event that could be dealt with more or less independently of previous and subsequent ones. In other words, one is left with the feeling that the primary parent phenomenon of military rule does not amount to more than a collection of singular regimes − a view that hinders any dynamic approach geared toward determining, beyond the immediate discontinuities, patterns of evolution, general uniformities, if not constant laws, in the 'total phenomenon'.

However, the variations between regimes and the distribution of each dominant type across time clearly suggest that they should rather be considered as phases of what could be conceived as the life-history of a praetorianism that began in the mid-1960s; thus radical military regimes can be viewed as one of these phases. Further, given the evidence available, this history is not erratic. The evolution of the political nature of the various regimes, that is the political content of each phase, and the pattern of their succession (for example, the historically recent appearance of radical forms of regimes) implies a cycle whose shape − and this is the underlying hypothesis − evokes what has been described as the 'natural history of revolution'.[2]

Briefly summed up, the political history of African states following independence reveals two distinct types of military intervention. One of them, the first to appear, is generally temporary and reactive: intervention is a matter of holding the ring, or is *arbitral* in nature. The military, generally in the shape of its senior ranks, is dragged into the political arena, rather than taking power on its own initiative: it still acts as the 'objective client' of the state, filling a momentary political vacuum. This kind of militarism was frequent in the late 1960s. The second type of intervention, more common since the mid-1970s, is truly stratocratic in that the army, often through its more politicized middle and junior ranks, decides to invest the state apparatus and to assume itself all political responsibilities. While the first mode conceives itself as a provisional interference in the civilian management of the state, the second implies a militarization of the political system that goes deeper and is not restricted in duration.[3]

Another key dimension of praetorianism is revealed by a more attentive analysis of the organization of military rule itself and its evolution. With only a few exceptions, three phases can be observed. At first, military rule is moderate, apolitical, with a little-differentiated mode of government that pays scant regard to constitutionalism, its official texts being laconically formulated. Military rule here acts as a sort of governing bureaucracy, made up of *ad hoc* organs or structures partially derived from the previous political regime. Power is concentrated in the hands of one man, or of a small group with a *primus inter pares*. This individual or group legislates by ordinance with the co-operation of civilian technocrats under the control of the armed forces. The governmental function is conceived and handled in strictly technical terms. In general, the level of political participation by the governed is reduced to a minimum and there is only a limited concern for change. Then, more or less rapidly, usually following a shift in the leadership structure, in the course of which generally apolitical senior officers are replaced by their politically more militant juniors, the nature of military rule changes. New types of regime emerge, that are politicized, mobilizing and committed to an ideology, more or less radicalized, of social transformation. Patterns of government grow more authoritarian and centralized, but at the same time regimes come to be afflicted by instability. At a certain point, however, more permanent principles of government are laid down, concern for the framing of a new constitution grows, and praetorianism, operating now within a more differentiated political structure, enters a third stage. Characterized by what could be defined as a 'thermidorian' outlook, this phase is marked by a return to stability and greater political realism. The ideology, previously 'situationally transcendental', to use Karl Mannheim's terminology, becomes 'situationally congruent'. Because of the increasing co-operation with the civilian political-administrative elite and the greater interplay with various social forces, the leadership tends to 'de-militarize'. A formal return to civilianized, if not civilian rule, either in a sort of Kemalist manner or simply via the restitution of power to civilians accompanied by a withdrawal to barracks, marks the 'end' of the praetorian life-cycle, in the sense that the emerging system of rule is no longer stratocratic.[4]

If the various political and military manifestations that have occurred in Benin since 1963 are approached in this light, clearly the rise of Colonel Mathieu Kérékou to power after the coup of 26 October 1972 and the political line pursued since 1974 represent the radical phase of military rule in Benin.

It thus constitutes the central issue of the present analysis. That said, however, the vicissitudes of this period cannot be properly treated without at least summary reference to previous moments in the cycle taken as a whole, but more importantly, without examining those subsequent events that obviously reveal a clear ebb in the tide of radicality. In many ways, this later stage is inseparable from the preceding radical one. They relate to one another very much as routinization of charisma relates to pure charisma. The radical element of praetorianism, as of revolution, is, like charisma, too volatile to last and must lead to an institutionalization that in turn affects its nature. The third stage cannot be dissociated from the second one since, though modified in form, it incorporates the principles that emerged in the second phase.

The Pre-Radical Phase of Praetorianism

The first military interventions were undoubtedly of an arbitral nature. In October 1963, then in November and December 1965, the military acted as mediators with the intention of breaking a political deadlock brought about by problems of regionalism and economic disarray.[5] It intervened with the assent, if not the encouragement, of public opinion, but with no expressed intention to stay in power. In other words, militarism was of a reactive nature in general, although personal ambitions, as in the case of the then Colonel Soglo, could not be discounted.

From the institutional point of view, the techniques of military arbitral rule as it occurred in Benin fell into two categories. The first consisted of a superficial interference with the political process. Admittedly, the existing institutional apparatus was dissolved after the abrogation of the constitution currently in force, but it was simply replaced by a new one, more appropriate, elaborated by the civilian politicians themselves. These, moreover, participated in a provisional government that military leaders merely presided over (as after October 1963) or kept alive without actually participating in it (as after November 1965 with the Congacou government). The uniformed rulers showed very little concern for change, seeking only to push for a new constitution and new elections before stepping down from power.

The second form of arbitral government involved a deeper interference with the political system, as was seen after the coup of 22 December 1965. It was a less ephemeral occupation of power than before and it resulted in greater political control arising from the establishment of *ad hoc* structures of government. The military ruled with the peripheral co-operation of civilians and set itself more ambitious and more global political objectives: not only a return to political stability, but also the restoration of economic and social normality. However, the levels of participation and mobilization were very low. Colonel Soglo's government, born from the intervention of December 1965, illustrated such a pattern of arbitral rule.[6]

The coup of 17 December 1967 has no great relevance from the standpoint of institutional change. It could be interpreted simply as a palace affair. The Soglo cabinet proved unable to find adequate solutions to the economic issue, unable also to maintain order, judging from the increasing number of strikes and rising political tension throughout the country. The coup also reflected the fact that cleavages among the military (essentially generational and professional, complicated by ethno-regional tensions) had become conflictual and had prompted the emergence of a group of younger and more politicized officers. The influence of these men had begun to be felt as early as 1966 with the creation of the Military Committee of Vigilance, which acted as a supervisory agency of the government. This trend indicated also the strengthened control of the military over public affairs (the committee was exclusively composed of officers and NCOs), which led to the dissolution of the civilianized Committee of National Renovation elected by representatives of different national interest groups and holding legislative competence in economic and social areas.

Yet the army did not seem to intend to stay in power. A timetable was soon prepared for a return to civilian rule. On the whole, the regime born from the 17 December 1967 coup appears to stand at the point of articulation between the arbitral and the praetorian phases. It also indicates the end of apoliticism and moderate ideological attitudes on the part of the military rulers, prefiguring in some way the subsequent radical turn.

After the electoral fiasco of May 1968 and the annulment of the elections, tensions appeared between partisans of political neutrality (that is, a return to civilian rule) and partisans of a military regime. The agreement that emerged over the candidacy and the five-year presidential mandate of Emile Derlin Zinsou did not relieve these tensions, as was shown by the nascent conflict between Lieutenant-Colonel Alley (favourable to civilian rule) and Major Kouandété who favoured a fully-fledged extension of military rule. The conflict, which reproduced the main factional cleavage in the Dahomeyan armed forces, lasted several months and turned to the advantage of Major Kouandété. Kouandété became chief of staff while Lieutenant-Colonel Alley was arrested and the whole Abomey group purged from the military. The position of the young politicized military faction thus seemed consolidated and Major Kouandété, whose disagreement with President Zinsou had meanwhile become more serious (notably over the status and the autonomy of the armed forces), decided to precipitate things by having the president arrested.

This operation proved premature, however. Not all officers were behind their chief of staff despite his influence, all the more so as he had acted without preliminary consultations with his peers. But the mainstream opposition came from the Fon segment and a few moderate officers who took advantage of Major Kouandété's over-hastiness, and the subsequent hesitations of military opinion, to regain their lost power. Lieutenant-Colonel Alley was then reinstated in his functions with the rank of Colonel, as were Captain Hachémé and Major Chasme. Colonel de Souza was nominated head of the provisional military Directorate which was to rule until new elections could be organized. These collapsed in utter confusion and threats of secession, before a compromise could be reached in the setting up of a rotating presidency and with the Presidential Council being shared by the three perennial regional contenders.

The regime established after the removal of President Zinsou has a peripheral status in the institutional cycle of military rule as analysed here. It was neither arbitral nor praetorian since the military did not remain in power (though had the army been able to agree on one man in its ranks, it might have assumed power for itself). The regime exhibited all the traits of a transitional emergency regime. The Ordinance of 26 December 1968 set up a system in which power was concentrated, semi-institutionalized, resting on a directorate, responsible to the supreme council of the armed forces. The directorate functioned as a cabinet, but it held legislative competence in addition to executive power. The head of the directorate disposed of special powers, but their exercise had to be countersigned by the two other members. A supreme court and an economic council completed this ensemble.

With this intervention, the ascent of Major Kouandété ended. A mere associate member in the directorate, he ironically became, after the military reorganization of July 1970, the deputy of Colonel Alley, nominated General Secretary of National Defence, and lost his post as chief of staff to Colonel de Souza. The plot of February 1972 in which Kouandété was implicated, and for which he had been sentenced to death, definitively ended the political ambitions of this officer (the sentence was commuted and he resigned from the military in 1973). But if the moderates had apparently become influential again, Major Kouandété's aggressive interventionist style gained adherents, especially among the young generations, and it paved the way for the praetorian drift of 1972. The reorganization of the armed forces in 1970 had in the end only a corporate significance, aimed at procuring material gratification for the military elites; it did little to appease internal tensions. The various military plots and mutinies of 1971 and 1972, often bearing political implications, amply demonstrated this. The most serious affair occurred on 26 February 1972 during which Colonel de Souza escaped an attempt on his life. It appeared to be linked to a conspiracy aimed at preventing Joseph Ahomadegbé to succeed Hubert Maga as head of the Presidential Council and probably to allow Major Kouandété to take over; three of the plotters, Captain Glélé, Captain Josué and Lieutenant Kitoy, were close associates of the former chief of staff.[8]

The Rise of Radical Praetorianism

The coup of 26 October 1972, led by Major Mathieu Kérékou, could at first be viewed, given the nature of ethnic and professional loyalties, as another operation undertaken to salvage Kouandété's position. In fact, however, even though he was freed, Kouandété was also forced out of the ranks of the armed forces. Thus, if one considers the ideological motives and orientations of the authors of the coup, especially those of Major Alladaye and Captains Assogba, Badjogoumé, and Aikpé, known for their political militancy, the coup can certainly be seen as an operation of a praetorian kind in the sense that it marked the emergence of the armed forces as an autonomous political force, acting on its own and according to its own political vision. This is perfectly summed up in the claim of Major Koffi (a member of the new 'junta'): 'This time the armed forces have assumed their responsibilities. We do not intend to give up power to anyone ... we must have time to show our abilities.'[9]

I

As suggested above, military rule, viewed as a whole series of differing regimes of martial origin, seems to evolve according to a natural cycle reminiscent of that of revolutions, a moderate phase being followed by a radical period and that in turn leading to a thermidorian change. Considering the personality of its leaders and the nature of its orientations, the regime established after the 26 October coup undoubtedly constitutes the radical phase of military rule in Benin, symbolized by — to use the neologism in fashion in Cotonou during the mid-1970s — the *révolutionnarisation* process. However, the onset of radicalism was not sudden. As if recapitulating the overall natural cycle, the history of the new regime had its own moderate period. Similarly, if we look at the last few years, it has seemed to evolve towards a thermidorian phase.

From October 1972 to early 1974, the regime was not significantly different from the kind of martial rule encountered up to that point, despite perhaps a greater emphasis on ideological rhetoric. From the viewpoint of political organization, it was typical of the semi-institutionalized state of emergency commonly observed under military auspices. Major Kérékou took over the presidency and the direction of the cabinet — the Revolutionary Military Government, composed of 12 officers — with full powers. A committee, the Military Council of the Revolution, comprising 15 officers and NCOs took charge of advising the government and supervising the administration. Besides this powerful militarized executive, an assembly was instituted as a consultative body; it adopted at first the name of National Consultative Committee, becoming the National Council of the Revolution in January 1973. Divided into three commissions and composed of 67 members, a majority of whom were military professionals, it represented the interests of the people and popular sovereignty and was intended to inspire the activities of the government.

As for its orientations, an element of political militancy was evident; nevertheless, although it could be viewed as the framework for later radical changes, the *discours-programme* of 30 November 1972 which defined the new regime's policies on the whole displayed ideological restraint. The dominant themes — corruption, order, national unity and independence, or inter-tribal dissensus and its politicization — did not differ from those of the current military discourse in a classical law and order system. Neither the emphasis on the so-called 'new national independence' nor the denunciation of 'foreign domination' actually embodied a radicalism specific to the regime. Rather, they illustrated an Africa-wide phenomenon, known as 'return to authenticity' — the reacculturation to the historical and cultural self: in this respect, it seems that the new Benin leaders have been influenced by Mobutu's own authenticity doctrine. 'Dahomeyization', more than revolution, would sum up the new orientation immediately following the coup. Standard ideologies of change, socialism and communism in particular, were viewed with distrust as foreign models and rejected.[10]

Although plans for an economic take-over by the state were drafted and there was talk of substituting for dependence on the West, very little changed. Dahomey remained, for example, in the French currency zone and avoided breaking with countries such as France and the United States.

II

The radical nature of the regime began truly revealing itself a year or so after its establishment, and the decisive radical turn in the evolution of Benin military rule occurred in 1974. This change appeared to take place in response to pressures emanating from the most militant sections of society, high school and university students in particular, who were unimpressed by the scope of change; in this regard the role of the United Democratic Front was conspicuous. During the earlier phase the regime seemed limited in its political and ideological claims, and appeared non-participative and non-mobilizing – in other words more caretaker than reformist; however, practically the opposite situation developed afterwards.

The paramount fact was the adoption of Marxism-Leninism as the fundamental tenet of the new regime. In an eight-point speech read on 30 November 1974 at Goho, President Kérékou declared that Benin was to enter on the socialist path of development and that Marxism was to be its guiding philosophy. Concomitantly, mobilization and the penetration of society were systematically organized through the state monopoly of the means of information and education of the citizen. A new educational system was set up: the *école nouvelle* henceforth alone assumed responsibility for education and for preparing youth for professional realities. It operated according to a radically new programme: it was linked to the production cycle and examinations were phased out and replaced by continuous assessment of students. To this programme was added civic, physical and military training; for that purpose a one-year period of national service comprising military, ideological and economic duties was introduced and made compulsory for both men and women. Continuing adult education was also established with the creation of the People's Centre for Education, Training and Initiation in Production. Political and ideological seminars were instituted for educators, magistrates and military professionals. Private associations and youth organizations were regrouped into unified national movements. The mass media passed under the control of the state, which, moreover, created its own instruments of propaganda such as the Voice of the Revolution and the publishing of a new daily, *Ehuzu*. This effort at controlling the socialization of the population had a moral side to it: measures were taken, for example, to reduce the opening hours of cafés and night clubs and to lay down proper codes of social behaviour.

Furthermore, the government enacted a profound transformation of society, embracing both administrative and economic spheres. The administrative reform breaking with the old French-styled system was aimed at granting greater social, economic and cultural autonomy to local units which were to be run by elected bodies and revolutionary committees. Interestingly, the cultural-ethnic geography served to define the new administrative organization. Reversing its earlier stand on regionalism, the regime recognized the multinational character of the country as well as its multilingual structure. The French language was replaced by indigenous tongues. The state moreover took over the direction of the economy through economic planning and moved toward its monopolization by reducing the realm of private (domestic as well as foreign) enterprise. This programme first affected the agricultural sector and primary industrial and commercial businesses; it was then extended to the banking, trade, insurance, transport and entertainment sectors. The state was thus able to control investments and credit while assuming a monopoly over import and export operations. Foreign interests, such as a French tele-communications business and various oil companies, were nationalized; the state actually took over both the sale and transporting of all petroleum products.

Foreign policy also witnessed important changes. It saw itself as a diplomacy of rupture and independence. In fact, though non-alignment was pledged, policy was deliberately oriented toward socialist states – Cuba, Vietnam, China, North Korea and East Germany, with which agreements were made; Benin, moreover, backed the Soviet Union over various issues, such as the intervention in Afghanistan. In Africa, Benin established relations with Libya and Sékou Touré's Guinea. It proclaimed solidarity with progressive states and peoples engaged in the struggle for liberation. Support was expressed for the Angolan MPLA leadership, for SWAPO, the ANC and the Polisario Front; and Benin was one of the first countries to recognize the Democratic Arab Republic of the Sahara. At the same time, the regime took its distance from Western states, France in particular, as well as from their clients. Relations with Taiwan and Israel for example were phased out; and in Africa, Benin dissociated itself from members of regional groups such as the OCAM, the CEAO, and the Conseil de l'Entente, which were accused of being too close to Western and French imperialism. Agreements with the United States were ended in 1976, after two years of tension which began with incidents concerning the US embassy. In the words of its leaders, time had come to put a stop to years of 'grovelling diplomacy' for Benin.

III

The political organization of the regime and its authoritarian outlook also demonstrated the post-1974 trend towards radicalization. Up to 1979, when the constitution elaborated in 1977 came into application, political power offered a semi-institutionalized, undifferentiated, and monocentred structure on the model of the one-party state. At the same time, Dahomey became the People's Republic of Benin (*République populaire du Bénin*) on 30 November 1974, and the Benin People's Revolutionary Party (*Parti de la Révolution populaire du Bénin*) was established. It had been prefigured by a 13-member National Political Bureau, created in 1974 over the National Council of the Revolution to pre-empt the formation of competing factions at the elite level and to reinforce the centralization of control. In contrast to most African examples, the party in Benin was organized along Marxist-Leninist lines, as a vanguard party with restricted membership, against leftist groups' preferences for a mass formation. Access to the party leadership posts operates on a discriminatory basis. At its head is the Political Bureau composed now of 6 members (all close friends of the president) and the 27-strong Central Committee, elected in May 1976 by the first extraordinary session of the party congress. The Central Committee constitutes the nerve centre of the state political institutions; directing and controlling all state action, it is the source of revolutionary *élan*. It oversees the National Council of the Revolution, which plays the role of a revolutionary assembly.[11] All nominations are made by government decree and the principles of selection work in such a way that not only are all ministers members of the National Council but both the Central Committee and the Political Bureau also are composed of members of the National Council. The result is a concentration of power, if not an organic fusion between the party and the government, with a high degree of militarization.

If it introduced a more pronounced differentiation of political structures and a wider breakdown of power among them − admittedly on the purely legal level − there is no question that the *Loi fondamentale* (the new 160-article constitution, enacted on 9 September 1977) appeared because of its general orientation and structure to maintain the radical line.

Codifying the various principles that had been elaborated after 1974, notably in Kérékou's speeches of Goho and Cotonou on 30 November 1974 and 1975 (the first announcing the adoption of Marxism-Leninism as the guiding philosophy of society and the second the establishment of a single revolutionary party), the text of the constitution clearly adopts a revolutionary perspective. Its provisions include a number of features common to the constitutional systems of most people's democracies based on the Soviet model. These are the ideological monopoly of a system of values and beliefs that defines the legitimacy of social action; solidarity with the anti-imperialist community; the application of democratic centralism; the leading role of the party and its massive intervention in the organic, functional and decision-making spheres of state power; a highly collectivized economy; and a particular definition of citizens' rights and duties.

It is not the purpose here to analyse the new constitution in detail; this has been done elsewhere.[12] Let it be said that technically it establishes an assembly type of regime in the Soviet style, without any separation of powers, whose central institution is the Revolutionary National Assembly, whose standing committee acts as a sort of presidium. Contrary to current African constitutional practice the president, elected by the assembly, has only limited powers and is responsible to the assembly. Moreover, a part of the power of the state is exercised by decentralized, locally elected bodies, and the judicial system, which functions essentially as the instrument of the revolution, remains responsible to deliberative and executive institutions.

In reality, however, the centre of the decision-making process is located in the executive authorities, and in the president in particular, because of the constitutional status of the party and of its role in the organization of the state. The party, which becomes the dynamic focus of the nation's political life, intervenes at every institutional level via the nomination and control of political personnel, who are responsible to it and whose electoral mandate can be rescinded by the party acting as a disciplinary agency. In addition, because of the logic of democratic centralism and the vanguard nature of the party, all power in the latter is concentrated at the top, above all in the Central Committee, which remains shielded from popular accountability and control. Now, since the Central Committee not only intervenes in the nomination of the power elite, but its members, and in the first place its head who, constitutionally, is Head of State, also control the branches of the executive, they are the repository of the quasi-exclusivity of political power. Thus the president, who through the party exercises sovereignty on behalf of the people, is constitutionally present at every level of the administrative and political structure. In other words, the interlinking of the party and the state, the functional and organic osmosis between them, induces a high concentration of power in the executive and a subordination of the deliberative organs. The Benin regime remains therefore within the pattern of a single-party state system, non-participative and potentially authoritarian to boot.

IV

As is generally the case with regimes of this kind during their most radical phase, the political life of Benin was characterized by a great deal of instability paralleled by a pronounced process of repression. Throughout the second half of the 1970s the regime was the object of a twofold opposition. The first originated outside Benin and came from groups of exiled politicians such as the Brussels-based Front for the Liberation and Rehabilitation of Dahomey; this group seems to have been involved in the troubles of October 1975 (the abortive plot to reinstate Zinsou who had been sentenced to death in March 1975) and, supposedly in collusion with other countries, notably France and Gabon, in the mercenary air and land operation of 16 January 1977. Within the country, political opposition built up in various civilian and military circles. There was unrest in rural areas, apparently provoked by the agrarian reform (notably, the *groupements villageois* and the *groupements révolutionnaires à vocation cooperative*), and in business groups opposed to the nationalization of the economy, the results of which left much to be desired. Intellectuals, though divided, increasingly criticized the regime, the most radical for its moderation (leftists from the communist party and the Benin Workers' Union were to form the Democratic and Anti-imperialist Front of Dahomey), others for its infringing of civil liberties. Most of them moreover resented certain reforms such as those relating to the *école nouvelle* programme. On the whole, the people of Benin, accustomed in the past to participating freely in the political debate, found it difficult to accept having their compliance coerced through a mobilization programme that they viewed as demagogical and non-participatory.

But it was in the military dimension that opposition was most tangible – though it was not necessarily distinguishable from civilian opposition, since the military has at times sought the co-operation of civilians in order to increase its influence. Military opposition arose from a complex process of internal factionalization that developed despite the purge of late 1975 during which senior officers from the older Fon generation were eliminated: men such as Colonel Alley and Major Hachémé, for example, had been sentenced to twenty years' imprisonment for conspiring against the security of the state. It was linked, in so far as it had a simple explanation, to the effect of fragmentation that the take-over and the exercise of political power had had on the internal cohesion of the military, a fragmentation that the institutional norms of discipline, obedience, and *esprit de corps* could no longer control.

The occupation of the state apparatus, in effect, inevitably arouses political expectations among men not included in the ruling structure, at the same time as it exacerbates the power ambitions of the leaders; this all the more so when economic and statutory privileges are also at stake. Because of status inconsistencies resulting from cases in which people belong simultaneously, but at different ranking levels, to the government and military hierarchies, it also multiplies the occasions for disputes. Further, it encourages corporate claims and inter-service rivalries over the budgetary, organizational, and professional opportunities that seem now to be readily available. In Benin, the consequent instability of the military was rendered all the more acute by the fact that these tensions often coalesced with 'natural' ethno-cultural cleavages, not to mention frustrations felt by many army units with regard to the highly northernized gendarmerie and other paramilitary groups more closely associated with the centre of power.

These tensions often took the form of competing ideological conceptions and outlooks over how the revolutionary design should be realized. They also materialized into frictions between military personalities and their clientèles; the clashes between Captain Béhéton, then Minister of Telecommunications, and Major Rodriguez, the Commissioner of the Cotonou Port Authority, were one example among many.[13] In some cases, they jeopardized the very existence of the regime. Two such occasions were especially serious. The first was in January 1975 when Captain Assogba, the Minister of Labour, publicly castigated the government for giving in to corruption, and President Kérékou himself was accused of embezzlement. Soon afterwards, in view of the strong public reaction, part of the armed forces and a number of senior officers asked for the president's resignation. It was only because these men hesitated to use force (though a coup seemed to have been planned) that Kérékou was able to politicize the affair: in his turn he accused his minister and his military followers of being the agents of imperialism and had them arrested and sentenced by a hastily convened revolutionary court for rebellion and threatening the state security. The second crisis was sparked off by a group of militantly radical officers who took advantage of rising dissatisfaction with what was considered as the too reformist character of Kérékou's rule in leftist and Marxist civilian circles, with which these officers had allied. The popularity of its leader, Captain Aikpé, at the time the Minister of Interior and Security, led the government to believe in the threat of a coup d'état. Fearing for his own leadership, President Kérékou moved quickly and succeeded in trapping Aikpé in an embarrassing situation, to have him shot by the presidential guard. This event provoked a wide popular demonstration and led to a general strike. Very many members of the armed forces took the side of the strikers and the army agreed to suppress the demonstration only at the price of a compromise which could for a time have jeopardized the president's independence, notably *vis-à-vis* Majors Azonhiho and Alladaye.

V

The swiftness of the government's reaction and of its move to institute repression during these crises, together with the considerable size of the prison population, underlined the repressive and authoritarian character of the regime. For several months, Kérékou dispensed with the government and ruled alone from military quarters. The efficiency of the coercive and judicial apparatus well illustrated these tendencies. The highly differentiated internal security system, composed of a militia, the gendarmerie, a police and various services of the Ministry of the Interior, showed a great versatility that allowed it to control the whole sphere of the private and public activities of the citizenry.[14] The structure of the judicial system, moreover, reinforced this apparatus. For example, the constitution explicitly authorizes the setting up of an emergency system to judge special cases, in addition to the fact that the absence of judicial independence and appeal processes offered only precarious protection to the citizen and operated favourably for the regime.

The particular character of citizens' rights and the status of public liberties defined by the constitution further accentuated the authoritarian dimension of the Benin regime. These rights and freedoms were in fact derived from the philosophy and the doctrine on which the regime and national action were based; as such, they could be exercised only within this frame of reference, and enjoyment of them could accrue only to those who fully adhered to the founding doctrine. The encouragement of informing, moreover, allowed anyone to denounce violations of the law as well as 'lapses from duty'. Together with the notion of 'the abuse of democratic freedom', such ambiguous clauses, being susceptible of wide interpretation, set limits on the rights of the citizen. And Benin, during this period, had thus the sad privilege of being mentioned among the world's violators of human rights in an Amnesty International report which estimated that the political trials of 1973, 1975 and 1976 were cases of flagrant injustice and that conditions of incarceration were particularly bad.

Yet, as has been the case in similar situations in the past and at present, the intensity of this radical stance assumed by the praetorian regime since late 1973 declined and entered into a new period.

The Thermidorian Phase of Praetorianism

No revolutionary phenomenon operating at an acutely radical level can be sustained for long. Ineluctably it tends to secularize − that is, to enter a process by which it becomes more moderate and less chiliastic. This does not mean that there is a return to the *status quo ante* nor that the revolution ends. On the contrary, this process integrates the radical phase and in fact enables the routinization of the changes brought about by the revolutionary movement to take place. As was argued above, the thermidorian phase is to revolutionary phenomena what the routinization of charisma is to pure charisma; it cannot be dissociated from an analysis of the radical phase itself.

I

It is impossible to date with precision the secularization of Benin radical praetorianism. Nor has it been a massive phenomenon affecting all sectors of the political system simultaneously; its contours have been blurred and it has advanced at asynchronous paces in different areas of political life. Yet there is tangible evidence indicating that the watershed was reached by the turn of the present decade. Political instability and the attendant process of repression have eased off significantly in the early 1980s. A greater moderation in the regime's political output was noticeable, which is clearly illustrated by the increasing realism and pragmatism of its leadership. Obviously, the general political discourse, the ritual Marxist-Leninist reference aside, became less absorbed with transcendental issues and the formalities of ideological orthodoxy, to focus on more immediate questions of nation-building. These still constitute fragmentary elements rather than a definite trend. But they are sufficiently numerous and explicit not to be ignored or considered as random events. Calling thus for an explanation, they could be viewed as representing both a new stage in the political evolution of praetorianism in Benin, and a validation of the hypothesis of a thermidorian change.

An examination of Benin now and in the recent past shows with little ambiguity that almost all the policy orientations adopted earlier have been altered or adjusted, generally in the direction of moderation. In the economic domain, for example, nationalization and the development of the public sector nearly came to a halt. The results of the policy were judged negative in terms of efficiency, productivity and cost (as shown by the decline of agricultural production, the flagrant lack of interest of the workers, not to mention widespread corruption to which president Kérékou himself alluded in September 1980, charging the unions with this). Placing the emphasis henceforth on productivity and rationalization, the government was led in the early 1980s to prepare a new programme restructuring the whole public sector, the key characteristic of which was a significant decrease in the number of production units. Moreover – and this clearly appeared from official statements such as the interview given by President Kérékou in 1982 – the role of private initiative in economic development was insisted upon. Recently, the government set aside funds for boosting small private businesses (seven billion francs CFA were appropriated towards this goal) and planned to denationalize some ten enterprises. If it was found ambitious in some regards, the 1983–87 development plan has however attracted the attention of various financial backers who have promised more than 100 billion francs CFA in assistance to Benin – proof again of the better viability of the new economic climate in the country, as well as of the pragmatism of Benin's emerging financial elite, attached to a more restrained economic programme.[15]

The fact that foreign investors and backers have been attracted to Benin resulted also to a large extent from the re-orientation of its foreign policy. Motivated by the ideal of socialist solidarity until the end of the 1970s, it has since then demonstrated a good deal of realism scarcely concealed by the façade of the revolutionary rhetoric. Admittedly relations with socialist states are maintained, yet Benin resisted signing any friendship treaty with the USSR, which was seeking to compensate for the loss of influence in West Africa following political changes in Equatorial Guinea and Guinea (Conakri). Moreover, there has been an increasing dissatisfaction with the poor returns drawn from these relations, except perhaps from those with China.

Although the severance of relations with the capitalist Western world could not be seriously undertaken and had to be traded for lesser measures, the continuous emphatic demands for it had been a favourite source of high radical yields for Benin. This is why, whatever their relative technical import, the shifts observed in this domain at the turn of the decade were all the more significant. These have taken the form of new investment and assistance agreements with various European countries, such as West Germany or Denmark, and Canada. But the formal resumption, if not the renewal, of relations with the United States and France constituted the most symptomatic demonstration of the new trends in Benin's diplomacy. The years 1982 and 1983 witnessed the progressive normalization of relations with Washington, marked by the visit of the under-secretary for African affairs at the State Department. Today, American aid to Benin is higher than that provided by Eastern European states. The agitated partnership with France – the latter for a while being violently denounced for its complicity in the aborted mercenary invasion of January 1977 – was at last restored to peacefulness. This process began in 1980 and was consolidated in 1981 with a visit of the French Minister for Co-operation to Cotonou. The political change of May 1981 in France gave Benin the opportunity to tighten its links with that country, which President Kérékou visited in September 1981 – a visit that was followed in November 1982 by a French mission to Benin and President Mitterrand's trip to Cotonou in January 1983. Today France, with financial assistance amounting in 1981 to 1.2 billion francs CFA, is the main supplier as well as the privileged partner of Benin.

On the inter-African level, a radical policy has apparently continued to guide Benin's diplomacy. Relations with Libya are symptomatic in this regard. In 1980, Libya offered Benin 100 million dollars in aid and both countries maintained a tight co-operation, exemplified by the establishment of joint businesses. At the same time Benin, still professing its commitment on the side of the progressive camp in Africa, gave all manner of assistance to Goukouni Oueddei's forces against Hissène Habré throughout the civil war in Chad; it is also said that Benin provided men to Libya's Islamic Legion in the 1983 operations in Chad.[16] Yet behind this façade, one notices that Benin also increased its participation in regional co-operation – either bilaterally or within multilateral economic groupings, as the ECOWAS or the Monetary Union for West Africa – with moderate francophone states such as Gabon (accused in the past of imperialist complicity in the plot of January 1977) Niger and Burkina Faso (with which Benin sought to solve certain border problems) as well as with other states in the area, notably Nigeria.

In sum, if radicalism continues to inform Benin's foreign policy, it is now in a more residual manner. Moreover, motives seem far less guided by a truly ideological commitment than by pragmatism: to secure another source of assistance while offering inexpensive tokens to preempt any possible leftist discontent from within.

II

Important changes also emerged in the areas of domestic politics, making it tempting to speak of liberalization. Since 1981, the focus on nation-building and the search for a consensus has led the government to engage in a policy of national reconciliation. This began to materialize with the freeing of the three former leaders of the country, Apithy, Maga and Ahomadegbé, on 19 April 1981. Then, in a speech delivered in January 1983, President Kérékou called upon all Dahomeyans in exile to come back to Benin with their safety guaranteed. This trend culminated in the general amnesty extended on 1 August 1984 to all political prisoners (except, however, for those involved in the January 1977 mercenary raid on Cotonou) and in the liberation of Colonel Alley who had been sentenced to twenty years' imprisonment in 1973. The level of repression and arbitrary justice subsided significantly. Reliance on coercion was progressively displaced by patronage-based strategies, in which, it should be noted, paramilitary institutions played a far from negligible role.[17]

The government did not hesitate to recognize the inadequacy or even failure of various reforms it had undertaken, nor to proceed with extensive readjustments. Such was the case with the *école nouvelle* which had caused a significant decline in the level of education of the country's youth and which the government had the courage to bring into question, returning to traditional patterns in both form and content.[18]

More significant was a twofold transformation of the composition of the government and of the executive structure of the party. This transformation began with the marginalization of the most ideologically militant (and the most stratocratic) officers, and was followed by an increase in the number of civilian technicians. After the cabinet reshuffle of 9 April 1982 there were only nine officers left out of 22 members of that body. The Aikpé affair had been the first occasion for the president to get rid of the most extreme groups; it has been succeeded by a gradual shelving of all officers opposed to the participation of civilians in government. In this respect, tensions had appeared as early as in 1977 in connection with the way in which members of the assembly were chosen, then again in 1979 with the establishment of the new National Executive Council that replaced the revolutionary military government in accordance with the constitution; four officers (who had assisted Kérékou in October 1972) twice attempted to put the state's leader in the minority, the last time in 1980; they were either shunted to minor posts or simply dismissed. This was the case with Major Azonhiho. Furthermore, the cabinet reshuffling not only introduced more civilians into the Benin leadership. It also marked the rising influence of the moderates and technocrats (also called the *syndicalistes*) over the ideologues (called the *ligueurs*) who have been the object of President Kérékou's invective since late 1981.[19] The dismissal of the pro-Soviet Minister of Foreign Affairs, Simon Ogouma, and the return after his rehabilitation of Captain Akpo as Minister of Health, are evidence of his new orientation.

The composition of the present government, renewed after the last presidential election of 4 August 1984, and now comprising 15 members instead of 22, confirms this trend.

Moreover, even if they had a non-competitive character, the legislative elections which took place first in 1979 then in 1984 have permitted civilians to enter and participate in the political arena. All members of the Revolutionary National Assembly are elected civilians. This was undoubtedly a key indicator of a willingness to proceed with the political integration of the civilian elite.

III

Several factors can be said to account for this process of deradicalization of military rule observed in Benin during the past years — although our earlier analogy with pure and routinized charisma could suggest that, because of the implied inherent climactic nature of revolutionary radicalism, such a trend is ineluctable. To avoid labouring here a point that might be viewed as secondary to the topic of this study, some brief remarks on a few of these factors must suffice.

The first set of variables relates to the 'institutionalization' and thence the legitimacy of the governing role of the military in a context of polarized pluralism.[20] The acceptance of military rule at its inception is actually the reverse image of the illegitimacy of the previous overthrown regime. Thus the viability of such a situation is of short term and rests only on the declared transience of the military government. When the praetorians claim to be eligible for longer-term involvement in the political process and eventually for exercising state power, radicalism seems an adequate means for overcoming this limitation. By demonstrating their progressive character, they offer, especially in a context of economic underdevelopment, tokens of their political credibility as a governing elite. At the same time, however, the long-term political viability of radical policies in a polarized social environment is highly hypothetical; in effect, it tends to correlate with the level of the potential for consensual or that of, to use Durkheim's formula, the 'precontractual solidarity'. Hence, sooner or later the acceptability, if not the popularity, of military rule tends to be best promoted by programmes with the lowest antagonistic coefficient, and these naturally exclude a highly radical stance.[21]

This need to fall back on the smallest common political denominator, moreover, is all the more urgent for the fact that a key area of potential destabilization — the military establishment — is too factionalized. This point is critical. The temptation for praetorian leaders in search of a power base is to bypass the military institution, which they can maintain in a state verging on fracture. Such a situation however presents also numerous dangers for law and order — one extreme being the 'Ugandan syndrome' in which the army dissolves into competing predatory autonomous bands. The trade-off, then, is to ensure a minimum of organizational coherence, with a greater dependence on the various corporate interests within the military establishment. Thus dependence in turn implies a reduction in radicality.

These observations apply also to radical techniques of government. A populist style of direct or quasi-direct rule and expanded mobilization tend to give way to pragmatic techniques of clientelism and patrimonialism that are more adapted to eliciting support in a fragmented polity. Brokers can thus be co-opted as political allies in the power structure in return for their clientelist support, and parties, far from serving as the expression of grass-roots interests and autonomy, operate as bureaucratic-patrimonial machines at the leaders' service.

The second set of factors explaining the thermidorian shift derives from the nature of the country's political economy. There is, first, the impossibility of obtaining sustained economic and political mobilization, and identification with and interest in radical collective programmes, when individual returns come to be perceived as negligible. In other words, Benin's progressive policies fell prey to the classic paradox of collective action.[22] Given its tradition and structure, the peasantry, without being conservative, could not be enlisted willingly for too long to support revolutionary policies, unlike elsewhere where peasants' interests were more naturally served by such reforms. The same can be said of the urban middle-class, and this leaves in the end the small and isolated left-wing groups — by definition a brittle and volatile support.

The second element of this category of factors has to do with the limits of enforced state-planning arrangements and of the modern equivalent of what has been defined as 'military Keynesianism'.[23] In effect, the economic structure of Benin being predominantly agrarian and not yet sufficiently concentrated, the multiplier effect generated by a centralized quasi-coercive system of production is not operative.

Finally, precisely because of the lack of key resources and these difficulties in finding means to increase production, the country is incapable of breaking out of the circle of external dependency. So the need to secure assistance on an international market, rendered, moreover, less prodigal by a decade of crisis, has forced the government to evolve more low-key economic programmes and to make greater room for those advisers who have demonstrated the urgency of bringing some measure of realism into economic policy if the country is to survive and grow. In a way, the thermidorian process arises from the need to harmonize politics and economics, in other words to readjust the political discourse in order to reduce the economic cost that the radical political stance necessarily entails.

Other variables would deserve to be taken into account should this analysis be continued and completed. The shift in the governing elite's value system to which we alluded above[24] is one of them. Another is linked to the restoration of the constitutional order under military rule. Praetorians have been led in this direction because of the *ex parte titulo* and *ex parte exercitium* precariousness of their political authority. Given the dominant accepted standards in this regard, given also the limited choice at their disposal, only legal-rational principles could provide a more enduring form of legitimacy, at least externally. Then, proceeding from such principles, the process of constitutionalization tends inevitably to evacuate all other patterns of legitimacy, in particular the charismatic nature of revolutionary radicalism, as well as its antinomian and extremist outlook.

Conclusion

Within the last decade, the praetorian life-cycle in sub-Saharan Africa entered a radicalized phase that saw a proliferation of socialist and populist regimes. The 'Leninist' claim of the military to direct the revolutionary process can be seen as the legitimation of its pretentions to form a governing class.

It is still too early to assess the full impact of the regimes born out of such ideologies. Considering the scope of socio-economic change, they are less encompassing and less radical than their Nassirist or Velascoan cousins. Politically, claims to be achieving popular democracy and participation remain lofty ideals and a matter of rhetoric. These regimes are monocentred praetorian party-states. They are revolutionary only insofar as the mode of governance bears some resemblance to Leninist techniques of power. The people's political participation is restricted to plebicitary functions and continues to fall short of the selection of political leaders. Admittedly, there is, behind the non-competitive character of electoral consultations, a sphere of contest, as for example at the level of the party structures when candidates are discussed and adopted.[25] This, however, is on the whole pseudo-competition. These false 'primaries' constitute a form of contest that, in contrast with that which takes place in open elections, forbids the formulation of heterodox programmes since, precisely to increase their chances of being accepted, candidates tend to avoid stepping beyond narrow ideological conformism. If there is any competition at all it is limited to considerations of persons, professions, or regions, and even here the effects of democratic centralism or that of the voting system (for a single national list in the case of Benin) further circumscribe the field of competition. Any form of opposition, in the sense of offering an alternative ideology, is thus muted or forced to operate illegally.

This said, the balance sheet should not necessarily be read as entirely negative. In Benin, the political leadership has remained the same since 1972, which, compared with former times, constitutes indisputable progress. Again, since the end of the 1970s, the regime has faced no major crisis, although this does not mean that there have been no signs of opposition or malaise. The political institutions have functioned normally, and elections were held as planned in 1979 and 1984 (a decision of the Assembly in February 1984 extended the length of the mandate of its members and that of the president to five years). Recognition of the multinational character of society seems to have neutralized the more negative effects of regionalism. President Kérékou, who has proved to be a shrewd and able leader, appears to have been capable of generating a modicum of cross-regional consensus and legitimacy.

If the military seems to have taken the 'institutionalization' road, rendering improbable abdication from power and the wholesale transfer of authority — despite one allusion of President Kérékou to a possible return to the barracks — it has sought greater collaboration with civilians. As pointed out above, the National Executive Council, which succeeded the revolutionary military government, has always been mixed in its composition and today civilians out-number military members. The National Revolutionary Assembly is entirely composed of elected civilians. The idea of a civilian–military collaboration is now fully accepted by military leaders and President Kérékou has proved his willingness to defend such a principle.

Uncertainties, however, remain; the metaphors of life-cycle or thermidor used here cannot be taken *stricto sensu*; immobilization, slowing down, setback and regression are always possible. The obvious factor capable of frustrating the evolution described here is naturally a coup by a faction of the military, perhaps NCOs or junior officers (this last sector of the hierarchy having not taken its turn in the seats of power) influenced, for example, by the populist model of neighbouring Ghana or Burkina Faso;[26] or a preemptive coup by more conservative seniors against precisely such a populist threat.

The process of constitutionalization with its reference to the principle of popular sovereignty, which establishes the leadership as the expression of the people's will, provides a deterrent against extra-constitutional contestation by exposing the latter as an automatic violation of legitimacy. And by subordinating the armed forces to the party and the head of the state, the constitution provides for legal-rational control of the military (see article 10).[27] But, in a context that assumes a relationship between politics and the army, making the military an integrative part of the revolutionary process and of its success, there is always room for coup legitimation.

Another possibility is the personalist temptation *à la zaïroise* as already exemplified by one of Benin's neighbouring rulers, General Eyadema. But of course, any prediction in this domain is only shaky conjecture.

Before concluding, it must be pointed out that all the reflections made in this study of Benin's military regime are tentative, given the fragility of the empirical evidence. The study does not claim to exhaust the issue of militarism in its radical version. This certainly deserves more than the superficial treatment it has received until now. Our remarks have simply sought to offer a preliminary response aimed at establishing elements of a hypothesis for further research.

NOTES

Michel L. Martin is director of the Centre William I. Thomas and Professor at the Institut d'Etudes Politiques, Université de Toulouse I, and Guest Scholar at the University of Chicago.

1. On this general issue and its treatment in non-Western cases, see Barrington Moore's *Social Origins of Dictatorship and Democracy* (Boston: Beacon Press, 1966); and Ellen Kay Trimberger, *Revolution from Above: Military Bureaucrats and Development in Japan, Turkey, Egypt and Peru* (New Brunswick: Transaction Books, 1978); also Alain Rouquié, *L'Etat militaire en Amérique latine* (Paris: Seuil, 1982), Ch. 10.
2. This concept, which has been used by various writers (Crane Brinton, *The Anatomy of Revolution*; Max Lerner, 'The Pattern of Dictatorship'; J. O. Hertzler, 'The Typical Life-Cycle of Dictatorships', André Joussain, *La loi des révolutions*, etc.) was put forward by Robert E. Park's student, Lyford Edwards, at Chicago in a book published in 1927 by the University of Chicago Press under the title: *The Natural History of Revolution*. The idea of applying it to military rule was suggested by Morris Janowitz in a new introduction to his classic on the military in non-industrial societies, re-edited as *Military Institutions and Coercion in the Developing Nations* (Chicago, Il: University of Chicago Press, 1977). I have tried to expand

this idea further by applying it to successions of military regimes approached as wholes; see also Luc Cambounet's doctoral thesis 'Le pouvoir prétorien africain: une interprétation de sa dynamique'. Mimeographed, Centre William I. Thomas, Toulouse, 1983.

3. This shift simply corresponds to the rise within the hierarchy of younger officers whose mentality differs from that of older officers, who, because of natural and organizational attrition, are becoming less numerous. While the latter had been socialized to the principle of apolitical subordination to civilian power (in the Western tradition, during their service in Euro-colonial units or their training in European schools), the former had been far less exposed to European professional values (many did not attend European schools but went to newly established military facilities and academies in Africa).

Moreover, it should not be forgotten that these younger generations have been growing up in an era, the late 1960s, in which liberal ideologies permeated the value system of most societies of the world and were lived in quite a militant fashion. Radical praetorianism is to some extent part of a larger process and so has many functional ideological equivalents: it is to the non-Western military what liberal theology was to the church, Marxism to universities, radical feminism to womanhood, etc.

4. The reality is, needless to say, far more complex than this rendering which is intentionally ideal-typified. Firstly, though each regime/phase has one dominant character, it evolves through its own cycle, which actually appears to repeat the parent one; to use a rather old-fashioned formula, it is as if each regime's ontogeny was recapitulating the overall praetorian philogeny. Secondly, some interventions, given their nature, set back the cycle to an earlier phase (especially when the regime they introduce recapitulates the overall natural history) or when, on the contrary, one phase (the moderate one) is skipped. But, on the whole, it is difficult to miss the emerging uniformity. Besides, one has to take into account the demonstration effect created by the dominant form of ideological and political organization then in force on the continent, which tends to correspond to a specific phase of the evolution of the praetorian cycle. In effect the phases of the evolution seem to appear at specific moments: the 1960s would correspond to the period of greater frequency of arbitral military rule, that is, the moderate phase of the praetorian cycle, the mid-1970s to that of praetorian radical rule, and the present period to its thermidor.

We should note that the thermidorian phase, if we follow the reasoning of note 4, correlates with the secularization process affecting the parent social revolution that had occurred everywhere by the end of the 1970s.

5. It is not the purpose of this article to examine the nature or the causes of Benin's socio-political situation after independence, notably its perennial political instability; one key element is that the emergence of a civic sense and a popular consensus has been blocked by the vitality of regionalism and the consequent lack of one legitimate national founding leader (three of them concurrently share such a legitimacy) at the sub-national level. On this, as on other issues, see *inter alia*, Maurice A. Glélé, *Naissance d'un Etat noir: l'évolution politique et constitutionnelle du Dahomey de la colonisation à nos jours* (Paris: LGDJ, 1969); Dov Ronen, *Dahomey: Between Tradition and Modernity* (Ithaca: Cornell University Press, 1975); Samuel Decalo, 'Regionalization, Politics, and the Military in Dahomey', *Journal of Developing Areas*, Vol. 9 (April 1973); Michel L. Martin, 'Note sur le changement politique et constitutionnel en République populaire du Benin depuis l'Indépendence', *Année africaine 1982* (Paris: Pédone, 1984), pp. 91–127.

6. The cabinet presided over by Soglo was composed of three officers and ten civilians. It was not entirely cut off from society since there existed also the Committee of National Renovation whose members had been elected by a group of electors representing the various national interests and by a group of senior officers. The committee held a number of legislative and economic responsibilities.

7. The ethnic tensions could be summed up, although the reality is more complex, in a north-south polarity (Fon and Yoruba, on the one hand, Basila, Bariba, and Somba on the other) which corresponded for a long time to the cleavage between officers and enlisted men. This tension, because of the acuity of regionalism in the political sphere, progressively affected the officer corps itself, in which northerners (25 per cent of the total) grew aware of their minority status. Yet, it is noticeable that this category of cleavage was not necessarily coupled to that of the parent regionalism: thus, during the 1965 crisis Colonel Soglo refused to help

Ahomadegbé, to whom he was close, to evict Maga from the north. The effect of institutional norms or of leadership has moreover sometimes diminished dissensus brought about by ethnicity: see, for example, the popularity of Lieutenant-Colonel Alley, a Basila, among Fon officers (with Soglo notably) or, conversely, his disagreement with Kouandété, although not a southerner. When they have operated in the military, ethnic cleavages have done so in an autonomous manner and often as an *a posteriori* legitimation for conflicts of another origin.

8. On these events, see sources cited in note 6, and also Chapter 2 of Samuel Decalo, *Coups and Army Rule in Africa: Studies in Military Style* (New Haven, CT: Yale University Press, 1976), pp. 39–86; Dov Ronen, 'Benin: The Rule of the Uniformed Leaders', in I. J. Mowoe (ed.), *The Performance of Soldiers as Governors: African Politics and the African Military*, pp. 101–49 (Washington, DC: University Press of America, 1980).

9. *Bulletin quotidien de l'Afrique noire*, no. 712, 15 Nov. 1972.

10. Cf. President Kérékou's interview of June 1973 to the *New Nigerian*; see Andrew Racine, 'The People's Republic of Benin', in Peter Wiles (ed.), *The New Communist Third World: An Essay in Political Economy* (New York: St Martin Press, 1982), p. 209; Ronen, 'Benin: The Rule of the Uniformed Leaders', pp. 132–33.

11. The status of the party appeared in *Ehuzu*, no. 456, 5 Aug. 1977.

12. See Dmitri-Georges Lavroff, 'La République populaire du Benin: La constitution du 9 Septembre 1977', *Année Africaine 1977* (Paris: Pedone, 1979), pp. 109–58; Alexandre Paraiso, 'La Loi fondamentale et les nouvelles institutions de la République populaire du Bénin', *Recueil Penant* (1980), pp. 288–306 and 403–40; also my 'Le cycle constitutionnel béninois depuis 1960 et la Loi Fondamentale du 9 September 1977', in F. Reyntjens (general editor), *Constitutiones Africae* (forthcoming).

13. Decalo, *Coups and Army Rule in Africa*, p. 83, note 81.

14. The establishment of these institutions helped to relieve the armed forces of having to handle this sort of task, for which they are not prepared. These tasks entail moreover expensive logistical back-up and budgetary surplus, which in any case do not guarantee operational success. Military forms of social control are far more limited in efficiency than is usually believed: on this issue see Michael Mann, 'The Autonomous Power of the State', *European Journal of Sociology* Vol. 25 (1984), p. 200; Owen Lattimore, *Studies in Frontier History* (Oxford: Oxford University Press, 1962). In rural societies, in particular, paramilitary forces have revealed themselves to be far more operational and useful for penetrating society: on this issue, still little investigated, see Morris Janowitz, *Military Institutions and Coercion in the Developing Nations*, Ch. I.

15. These backers, who met in Cotonou in early 1983, were the World Bank, the EEC, the African Bank for Development, the OPEC, France, Belgium, West Germany and Japan. On this question, see Roger Jouffrey, 'Le Bénin depuis 1981', *Afrique contemporaine* 22 (July–Sept. 1983), pp. 42–3.

16. In 'Spartacus', *Les documents secrets: Opération Manta, Tchad 1983–1984* (Paris: Plon, 1985), p. 190.

17. This role, performed by paramilitary agencies that are organizationally (from the professional as well as the logistical standpoint) adapted to day-to-day interactions with the population, urban or rural, calls for more systematic research.

18. Jouffrey, 'Le Bénin depuis 1981', pp. 37–9.

19. Cf. his attacks on the *'anarcho-syndicalistes'* and the *'démagogues'* of the national teachers' union in late 1981, and his speech to the nation of February 1982.

20. The term 'institutionalization' is understood here simply as the process by which the military gives to itself the means to routinize its political role either as leader or at least as participant in the running of the state. For Samuel Finer, this is 'quasi-institutionalization'; 'institution-alization' proper implying only a support role after the return to the barracks; see Samuel Finer, 'The Retreat to the Barracks: Notes on the Practice and the Theory of Military Withdrawal from the Seats of Power', *Third World Quarterly*, Vol. 7 (Jan. 1985), pp. 18–22.

21. For further remarks on the issue of legitimacy see Gus Liebenow, 'The Military Factor in African Politics: A Twenty-Five Years Perspective', in Gwendolen M. Carter and Patrick O'Meara (eds.), *African Independence: The First Twenty-Five Years* (Bloomington: Indiana University Press, 1985), pp. 143–7 *et passim*; and Michel L. Martin, 'Réflexions sur

la nature et la légitimité du pouvoir martial en Afrique noire contemporaine', in Maurice Duverger (ed.), *Dictatures et légitimité* (Paris: Presses universitaires de France, 1982), pp. 443–62.

22. As brilliantly argued by Mancur Olson, *The Logic of Collective Action: Public Goods and the Theory of Groups* (Cambridge, MA: Harvard University Press, 1965).

23. Michael Mann, 'The Autonomous Power of the State', p. 204, and his *History of Power in Agrarian Society* (forthcoming).

24. See note 5.

25. See some of the papers collected in Centre d'Etude d'Afrique noire, *Aux urnes l'Afrique: Elections et pouvoirs en Afrique noire* (Paris: Pédone, 1978), and Yves-A. Fauré, 'L'évolution politique: élections et partis en Afrique noire', *Année Africaine 1978* (Paris: Pédone, 1979), pp. 214–50.

26. Also noted by Henry Bienen, 'Populist Military Regimes in West Africa', *Armed Forces and Society*, Vol. 11 (Spring 1985), p. 375. Incidentally, Bienen argues in this article that populist regimes have a specificity of their own, one at least that makes them different from conventional radical regimes. This seems true only to some extent. Our own contention is that populist military regimes are only one radical manifestation of the praetorian life-cycle in Africa. Populist forms of military government have in common with a regime like that of Benin a politicized judiciary (as we have seen), and an armed force involved in the process of revolution, for example. Mobilization might seem more direct and more expanded in populist regimes, yet it remains that the autonomy of the people and its political participation is no less restrained than in other radical systems. The difference resides rather in the personalities of the leaders; populist leaders come from the third generation of the post-independence military establishment, men placed in the lower rungs of the hierarchy (junior officers, NCOs) – in other words, the youngest age-group of the politicized generation of the military (see note 4). They also come from a more disintegrated military establishment (that they often purposefully maintain in that state). We should note also that, as shown by the recent developments in Ghana, Liberia and even Burkina Faso where populist regimes have developed, there is a change in the leaders' attitudes and policies that could indicate an attenuation in radicality.

27. In this respect again, the role of the paramilitary institutions in ensuring efficient civilian control of the military would be worth exploring, notably the extent to which they help prevent or pre-empt the development of factional cleavages, their intensification and their eruption on the political scene. The fusion of 1977 between, on the one hand, the armed forces and the gendarmerie and, on the other, the remaining paramilitary forces and the police under the control of the party in Benin, originated in just such a preoccupation.

The Revolutionary Process in Burkina Faso: Breaks and Continuities

René Otayek

With Captain Thomas Sankara's seizure of power on 4 August 1983 the Upper Volta, which became Burkina Faso[1] one year later, plunged headlong into a period of political and ideological radicalization. It thus broke with the institutional stability that had characterized its evolution since gaining independence. In an Africa where changes of leadership so very frequently take place through a coup, the relatively democratic functioning of Upper Volta's political system was seen as an object of true sociological originality or, for proponents of a narrow developmentalist view that mechanically links democracy with level of economic development, as an aberration. In fact the Upper Volta, or rather Burkina, was marked up until 1980 by the existence of a political life that had no parallel in francophone Africa: multi-party and trade union pluralism, competitive elections, freedom of opinion, tolerance, etc.; and when a change of political leadership did involve recourse to arms (as in January 1966 when General Sangoulé Lamizana, at the prompting of the trade unions, had to make up his mind to gather up the tottering power of Maurice Yaméogo, head of state since independence), it had all the appearances of a peaceful transfer of power with only the sanction of constitutional legality missing.

But the succession of three coups d'état that Burkina has had since 25 November 1980, marking the end of the Third Republic and with it the abrupt entry of the military into the political debate, spelled the break with this sort of gentlemen's agreement that had protected the struggle for power from bloody political settlings of accounts. At the same time it threw Burkina into the 'age of the praetorians'.

It is well enough known that the militarization of power is the dominant tendency in the historical evolution of African political regimes. Nor is the phenomenon of very recent date. Since the mid-1960s, in all parts of Africa and whatever the ideological orientation of the civilian ruling elites, African armies have intervened in political life on innumerable occasions. However, one of the most marked differences between the post-independence *pronunciamentos* and the most recent coups d'état lies in the nature of the political, economic and social designs of the coup-makers. The coming to power of the National Council of the Revolution (*Conseil national de la révolution*) in Burkina is one of these 'second generation' coups d'état.

BURKINA FASO

Burkina Faso (Upper Volta until 1984) is a land-locked country. Wooded savannah in the south gives way northwards to the plains of the Upper Volta, which dry out into sand and semi-desert. The majority of the 6.6 million population are Mossi, the rest being made up of Fulani, Gourmantche, Bobo, Lobi Senoufou and Bissa.

Independence was obtained on 5 August 1960, when Maurice Yaméogo became the first president, elected by universal suffrage in December 1960, and re-elected in October 1965 with 99 per cent of the vote. Yaméogo ruled autocratically and opposition parties were either banned or absorbed. Even this, however, did not enable the government to deal with the pressing economic problems that faced it.

In January 1966 the military intervened and assumed power under the leadership of Lieutenant-Colonel Sangoulé Lamizana. The military government succeeded in implementing the austerity measures that had created the crisis leading to Yaméogo's downfall. The events leading from this initial military intervention to the radical turn under Captain Thomas Sankara in August 1983 are included in the analysis given here of the Sankara regime.

The Revolution of 4 August 1983 and its Origins

The 'Sankara phenomenon' appears today, with hindsight, to be the logical and fateful conclusion of a sequence of events that had been developing over a number of years. In fact, as time receded, the experience of the Military Restoration Committee for National Progress (*Comité militaire de redressement pour le progrès national*) which brought the period of Lamizana's power to an end, and even more so − that of the Council of the Safety of the People (*Conseil du salut du peuple − CSP*) which succeeded it on 7 November 1982, can be analyzed as simple periods of transition, during which conflicts crystallized and ideologies matured.

A Society in an Impasse

The seizure of power by the National Council of Revolution (NCR) has often been analyzed as the final act in a crisis of authority at the apex of the state apparatus, between Thomas Sankara and Jean-Baptiste Ouedraogo, respectively prime minister and head of state in the CSP government that governed the country from 7 November 1982 to 4 August 1983. This approach is not entirely erroneous. But the mutual hostility between the two men and the double-headed structure of power that resulted from it were more a reflection of the accumulation of a number of political deadlocks than the cause of the trial of strength of the summer of 1983, which ended in Sankara's triumph. In fact the origins of the revolution of 4 August are diverse. The principal ones are as follows:

(1) The discrediting of the civilian elites. One of the reasons that explain the coming of power of the army in a country that had a reputation for its stability, governed as it had been for over fourteen years by the same man – General Lamizana – is the profound discredit with the people into which the Third Republic and its leadership had fallen. When Colonel Saye Zerbo put an end to the civilian regime on 25 November 1980, the Upper Volta was passing through one of the most serious crises of its history. The authority of Lamizana, even though he had been re-elected head of state in 1978 after an election that was without doubt the most open in independent Africa,[2] was more and more challenged. Elected to be president of all citizens of Upper Volta, he made the mistake of joining the Democratic Volta Party – Democratic African Rally (*Parti démocratique voltaïque – Rassemblement démocratique africain* – *PDV – RDA*). This decision, rather than rallying new sources of support behind him – which was the aim – on the contrary damaged his image as 'focus of the nation'.[3] On top of this had come a severe crisis in the state apparatus where prevarication, nepotism and corruption had become the order of the day at every level. The administration was being turned into the hunting preserve of the president's party and, with the help of a weakening of governmental power, the political stalemate deteriorated daily. In this context the MRCNP's taking affairs in hand was welcomed favourably by the population. Given the extent to which political society had crumbled and the traditional politicians were compromised, the army appeared as the only organized institution capable of ensuring efficient government. However, far from bringing a solution to the deadlocked institutions of the Third Republic, the coming to power of the MRCNP was to provoke a deterioration of the situation. This manifested itself on the one hand in an increased politicization of the army and on the other in a sharpening of the political and social climate.

(2) The end of unity in the army. The military profession has always enjoyed an unrivalled prestige in the politics of Burkina. Since the army enjoys a great many privileges there, embarking on a military career is a valuable means towards social advancement. Aware of its influence the army had managed to preserve its cohesion until 1980. But from the moment when the political plans of the MRCNP began to become clear, the latent differences within it gradually emerged into the light of day. If the army, as an institution, was unanimously in favour of putting an end to the 'incompetence' of the civilians, it did not display the same unity when the exercise of power called for clear choices in political and ideological matters. In order to govern, the military has to be united as an institution. But from November 1980 it no longer was; below the officers of high rank who occupied the front of the political stage a whole cohort of junior officers with more radical ideological preferences was in ferment – officers for whom, moreover, strict lines of hierarchy meant the blocking of promotional prospects. The way was thus open henceforth for the 'waltz of the praetorians'.

(3) The deepening economic crisis and the end of the dialogue with the trade unions. When the army decided to put an end to Lamizana's regime the national economy was in a parlous state. The developmental strategy that had been adopted, resting on a liberalism bordering on anarchy and symbolized by the slogan '*enrichissez-vous*', had resulted in a widening of socio-economic differentials, whilst clearing a path for the emergence of an embryo business-oriented bourgeoisie. Popular discontent coincided with a continued drop in the standard of living. Very significantly, the MRCNP saw as its first task putting the economy back on its feet along established lines through budgetary austerity and bringing order into the management of state corporations and the administration. At the same time it was decided to clean up political morality and to take action against those who had embezzled public funds under the previous regime – the kind of measures that would rally the people, especially as they included an announcement that the primary teachers, who had been on strike during the last two months before Lamizana's fall, would have their salaries paid in full.

These measures, aimed first of all at placating the trade unions, only partially achieved their object. For it was in relations with the trade unions that, paradoxically enough, the first signs of a rejection of the MRCNP appeared. What brought about a crisis between the two really structured forces of society – the army and the trade unions – was the MRCNP's wish to bring in a new and extremely stringent regulation of the right to strike. But in fact, the conflict revealed a contradiction between two opposing logics: that of the trade unions, pluralist and anti-centralist, and that of the military: authoritarian and integrationist. A trial of strength was thus inescapable. At its close the MRCNP lost that support which is (or rather which was) of the greatest importance for the survival of any political regime in Burkina.[4]

More serious still, this crisis had repercussions even inside the MRCNP, which split between those who were for and those who were against the trade unions. It was, incidentally, this that caused the MRCNP's secretary of state for information to resign in protest, that secretary of state being a certain Captain Sankara. Apart from its relevance to these particular events, this resignation suggested that sharp ideological cleavages existed within the army, and announced that upheavals were in the offing. When the MRCNP collapsed, the hour of the captains sounded.

(4) The power vacuum of the CSP period. On 7 November 1982 Colonel Zerbo was overthrown and the CSP was established in power. As in November 1980, the people, and particularly trade unionists, welcomed this. However, despite this initially favourable atmosphere, the new regime very soon turned out to be incapable of putting forward coherent plans with any chance of sustaining the mobilization of the people that its arrival in power had set in motion.

Despite a few attempts at establishing a certain form of direct democracy (the organization of large mass demonstrations, frequent visits to the regions by the principal political leaders, etc.), the CSP, several months after assuming power, presented a balance sheet that was singularly uninspiring.

The source of this failure must be sought in the very composition of the CSP, a 'heterogeneous coalition',[5] the power relations within which were symbolized by the association in office, at the summit of the state apparatus, of two such disparate personalities as Thomas Sankara and J. B. Ouedraogo. In fact, whilst the youthfulness of its members (34 years old on average) was one of the chief features of the CSP,[6] the harmony among them was far from perfect. The creation of the body that succeeded to the MRCNP marked the ousting of the high military hierarchy that was linked to the traditional political forces; it also produced a subtle dosage of young nationalist and populist officers of middle rank who were often close in their social origins to the civilian elites that had governed the country since independence. And among the youngest officers a second line of cleavage separated those who were more moderate from proponents of a thorough transformation of political and social structures, supported by the more radical political and trade union organizations. Captain Sankara was the spokesman of this faction.

Riven by its internal contradictions the CSP was, moreover, paralysed by the rivalry that became daily more clear at its summit. Captain Sankara swiftly asserted himself as the true fount of decision-making, leaving the head of state, J. B. Ouedraogo, a purely symbolic role to play. The latter owed his continued occupancy of his post only to his weakness and to the fact that he was situated at the meeting point of a number of tendencies that coexisted within the CSP, and was therefore the most acceptable compromise candidate. But in fact, in internal politics and at the diplomatic level, Thomas Sankara behaved as the only true policy-maker of the CSP. From then on a trial of strength was yet again inevitable. It was to take place in 1983 and to result, on 4 August, in the formation of the National Council of the Revolution (NCR).

In the light of these events, it can be said that each of the three coups d'état that took place between November 1980 and August 1983 marked a further settling into place of the forces in contention for power. The coming to power of the MRCNP, which constituted the first real military intervention and was supposed to put an end to the political and social stalemate, brought about not a lessening of tensions but, on the contrary, an exacerbation of them; and in so doing it unleashed forces that until then had been contained. From this point of view it carried within itself the political and social seeds that were to germinate, less than three years later, in the revolution of 4 August.

The Revolution of 4 August, or the Period of Rupture

The proclamation of the People's Democratic Revolution marks conclusively the end of the bi-polar relationship between the civilian elites and the military hierarchy which, in turn or together, had governed the country since its accession to national sovereignty. In this sense it constitutes a profound rupture at a number of different levels.

The first concerns the verbal revolution. The NCR was to take on itself swiftly the task of answering, at least at the level of its discourse, the fundamental question of whether what had taken place was a simple coup d'état, of which Africa has witnessed so many examples, or a true revolution. It should

be said at once that this discourse was at first little different from the declar-
atory programmes that one normally hears after any coup d'état: the same
promise of a fight against corruption, the same economic purposefulness, the
same appeal to the people's will. In fact, the NCR's ideological output turns
around a few simple ideas contained in the Political Orientation Speech
(*Discours d'orientation politique* – DOP) that Captain Sankara delivered
on 2 October 1983 and that stands as a veritable ideological charter of the
revolution. The difference, and it is a big one, is that for the first time in the
political history of the country a regime was clearly asserting its intention of
transforming society by transferring power 'from the hands of the bourgeoisie
to those of the popular classes'. For the first time, too, a regime was proclaiming the need to count on its 'own resources' in order to realize goals of self-
sufficiency in food and of home-based development. From this point of view
the political change that got under way from 4 August 1983 can be called
'revolutionary' in the etymological sense of the term.

That said, it should be noted that no explicit reference is made to any precise
ideology. Moreover, when Captain Sankara was questioned on this he was
swift to assert that the revolution in Burkina was 'neither of the left nor of
the right' and that its goal was 'adequate food, clothing, shelter, medical care
and education' for the people.[7] Expressed in these terms, the content of the
movement of 4 August stems from a conception of social change that is more
Saint-Simonian than Marxist-Leninist: it is not to be excluded, however, that
this message was particularly for external consumption, designed to allay the
fears that Burkina's rapprochement with the more radical African regimes
(and with Libya in particular) arouses at the international level. For it is none
the less true that the constant reference in official speeches and the media to
anti-colonialism and anti-imperialism reflects a modification of the broad
political and ideological themes that predominated up to August 1983.

The second break with the past concerns the take-over of the state apparatus.
In contrast to earlier military governments that were content to make the post-
colonial state apparatus work for their own benefit, making only minor adjustments to it, the NCR at once embarked on a vast purge aimed at removing
officials compromised by working with previous regimes. Functionaries who
were judged to be unreliable were 'relieved' by the hundreds and replaced by
revolutionary cadres.[8] At the same time any opposition that might have
arisen from the deposed leadership was eliminated by setting up popular
revolutionary tribunals charged with bringing to justice politicians of the Third
Republic and the more prominent members of the MRCNP. The army itself
was purged and its general staff replaced by a 'high command' under one of
Captain Sankara's trusted followers, Commander Lingani. The Republican
Guard was dissolved and the *gendarmerie* was reorganized, as being potentially
putschist. In this way the NCR could claim to be offering proof of its political
purity whilst at the same time consolidating its power by taking over the state
apparatus.

A third sign of a break with the past was the emergence of the 'cadets'.
One of the most interesting sociological features of the NCR's arrival on the
scene is the way in which the 'cadets' arose with it. First of all military cadets,

because the NCR, the supreme organ of the revolution whose exact membership is a matter of secrecy, contains only young officers, non-commissioned
officers or soldiers, to the exclusion of any representatives of the upper
hierarchy. The former group, convinced nationalists, university graduates
trained in the best foreign military academies, was worlds apart from the latter,
who were often veterans of the French colonial wars and for the most part
bound to the traditional politicians and to the clientelist networks of the
Third Republic. But also *social* cadets: middle-level administrative personnel
in public administration, young underemployed technocrats, impatient for
positions of responsibility and power, who were among the most ardent
supporters of a revolution in which they discerned a means of replacing the
gerontocracy that had staffed the post-colonial state for decades.

Fourth, there is the rise of new social and political forces. The revolution
of 4 August was one of the rare cases in Africa of a military government
brought to power with the support of the political parties and the trade unions.
It is a situation that recalls, to a certain extent, that which obtained in Ethiopia
after the fall of the imperial regime. In fact once in the saddle Captain Sankara
invited the political organizations that had campaigned for his liberation to
participate in his government. What is interesting about this move is the fact
that it concerned organizations that claimed explicitly to be Marxist-Leninist.
Such were the LIPAD (*Ligue patriotique pour le développement*), created in
1973 from a schism inside the African Independence Party (*Parti africain pour
l'indépendence — PAI*) and very close to the Trade Union Federation of the
Volta (*Confédération syndicale voltaïque — CSV*) that later became the CSB.
Such also were the Union of Communist Struggle (*Union des luttes com-
munistes — ULC*), born in 1980 of a schism in the General Union of Voltese
Students (*Union générale des étudiants voltaïques — UGEV*); and the Volta
Revolutionary Communist Party (*Parti communiste révolutionnaire voltaïque
— PCRV*), set up in 1978 by a group that had left the Volta Communist
Organization (*Organisation communiste voltaïque — CCV*), a nebulous
Marxist-Leninist formation established in 1975 by militant students and trade
unionists.

Undoubtedly, Sankara's offer announced a transformation of the rules of
the political game. It marked in a spectacular way the total marginalization
of the old political structures of the Third Republic — mostly parties of local
power-holders — and the rise of radical and militant movements that were
close in their discourse to the world of labour and that hitherto had operated
clandestinely or were merely tolerated. The initiative of the leader of the NCR
had a double aim: on the one hand to give the military the means to widen
their popular base, and with it the bases of their revolutionary legitimacy, by
securing the support of the more dynamic social and political forces — that
is, the workers and the intellectuals; and on the other hand to give form to
the pronouncements of the NCR by conferring on the extreme left the task
of ideological formulation, a task that the military had shown they were not
competent to perform. However, only the LIPAD and the ULC were to
respond favourably to the offer. And the agreement sealed on 4 August 1983
was not long to withstand the test of power.

The break with the past took the form of an overturning of alliances. It is here, without any doubt, that the break has been most radical, since the formation of a new 'hegemonic bloc' underpins the entire political and economic project of the NCR. Ever since independence the social base of every regime, one after another, had comprised in the main the public administration, the traditional chiefs and the Catholic and Muslim religious hierarchies. This pact was subject to passing tensions (as when Maurice Yaméogo wanted to launch an attack on the privileges of the Mossi chiefs) but it was never brought into question, even by the CSP. But putting into effect the NCR's economic policy as it has been formulated in the DOP and the People's Programme for Development (PPD − a sort of two-year plan decided in 1984) postulates the dismantling of this pact and the establishment of a new alliance, this time with the peasantry, to the detriment of the social strata normally associated with the running of public affairs.

Because of its many implications, therefore, the revolution of 4 August 1983 cannot be regarded as a simple coup d'état. In particular it is not a corporate movement specific to the army as an institution, nor does it express the sectional demands of one part of that army in a quest for power, even if the momentum created by the triumph of Captain Sankara has acted as a catalyst in the political assertion of a new elite centred on the youngest age groups. An analysis of the revolutionary process since 4 August 1983 will allow the extent of the changes instituted by the NCR to emerge. To this we now turn.

The Revolution and its Contradictions

Since nationalism is the dominant element in the NCR's ideology it is first of all at the economic level that the most marked change has occurred. On his accession to power Captain Sankara made clear his intention of freeing the national economy from its constraints by detaching it from 'neo-colonial and imperialist' domination. Achieving this aim implied a complete break with the policy of all civilian governments up until 1980, which neither the MRCNP nor the CSP had questioned. This policy revolved around a conciliation of French economic interests (for the most part industries concerned with processing agricultural products) with an attempt to create a national business bourgeoisie supported by an administrative apparatus that would function in the latter's interests. However, if the ultimate objective of the revolution of 4 August 1983 is clear, the means for arriving at it, on the other hand, are much less obvious.

The Economic Choices Facing the NCR, or the Revolution in Search of Itself

In fact, the economic programme of the NCR is still very vague. The PPD, moreover, reflects this incapacity to plump for a clear strategy of development. Conceived more as a catalogue of aims than as an instrument of real planning, the PPD can boast of no fundamental analysis, no long-term perspective, no global project. The most it does is to trace, up to a horizon of 1985, the needs in food products, water resources, housing and the basic socio-economic infrastructure.[10] In fact, its chief originality lies in the attention that it devotes to the mobilization of human resources. But this implies massive recourse to the labour power of the peasant population and to taxation of the salaries of those in the public service and the private sector. In addition, most of the financing of the PPD, that is, over 129,000 million francs CFA out of a total of over 160,000 million, depends on foreign sources and is therefore subject to the vagaries of diplomacy.[11] Finally, and yet another sign of the confusion that hovered over the elaboration of the programme, the NCR makes no distinction between productive investments (works on the agricultural, hydraulic and educational infrastructure) and unproductive ones (construction of villas for state officials, and of cinemas and stadiums, for example).

Despite its limitations and its technical shortcomings (very unsatisfactory feasibility studies, no rational methods of organization and management, a lack of co-ordination between the services responsible for carrying out the planned projects), the PPD none the less has the merit of expressing the intention of the NCR to insert the peasantry into the process of political and economic development. The reform of agriculture and agrarian property of 9 August 1984 is another extremely important manifestation of this.

In a basically agrarian country like Burkina, where the peasantry represents 87 per cent of the active population,[12] any change in the property law and in the social structures that it underpins cannot but follow a certain political logic. The logic that inspired the reform of 9 August 1984 was a categorical one since, according to the terms of the ordinance that sets out its content, it falls within the framework of the fight for economic independence that was initiated on 4 August 1983. It is with this struggle in view that the reform dispossesses the great landed proprietors and abolishes the traditional rules with reference to which the chiefs held their vast estates. The confiscated land was distributed according to the principle 'one plot of land for one person or one household'.

This reform is important for two reasons. First of all, it constitutes a frontal attack on the very foundations of the power of the traditional authorities, something that only Yaméogo had dared risk and with well-known results; second, because it laid the basis for a total reorganization of the system of land-holding and property in a collectivist direction, in so far as it provided for the organization of the peasantry in 'democratic structures' and for the launching of a 'strategy' for collective development' to make possible 'the scientific use' of the land.[13] Although the exact content of these arrangements was not made clear, it is none the less the case that if this reform were to be implemented in all its vigour, it would without any shadow of doubt mean the end of a social order in the countryside that is many centuries old. The reform, moreover, is the key-piece in the 'anti-feudal struggle' of the NCR; it crowns a movement that started in January 1984 with the abrogation of the laws giving the customary chiefs their political and administrative rights, their incomes and their privileges.

By stripping the chiefs of all their power, the NCR aspires to 'break' the traditional systems of inequality and domination and to clear the way for the emergence of social partners all the more receptive to its discourse for having been freed from their subordination to the hierarchy. But the latter, despite the attacks made on it,[14] still disposes of substantial influence. In certain cases it has even managed to recover its lost positions by taking control, especially in the countryside, of the Committees for the Defence of the Revolution (the CDRs). It is thus still in a position to resist the decrees of the central government, and therefore to block the transformation of social relations on which the success of the agrarian and property reform depends.

This is why the NCR has taken a number of measures in parallel that are favourable to the rural areas (in particular a rise in the official purchase price paid to the producer for cereals, but also a literacy campaign for adults, medical preventive care, irrigation projects and measures to prevent erosion) at the risk of upsetting urban workers by reducing their purchasing power. But if it is taking this risk of cutting itself off from a social base that applauded its arrival, this is precisely because its economic aim, as it appears from the PPD and the agrarian reform, involves a total overturning of the balance (or rather the imbalance) between the urban and rural worlds, a plan that depends on the reversal of political alliances mentioned above. This strategy, if it is to succeed, necessarily requires the voluntary support of the peasantry, and this in turn means launching, at the regional, departmental and local levels, small-scale developmental projects that are worked out and carried out 'at the base' and hence escape, if only partially, central control. This form of self-management − for that is what it is − is contained in embryo in the PPD which claims 'to count ... above all on the labour power of the popular masses'.[15] But the NCR hesitates to commit itself whole-heartedly to this course of action, as is witnessed by the pursuit of 'grand' projects bureaucratically decreed 'from above' (such as that concerning the Sourou Valley), the economic viability of which is doubtful. In these circumstances, and given that the nature of the farms that are supposed to be set up as part of the agrarian reform (state farms, co-operatives, or family holdings) has still not yet been decided, the question that arises with particular salience is that of the social base that the revolution will be able, or unable, to create for itself.[16]

A nationalized economy or a market economy? The debate concerning the industrial sector is just as far from being settled. True, Burkina's industrial base being what it is − that is, extremely slender − the choice of what strategy to follow does not arise in the same terms as in the agricultural realm. It is none the less the case that the ultimate orientation of the revolution will be determined by the answers given to problems that are awaiting a solution. Here too, as between heavy and light industry, the NCR has not made a choice, as can be seen from the case of the relaunching of the 'Tambao project' to mine manganese in the north of the country. This project, constantly being resuscitated and as often abandoned, requires an investment of some 7,000 million francs CFA and is of doubtful utility, given that the world market for manganese is saturated. But the NCR wishes to make of it the symbol of the Burkinese people's determination to 'rely on its own forces' − that is, a theme capable of rallying the energies of everyone.

However, priority is at the same time given in official statements to the small and medium enterprises (the SMEs) that are seen as the lever of development.

According to official figures the SMEs in Burkina employ almost 70 per cent of the active urban pupulation (and 80 per cent if artisans are counted).[17] Confronted with the crisis through which this sector is passing (prohibitive energy costs, excessive interest rates, over-heavy taxation, for example), the government has adopted a certain number of measures designed to reduce the overheads of enterprises (such as exemption from import taxes on raw materials, the creation of zones where firms can install themselves at reduced cost, the setting-up of a government office to promote the SMEs). But the effect of these measures has been cancelled out by the financing of the URCBA (the Revolutionary Union of Banks) in which the SMEs have to participate. This has aggravated considerably the financial difficulties of many of them. In addition the artisans − a particularly dynamic group − have been almost completely neglected, since they benefit, according to the PPD, from only 1.5 per cent of the 'support programme'.[18]

The manner in which the NCR has chosen to treat its economic problems illustrates the narrowness of its margin for manoeuvre, the inconsistencies of its policies, and its refusal from the start to engage in overall state *dirigisme*. In response to the fears that have been aroused in economic circles, the military constantly repeats that 'the private sector has its place in the revolution'.[19] Whether through prudence or tactical choice, French economic and financial interests in industry have indeed never been threatened. Even more significantly, the regulations concerning investments have been revised in such a way as to favour the creation of enterprises using national capital − a goal that has nothing 'revolutionary' about it, since it was already considered a priority under the Third Republic, but which is frustrated, and will continue to be frustrated, by the structural weakness of Burkina's economy. A break with the liberalism of preceding regimes is therefore hardly on the agenda. At the most the regime seems to be moving towards a mixed economy, comprising an enlarged public sector and a private sector governed by the law of the market. Ideological voluntarism has turned out not to be entirely compatible with economic and political realities.

The Limits of Revolutionary Power: Economic Constraints and Political and Sociological Impediments

The radicalism of the revolution of 4 August, whilst still alive, is none the less confined within certain limits deriving first of all from a number of economic constraints that stem in turn from structural and conjunctural factors.

Burkina is well and truly situated among the less developed countries and its per capita GNP hardly exceeds 200 dollars a year (210 in 1982).[20] It is a totally land-locked country, dependent on its regional environment for its external trade. Having no exploitable mining resources (with the exception of the manganese of Tambao) it derives most of its budgetary income from customs duties and from the sale of certain agro-industrial crops − principally cotton (40−50 per cent of registered exports), oleaginous products (peanuts and karite) and livestock (30 per cent of export receipts).[21] Being an agrarian country, Burkina suffers also from problems of water supply aggravated by the drought that is affecting the whole of the Sahel. Control of water resources is a major preoccupation, whilst the poor quality of the soil permits only modest yields. Finally, the production of foodstuffs caters only partially for a population growth that is too high for the available resources.[22] Paradoxically, however, the economic crisis that Burkina is passing through at present is not connected with bad results in agriculture. On the contrary, the harvests of cereals, cotton and oils have on the whole been good in 1982–83 and 1983–84.[23] It is more at the financial level that the situation has dangerously degenerated.

The fact is that exports of agricultural produce are far too small to cover requirements in imported goods. Year by year the deficit grows as concerns both consumer goods and manufactured articles, not to mention the growing oil bill. The deficit reached a record of 72,000 million francs CFA in 1981, with interest payments of 22 per cent.[24] Overall, every financial indicator is in the red: the balance of services, the public treasury, the external debt and the budget are all in deficit[25] and the banking system is falling prey to severe difficulties.

The NCR cannot, of course, be held responsible for a situation that is due chiefly to bad management in the period up until 1983 (useless expenditure, wastefulness, slack management, embezzlement of public funds). It is none the less obliged to do something about it, since it is clear that it is on its ability to deal with the crisis that it will be judged by the providers of foreign aid, whose help remains indispensable.

Like it or not, the NCR has therefore had to comply with the requirements of the IMF and to adopt unpopular measures designed to bring order to the country's economy and finances. This was a fundamental condition for obtaining the credits ($16 million Special Drawing Rights) requested in 1981.[26] Placed under surveillance, the Burkina government has adopted a policy of budgetary austerity based on a reduction of public spending, through such measures as a slimming-down of administrative personnel in the public service by mass dismissals and early retirements, reduction of wages, salaries and bonuses, 'voluntary' contributions, elimination of rewards in kind to senior officials, and increased tax burdens through the abolition of family allowances. But these measures having been judged insufficient by the IMF, yet others have had to be taken affecting the least favoured social strata – in particular an increase in taxation on items of current consumption and on oil products.

Relations with France are equally indicative of these constraints. The ex-metropolis is by a long way the chief provider of aid to Burkina. Year in, year out, its assistance amounts to over 40 per cent of the national budget (45.2 per cent in 1982 and 42 per cent in 1983).[27] Any change in the links between the two countries is bound to have serious consequences for Burkina. That is why, despite a certain tension connected with the role that the French government played, according to the NCR, in the arrest of Captain Sankara on 17 May 1983, co-operation with France has never been called into question, even if the NCR would doubtless prefer to see its content altered.[28]

The same thinking lies behind the fact that the NCR swiftly opted for an open policy towards Burkina's neighbouring states, particularly the Ivory Coast and Niger, which were apprehensive about Captain Sankara's pro-Libyan sympathies and fearful of the possible creation of a 'revolutionary axis' between Tripoli, Ouagadougou and Accra. This was considered by President Houphouet-Boigny in particular as a centre of destabilization capable of disturbing the geopolitical equilibrium of West Africa.[29] The NCR had no hesitation therefore in replacing its rather uncompromising relations with Libya in 1983 with the establishment of a veritable alliance with Algeria, whose moderation in inter-African affairs is well known.[30] Over a million Burkinese workers are employed in the Ivory Coast – a fact that Thomas Sankara could not ignore and which explains his desire to avoid a total break with Abidjan.[31] In the same way Ouagadougou has agreed to Mali's entry into the West African Monetary Union, although the border dispute between the two countries awaits a solution. Finally, relations with Niger, which had been tense for some time, were improved after a visit from Seyni Kountché (in his capacity as chairman of the Inter-State Committee to Combat Drought in the Sahel) to the capital of Burkina on 19 and 20 March 1984.

The NCR has offered proof of its pragmatism through this series of adjustments. But this pragmatism poses a number of questions, the most pregnant of which for the future of the regime is to know whether pragmatism is compatible, in the long run, with the many tensions caused by adaptation to the constraints facing the government. For it is obvious that the policy of austerity will conflict with the proclaimed goals of a better life and prosperity[32] and that, if it is to be accepted, it must rest on a minimum of political consensus. Yet, a little over two years after coming to power, the NCR appears extremely isolated, its principal supporters having abandoned it one after the other, victims of internal conflicts and of power struggles.

These supporters were drawn for the most part from the far left. But this has always been, and remains, deeply marked by the differences within the international communist movement. Ideologically, there is not much in common between the LIPAD with its 'classical' Marxism based on promoting the idea of the leading role of the working class, the ULC which is closer to a pro-peasant model inspired by the Chinese revolution, and the PCRV, which adheres to Albanian positions. Yet it is to this small – but activist – extreme left that the NCR has turned to broaden its popular base and to neutralize the hostility of the traditional socio-political forces. Relatively united as long as they were engaged in clandestine struggle these organizations have given evidence of their internal divisions and rivalries since 4 August 1983. The PCRV, for instance, was unable to maintain its unity when faced with an offer of participating in government, and a faction – styled 'the communist group' – broke away during 1983 and rallied to the regime, whilst the rest of the party adopted an extremely critical attitude towards the NCR. As for the ULC and the LIPAD, their presence in the government has sharpened the mistrust that they have for each other, the first accusing the second of hegemonism. All in all, the left front on which the RNC hoped to rely has collapsed, undermined from within.

To this should be added particular tensions that have arisen between the military rulers and the LIPAD. Of the three principal political formations of the extreme left it is the LIPAD without doubt that had the best chance of influencing the NCR: it possessed battle-tried cadres, a sense of organization, experience of political struggles and, above all, a strong presence in the Burkina trade union confederation, which gave it unique possibilities for mobilizing the people. Aware of its power, and wagering – perhaps wrongly – on the personal links that bound its leader, Adama Touré, to Thomas Sankara,[33] the LIPAD strove to set its imprint on the revolutionary process, profiting from its presence in the government to try to infiltrate the state apparatus. But its ambition conflicted with the plans of the military who, whilst anxious to have civilians by their side, intended to keep a tight grip on power. Since then, the tension between them and the LIPAD was to increase, punctuated in May 1984 by the dismissal of the 'Lipadist' Minister for Youth and Sports, who was accused of wanting to give his organization the credit for the 'anti-imperialist' demonstrations organized by the government on the occasion of the Festival of Labour, and culminating a few months later in the sacking of the other LIPAD ministers and the arrest of its principal leaders.

As a result of this complete break with the LIPAD the NCR is left virtually alone in power, the presence of the ULC in several posts of responsibility not giving anyone any illusions. In fact, power lies more and more, in real terms, in the hands of the followers of Thomas Sankara. It is they who hold most of the ministerial briefs (such as defence, the economy, information). Most of these followers are members of a clandestine organization that is very little known, the Communist Officers' Group, set up in 1979. More seriously, the conflict with the LIPAD provoked disagreements even within the NCR, where Captain Blaise Compaore, one of the chief leaders of the regime who is said to be close to the Soviet Union, could not accept the purge of the 'Lipadist' ministers.[34]

In view of the narrowing of its social base, which was further accentuated by the launching of its policy of austerity, the NCR found itself obliged to develop new political support. It found it in the Committees for the Defence of the Revolution (CDRs). Set up at first – that is, after 4 August 1983 – to defend the revolution, the CDRs swiftly became an instrument in the hands of the NCR to counterbalance the growing influence of the LIPAD and the trade unions. Inspired by similar structures in Cuba, Ethiopia and, above all, Ghana, the CDRs have been given the job of mobilizing the population and are to be found in all sectors of production, in the administration and in the army. Ubiquitous in Ouagadougou (but almost non-existent in Bobo-Dioulasso, for instance), they serve as organs of political and social control. But their functioning does pose problems for the NCR.

To begin with, the trade unions were not slow to see in them a serious rival, particularly in public enterprises and the administration, where the unions draw most of their support. This, together with certain statements by members of the NCR that have been taken as anti-union,[35] has led the unions to wonder whether the military does not intend to undermine the very foundations of their influence. Perceptible all throughout 1984, the tensions between the unions on the one hand, and the NCR and the CDRs on the other, reached a climax in October when the CSB took advantage of the policy of austerity to break spectacularly with the NCR.[36]

Another problem that the CDRs have experienced is in recruitment. Very soon, whilst they were supposed to be a creature of the NCR, the CDRs found themselves being infiltrated by elements that were totally foreign to the revolution: militants of the RDA − the old party of the Third Republic − customary chiefs who were using this avenue for seeking to recover their lost power, leftist leaders or 'Lipadist' marginals, careerists of all kinds. In short, the CDRs were eluding the control of the NCR when they were supposed to be its instrument.

In these circumstances, the regime had to resolve to take the CDRs in hand. They were disarmed for the most part, and their prerogatives, originally very vague, were more clearly defined by a general statute that was adopted on 17 May 1984.[37] According to the stipulations of this statute, the CDRs have the task of carrying out the directions of the NCR, and it is for the latter to appoint their main national and regional officers. They have thus become simple transmission belts at the service of the political leadership.

Apart from these internal dissensions, the NCR has had to face up to opposition from the social strata most affected by the policy of austerity, and first of all from within the public administration where the dismissals on ideological or economic grounds were very badly received. But the NCR responded with the utmost vigour to resistance from the trade unions, not hesitating in March 1984 to sack, purely and simply, some hundreds of teachers who had gone on strike.[38] There is the same problem in the army where there is far from unanimity concerning the reform programme and the creation of the CDRs. It might be asked whether the NCR, by deliberately encouraging a thorough-going politicization of the army, is not running the risk, paradoxically, of arousing a reflex of self-defence in an institution that is traditionally jealous of its privileges. As for the customary chiefs, the stock of their authority, though diminished, is still quite considerable in the countryside. Finally, political opposition coming from the governing classes of the Third Republic and the MRCNP has still not completely laid down its arms, even if it has had to go into exile in order to organize itself (in Togo, the Ivory Coast and France for the most part).

However, by neutralizing one after the other the poles of resistance, the NCR seems to have ensured its immediate future. But by adopting a strategy of systematic confrontation it restricts its possibilities of controlling political and civil society. It is hard to see how the NCR, isolated as it is and sustained only by the CDRs, can in these circumstances succeed in its aim of transforming society other than by authoritarian means. In other words, it is the very nature of the regime born on 4 August 1983 that has been brought into question.

Conclusion

Is this regime a military regime in the strict sense? Any answer to that question must be subject to qualifications. In so far as the NCR took power by force of arms and the army controls the political arena, then yes, the regime in power in Burkina is a military one. From this point of view the change in August 1983 is first and foremost the result of a coup d'état, conducted according to the usual techniques of staging such a coup. That said, the regime of Captain Sankara has certain characteristics that distinguish it from the usual praetorian phenomenon in black Africa.

The causes of military intervention in the political equation are too well known for it to be necessary to rehearse them in detail here. They can be briefly recalled: disintegration of the traditional political and social systems, inefficiency of the administrative apparatus, 'incompetence' (supposed or real) of the civilian elites, ethnic and regional tensions, instability – all these are factors that make the army, in a crisis situation, appear as the last resort.[39] It is, moreover, in many cases the only organized institution that has any discipline. The great majority of African coups d'état are to be explained by a coincidence of these factors, to which are frequently added demands specific to the army as a constituted body, and these give certain coups at times a corporatist dimension.

However, whilst there is a broad enough consensus among analysts of African political systems on the origins of the coup d'état in general, reflection is only just beginning on the exact nature of the military regimes that have appeared during the past decade in countries such as Ethiopia, Ghana, Madagascar, Libya or Burkina. Clearly there has been a break with the classical military model of the 1960s, a break whose chief characteristics are well illustrated by the NCR.

The first of these characteristics is without any question the age of the military men that have taken power. They have been, as has been pointed out very many times, young officers, non-commissioned officers or ordinary soldiers. The revolution of 4 August 1983, like that of Jerry Rawlings in Ghana, is a revolution of captains. If this coup d'état is to stand out from other run-of-the-mill coups d'état it has to have a novel political and social programme.

The ideology – the second characteristic – is thus a determining indicator of the nature of the regime. It has long been admitted, and quite rightly, that when it took power the military was content to run the state without attacking foreign interests or those of the dominant classes that were linked to them. This is not the behaviour of radical military regimes that claim to be reconstructing society on new ideological bases, even if it means extending their control over the whole of society. Yet very often, if not always, this transformation is accompanied on the diplomatic level by a more or less evident rapprochement with states that share the same radical convictions.

A third characteristic of these regimes is the symbiosis that they set up – or attempt to set up – with civilian counter-elites that are close to them in ideological terms: radical trade unions, political organizations, or student movements of the extreme left. The logic of this step is to arrive, though it might take time, at the creation of a single party that would in a way institutionalize the authority of the military. This is what seems likely to happen in the medium term in Burkina in the form of a probable 'revolutionary front' uniting the political groups that are in agreement with the NCR's programme.

The fourth characteristic is the investing of the coup with a special value. These young military people are in fact often convinced that they are engaged in a mission of salvation. The tendency of public pronouncements to resemble incantations and the prominence of slogans with a moral content are very revealing in this respect.

Finally, the fifth and last characteristic, closely connected with the last mentioned, is the appearance of a charismatic leader who concentrates in his person all the values of the change that has been brought about. His role is to transcend existing hierarchies. He is scarcely ever the highest-ranking officer, but nevertheless it is to him that power falls. He does not derive his authority from his post, but from his personality, his gift of speech, his capacity to elicit people's commitment and to communicate directly with the people. This was the case with Nassir; it is the case with Jerry Rawlings and with Thomas Sankara.

The regime in Burkina is of interest precisely because it unites all these characteristics. To adopt a Weberian concept, we would suggest that it represents the ideal type of the radical military regime.[40] Few other regimes correspond so perfectly to this ideal type, with the possible exception of that in Ghana to which, by a significant coincidence, the revolution of 4 August 1983 sees itself as being closest.[41] It should also be noted that non-radical regimes may adopt certain characteristics of Sankara's regime without thereby falling into the same category. Thus, General Murtala Muhammad in Nigeria was without doubt a charismatic personality (and his assassination greatly enhanced his charisma), but his regime had nothing radical about it; Sergeant Doe in Liberia comes from the same generation as Sankara and Rawlings but his regime has developed in a direction totally opposed to theirs; the Ethiopian Dergue has embarked upon a profound transformation of society without generation or charisma being obvious factors in the Ethiopian revolution. It appears, on the evidence, that we are confronted with an extrémely complex phenomenon that requires Africanist political scientists to revise their thinking and their methods.

NOTES

René Otayek holds a research post in the *Centre d'étude d'Afrique noire* (CEAN) in the Institut d'études politiques at Bordeaux.

1. The expression Burkina Faso, which means 'country of free people', was formed by juxtaposing two terms, one of them Moorish (Burkina) and the other Peul (Faso).
2. It required a second ballot to elect Lamizana who lacked by far an absolute majority in the first round and only just achieved one in the second.
3. C. Some, '*Haute-Volta: bilan de la politique de redressement national amorcé le 25 novembre 1980*', *Centre d'étude d'Afrique noire, Travaux et Documents*, Vol. 2, 1983, p. 2.
4. On the conflict between the unions and the MRCNP see Some, op. cit., and R. Otayek, 'Haute-Volta; chronique politique et constitutionnelle', *Année africaine*, 1983 (forthcoming).
5. L. Yarga, 'Les prémisses à l'avènement du Conseil national de la révolution en Haute-Volta', *Le mois en Afrique*, 213–214, Oct. – Nov. 1983, pp. 24–41.
6. For further details on the events of the summer of 1983, see Otayek, op. cit.
7. Interview in *Newsweek*, 19 Nov. 1983.

8. Over 350, according to *Le Soleil* (Dakar), 20 Feb. 1984.
9. *Carrefour africain* (Ouagadougou), Vol. 796, 16 Sept. 1983, p. 10.
10. See the 'People's Programme for Development 1984–85', Ministry of Planning and People's Development, Ouagadougou.
11. Ibid., pp. 3–4.
12. J. M. Derrien, 'Les salariés du Burkina font-ils partie des classes moyennes?', *Tiers monde*, Vol. 101, Jan. – March 1985, pp. 69–79.
13. *Carrefour africain* (Ouagadougou), Vol. 844, 17 Aug. 1984, p. 8.
14. According to certain members of the NCR, the customary chiefs are the 'number one danger of the revolution': *Bulletin quotidien d'Afrique*, Vol. 11, No. 290, 24 Jan. 1984.
15. 'People's Programme for Development', op. cit., p. 1. The holding of the Fourth World Congress of Young Farmers in Ouagadougou in December 1984, on the theme 'The role of peasant organization in economic, social and cultural development', also forms part of this strategy.
16. On the NCR's economic strategy, see P. Labazee, 'La voie étroite de la révolution au Burkina', *Le monde diplomatique*, Feb. 1985, pp. 12/13.
17. *Carrefour africain* (Ouagadougou), Vol. 877, 5 April 1985.
18. The 'support programme' is a part of the PPD comprising a list of investments spread out over the period from October 1984 to December 1985 and separate from the 'basic programme', which concerns each of the provinces. See the 'People's Programme for Development', op. cit.
19. See *Marchés tropicaux et méditerranéens*, 1989, 23 Dec. 1983, p. 3112.
20. Ibid.
21. Ibid., 1982, 4 Nov. 1983, p. 2602.
22. Average annual population growth for the country as a whole was two per cent between 1970 and 1980: see ibid., p. 2603.
23. Ibid., p. 2604.
24. Ibid.
25. Servicing the external debt alone amounted to 8,200,000 million francs CFA in 1983 and 12.5 thousand million in the following year, whilst the budgetary deficit was over 10,000 million francs CFA in 1984 as against 7,500,000 million francs the year before: *Le Monde*, 10 July 1984.
26. *Marchés tropicaux et méditerranéens*, 1982, 4 Nov. 1983, p. 2604.
27. Ibid., 1975, 16 Sept. 1983, p. 2205; and *Le Monde*, 10 July 1984.
28. On France and the arrest of Sankara on 17 May 1983, see Otayek, op. cit.
29. In May 1983 persistent rumours in Ouagadougou cast the head of state of the Ivory Coast as the chief instigator of the ousting of Captain Sankara.
30. The cooling of relations with Libya is due not only to a wish to allay the apprehensions of neighbouring states but also to Libyan demands to be reimbursed for military equipment delivered to Captain Sankara's supporters at the beginning of 1983. On the co-operation agreements between Algeria and Burkina, see *Carrefour africain* (Ouagadougou), Vol. 825, 6 April 1984.
31. This attitude was not affected by the alleged attempt on the life of the NCR's chief in February 1985 in Yamoussoukro (Ivory Coast) (a bomb had exploded a little before his arrival at the hotel where he was to stay during the conference of member-countries of the *Conseil de l'Entente*) nor, apparently, by the tension that existed between the two countries after the assassination in Abidjan, some weeks later, of an important Burkina businessman who was an opponent of the NCR's policies.
32. See, in this connection, the interview with Thomas Sankara in *Newsweek*, loc. cit.
33. Adama Touré in fact taught Thomas Sankara in the lycée where the latter studied.
34. See Labazee, op. cit., p. 12.
35. See *Carrefour africain* (Ouagadougou), Vol. 825, 6 April 1984.
36. Ibid.
37. For details of the CDRs' charter, see *Carrefour africain* (Ouagadougou), Vol. 833, 1 June 1984.
38. See Otayek, op. cit.
39. On military regime see, among others, W. F. Gutteridge, *The Military in African Politics* (London: Methuen, 1969); S. Decalo, *Coups and Army Rule in Africa: Studies in Military*

Style (New Haven: Yale University Press, 1976); A. Bebler, *Military Rule in Africa: Dahomey, Ghana, Sierra-Leone and Mali* (New York: Praeger, 1973); M. L. Martin, *La militarisation des systèmes politiques africains (1960–1972)* (Quebec: Naaman, 1976).

40. M. Weber, *On Charisma and Institution Building*, selected papers, edited and with an introduction by S. N. Eisenstadt (Chicago: University of Chicago Press, 1968); and idem, *The Sociology of Religion* (London: Methuen, 1964).

41. Apart from official statements, this is demonstrated by the existence in the two countries of identical institutions such as the popular revolutionary tribunals and the people's committees (CDR's in Burkina, workers' defence committees in Ghana), and by the joint military manoeuvres that took place at the frontier between the two states under the name 'Operation Bold Union'.

Madagascar: A Case of Revolutionary Pragmatism

Jean du Bois de Gaudusson

On 21 December 1975, the electorate of Madagascar voted on the following question: 'For the sake of a new society, and so that justice and social equality may reign, do you accept the charter of the socialist Revolution and the constitution that will represent its application, and Frigate-Captain Didier Ratsiraka as president of the Republic?' By responding to this referendum, according to official figures, with a vote of 94.66 per cent in favour, the electors approved far more than a simple change of a constitutional system or of a political team: at the same time as they endowed the country with definitive institutions and legitimized the position of a man who had come to power a few months earlier, they endorsed the choice of a new ideology and of a new type of state. Madagascar thus embarked on the 'resolutely socialist' path of revolutionary socialism. This sea-change surprised many observers familiar with the great island; it aroused, and continues to arouse, many questions about the origins and sources of a regime that seems in every way opposed to that which had been in power for almost 15 years. Ten years later, it still raises questions about the nature of the regime and its objectives. Madagascar has been subjected more than other countries to hasty and conflicting assessments: some see in it a state of socialist orientation gradually being integrated into the periphery of the international communist system,[1] others a bloody dictatorship and no more,[2] yet others an original regime that has managed to preserve, behind a phraseology current in the Third World, the central Madagascan values that remain, when all is said and done, close today to what they were under the previous system. The subtlety and complexity of the political processes of Madagascar,[3] and the pragmatism that has been elevated to the level of a policy, defy typologies and rule out categorical and definitive judgments.

An Unexpected Birth

Despite the difficulty in pin-pointing explanations, some light can be cast on the circumstances in which the Democratic Republic of Madagascar came into being in 1975 by examining the historical events. Three phases can be traced in the political history of Madagascar from 1959:

The first is that of the *First Republic* (1959–72). For 13 years Madagascar was exceptional among African countries for its stability and political moderation.[4] Subscribing to a liberal ideology that provided the under-pinning of the preamble to the constitution of 29 April 1959, the First Republic

MADAGASCAR

Madagascar, an island of 587,041 square kilometres, has a population of 9.4 million (1983 estimate). It became a French colony in 1896, achieving independence in 1960.

The colonial period saw the development of trade and railways, an import–export economy (based on coffee), the alienation of land to foreign settlers and companies, the formation of an intellectual elite and the exploitation of the peasantry (through taxation, forced labour, and insertion of the money economy). Politically, however, the Malagasy experience was marked, first, by the relative continuity of pre-colonial and colonial structures (which reinforced inequalities between the coast and the inland plateau, thus creating grounds for subsequent political tension) and, second, by the strength of the resistance to French rule by almost all strata of the population. This struggle for economic and political rights culminated in the 1947–48 insurrection, harshly repressed by the French army, when thousands of Malagasy died.

The failure of the insurrection demonstrated the gap between the aspirations of the elite and those of the peasantry, and also enabled France to offer independence in 1960 on its own terms.

was, it is true, endowed with a constitutional text that borrowed heavily from that of the Fifth French Republic, and was reinforced at the same time by the personality of President Philibert Tsiranana and by the existence of a powerfully dominant party – the Social-Democratic Party (*Parti social-démocrate – PSD*) – that gradually extended its influence over all sectors of public activity, both political and administrative. But there was none the less in the country a true political opposition, small but active, represented by the Marxist, and pro-Soviet, Congress Party for the Independence of Madagascar (AKFM). A lively press, moreover, made very good use of the freedom of expression that existed. As for the renowned Malagasy socialism that the leadership of the country referred to, it was, to say the least, diffuse and showed no great doctrinal consistency over the years; in practice it was used mostly to refer to agrarian relationships, and accommodated itself to the strong presence of private capital, mostly foreign, in industry and commerce. Another characteristic trait of the regime of President Tsiranana was the strength of its pro-Western alignment. This took the form notably of a strident anti-communism, illustrated by a foreign policy that ignored the socialist states and maintained close links with France. These last took many forms: the stationing of French troops in the country, strong French interests in the economy, and an extensive presence of technical advisers and assistants.[5] We should note, finally, the dialogue that Madagascar maintained throughout this period with South Africa.

A victim of the erosion of power, linked to that of its leader, and undermined by the sickness and dissension that were affecting the PSD,[6] the regime began to undergo a slow process of decomposition. The state appeared to be less capable of solving its problems, whilst resistance to it grew − peasant insurrection in the south of the island (April 1971) that revealed the poverty of the rural areas;[7] growing hostility from an urban and administrative bourgeoisie drawn from the upland plateaux that had lost its power to people of coastal origin; developing national aspirations fed by the ubiquitous French influence; the restlessness of young people faced with an educational system ill-adapted to an insufficient labour market, and so forth.

The regime could not withstand the insurrectionary events of May 1972 that were provoked by a crisis in schools and university poorly understood by the authorities, who showed a singular clumsiness in dealing with it. Deprived of military assistance that the French refused him, despite the terms of the co-operation agreements, the president of the republic was forced, on 18 May, to hand over full powers to General Ramanantsoa, leader of an army that up until then had shunned the political game entirely and showed little desire to participate in it.

With the arrival of the military in power the so-called *transition period* opened. It had a troubled history, and the event that marked its end − the proclamation of the Democratic Republic of Madagascar − could hardly have been foreseen.[8] At the outset this phase was seen as a technical interregnum of an apolitical nature. It was supposed to allow the new head of the government, confirmed in his position by the referendum law of 7 November 1972 that set up the new provisional constitutional framework, to restore order in the economy, to clean up the administration, and to preserve and strengthen national unity (programmatic speech of 27 July 1972); and also to prepare, within a maximum period of five years, a new liberal and parliamentary constitution. It was with this in mind that the new leadership, composed of military and civilian technical personnel, undertook a series of reforms that for the most part showed the political will to bring about a more real decolonialization: the country left the franc zone; the co-operation agreements with France were renegotiated (4 June 1973), leading to a marked slackening of the political and economic links between the two countries and to the end of the French military influence and presence in Madagascar; external relations were diversified by opening up foreign policy, under the Foreign Minister D. Ratsiraka, to the socialist countries; the state brought within its purview industrial production and commerce by creating state-owned companies and by a systematic policy of public participation in the capital of (foreign) private enterprises that were active in the 'vital sectors';[10] and the economy, the administration and the educational system were brought closer to Madagascar's traditions, with the administrative apparatus being reorganized, on the basis, chiefly, of *fokonolona* (see below).

Very swiftly − and this lay at the heart of the failure of the provisional government − disagreements arose over the content and the direction that should be imparted to the reforms. Many saw the policy of state intervention in the economy as a stage in a holding operation of localization until Malagasy private enterprise was ready to take over, whilst the AKFM, for example, which was the great beneficiary of this period, saw in it the beginnings of a socialist society. For yet others it was a matter of preparing to hand the economy over to the people in a form that could only be assured when peasant communities – the *fokonolona* – held the power of decision. But whatever the ultimate objectives were assumed to be, the intervention of the state had one certain consequence, which was also its cause: to allow a national bourgeoisie that was essentially political and administrative and still not extensively industrial to acquire a power of economic decision-making that had escaped it hitherto to the advantage of foreigners.

Another source of tension was ethnic. The Ramanantsoa government was perceived as discriminating heavily in favour of the capital, and it was because of demands violently expressed by military leaders of coastal origin that there was to open a period that is one of the most confused and agitated in Madagascar's political history.

Too indecisive to control a government that was more and more shaken by internal divisions, General Ramanantsoa was to give way, like it or not, to his Minister of the Interior, Colonel of the Gendarmerie Ratsimandrava, who professed a militant populism. He was sworn in on 5 February 1975, but was assassinated on 11 February in circumstances that a three-month trial was not able to elucidate. With this sudden death a contest for power took place between those that might crudely be termed bourgeois 'conservatives'[11] and the proponents of revolutionary schemes, although they were able to make common cause on occasion, despite their mutual hostility.

These tendencies were present within the Military Directorate (*Directoire Militaire*) that was set up immediately after Colonel Ratsimandrava's death. Led by General Andriamahazo, the officer with the longest seniority and the highest rank, and a minister in the Ramanantsoa government, it was composed of 19 military officers to whom the various ministers were subordinated. This was the only truly military regime that Madagascar has known. The confrontation between the different factions turned in favour of Frigate-Captain Didier Ratsiraka, thanks to the support of the coastal people to which he belonged and of the AKFM. He was the only person of a national stature, having acquired this during his period of office as Foreign Minister. He also seemed to be the person best placed for reconciling the conflicting interests of the political parties of the left and those of the bourgeoisie. This reconciliation was to be sealed by a programme[12] that envisaged the socialization of the economy and the assertion in all spheres of a Madagascan identity.

No sooner had he become chairman of the High Council of the Revolution (*Conseil suprême de la Révolution*) – a structure that replaced the Military Directory – and head of the government, than Didier Ratsiraka set to work to secure himself in power. He did this first of all by formulating the new social policies on which there seemed to be general, if at least only tacit, agreement, and by justifying in this way his accession to office at the head of the state. Spelled out first in a proclamation of 16 June claiming that 'the only way to achieve development is socialism', the ideological orientation of the regime was defined in a long speech that was broadcast by radio over several days (August – September 1975) and that, once edited, was to become 'the charter of the Malagasy socialist revolution', better known by the name of

Boky Mena – the red book – because of the colour of the cover of the standard edition of the document.

He secured his power secondly by preparing a new constitution. Unlike other comparable socialist states of the Third World (Algeria, Cuba) whose constitutions, when they were adopted, ratified in the light of experience a revolutionary process that had been in progress for several years, Madagascar in fact moved straightaway, from the birth of the new regime, to institution-alize the revolution, adopting a constitution of a rigid kind. This rapidity illustrates the intention of the leaders of Madagascar to endow the new commitment that had been proclaimed with an irreversible character, and to give the new power structure a legitimacy that in Madagascar requires a scrupulous respect for juridical procedures and legality.

A New Ideological Order

The most tangible evidence of the change that took place in 1975 is of an ideological kind. First of all, from being moderate in tone and structure under the First Republic, the discourse of the regime became radical; from being 'African' in the days of President Tsiranana, Malagasy socialism became revolutionary.

Justified at considerable length in the charter – its principal doctrinal source – the socialist revolution is presented as the only path capable of leading at one and the same time to national independence (against the 'imperialists'), to true democracy (against injustice and the 'reactionaries') and to economic development (against imperialists and their allies within the nation). Malagasy socialism was to be revolutionary, but also both original and autonomous. It rejects atheist materialism in the name of 'the fundamental values of the Malagasy people ... based on a certain primacy of the spiritual'. It allows for co-operation across classes since the national bourgeoisie – that part of the bourgeoisie that is not 'comprador' – can be revolutionary. No reference is made to the dictatorship of the proletariat.

These particularities are often used to demonstrate the endogenous nature of Madagascan socialism. It is none the less true that Marxism-Leninism inspires and shapes the discourse. The charter takes up the fundamental themes and enshrines its essential principles: the class war is acknowledged, as are the primacy of the struggle against imperialism and the public appropriation of the principal means of production; a model of development is outlined that makes agriculture the base and industry the motor of development; institutional reforms are proposed based on the principle of democratic centralism, and so on. As President Ratisiraka recognized, 'We are not exactly Marxist-Leninists, but we take from Marxism-Leninism the thinking behind our economic projects and all our philosophy, and we try to adapt it to Madagascan realities'.[13]

Madagascan socialism is a brilliant synthesis of the classic and Third World elements of Marxism-Leninism,[14] and a good illustration of the 'third way of development' represented by the idea of national democracy that the charter talks of at many points in order to describe the stage that Madagascar has reached in its evolution towards the socialist state.

Second, one of the first steps that embodied the new ideological commitment concerned the *constitutional system*. The constitution of 31 December 1975[15] introduced into the legal system of Madagascar notions and institutions hitherto unknown and directly imported from the constitutional theory of the socialist countries. Without attempting to exhaust the list one should note: the principle of democratic centralism, the distinction between state power and state administration, the principle of delegated powers as a substitute for that of the separation of powers, the insistence on the mandate of the people's representatives, the attachment to citizen status of duties, whilst rights are to be seen, in the final analysis, as only contingent, being reserved to those who work to support the charter and fight for the triumph of a socialist society.[16]

However, the influence of socialist constitutionalism by no means drove out other influences. The constitutional arrangements of the Democratic Republic of Madagascar (*République démocratique de Madagascar*) in fact draw largely on techniques − for example, that of 'rationalized parliamentarism' − of the First Republic, itself very close to the French Fifth Republic. Also, the organs that the Military Directory had set up to succeed itself in June 1975 have been retained; as in the case of many African and Third World countries, these in a rather surprising way make the political role of the armed forces official in constitutional law. But the maintenance of these institutions − the High Council of the Revolution and the Military Committee for Development (*Comité militaire pour le développement*) − has been accompanied by a modification in the description of their functions and even in their actual role.

The combination of these techniques borrowed from different constitutional systems yields results that defy classification according to classical typologies. This can be illustrated by the use that the Madagascan constitution makes of the distinction between state power and state administration. In the constitution of 1975 the first is held not by an assembly or its presidium but by the President of the Republic, whose office is described as 'the supreme organ of state power'. Elected on a universal suffrage, and independent of the National People's Assembly (*Assemblée nationale populaire*), he enjoys in addition most of the prerogatives of a presidium, including that of legislating, under certain conditions, between parliamentary sessions.

This combination has the effect − and is indeed also its cause − of strengthening the authority of the state and the power of the head of state. This pre-eminence is not diminished by the numerous other constitutional organs, most of which are dependent on the head of the executive: the High Council of the Revolution (HCR), two-thirds of the members of which are nominated by the head of state, is only a body for formulating policy, under the aegis of the President of the Republic;[17] the government, under the prime minister, is charged with carrying out the decisions of the President. Legislative power is exercised by the National People's Assembly, but the powers that the head of state has in this domain mean that he, too, is on occasion a legislator. The constitution makes provision for a responsible government − but only in exceptional cases. The National People's Assembly, elected by universal suffrage and on a system of proportional representation, meets only four months a year at a maximum and is unable to counter the power of the President, any more than can the High Constitutional Court or the Military Committee for Development that the constitution set up.

Strengthened by the idea of revolutionary socialism, the personal power of the President that is established in this way is reinforced still further by a weighty apparatus of political control, through the imposition of censorship and the creation of a political police.[18]

Foreign policy is a third special area where the socialist and radical orientation of the regime is particularly visible. The speeches of Didier Ratsiraka, first as Minister of Foreign Affairs and subsequently as head of state, call for a diplomatic stance open to 'all points of the compass' and in accordance with a policy framework that is not peculiar to Madagascar – one that combines non-alignment with an opening to the socialist countries. The latter figure as the objective allies of the Third World in its struggle for independence and development, as against the Western countries that are the historical incarnation of imperialism. In the name of 'positive neutralism', which the Military Directory proclaimed in April 1975, Madagascar has multiplied its links with the Soviet Union, North Korea, China, Cuba, Eastern Europe and revolutionary Africa, and has signed a number of co-operation agreements in the military and cultural fields, as well as in that of internal security. The DRM moreover systematically extends its support, especially within international organizations, to the various liberation movements in the Third World.

In parallel with this policy, the traditionally close relations with the Western countries and with the member countries of the major regional African organizations – now accused of being too close to French imperialism – are becoming more tenuous.[19] The deterioration of Madagascar's relations with the West has obviously concerned, above all, the erstwhile colonial power; but, although seriously strained, Franco-Madagascan relations have never been broken off.[20] In the fields of trade and culture France remains today by far the leading partner of the Malagasy Republic. The 'all points of the compass' policy has to this extent been modified, but with few concrete results. Thus, Madagascar is now only the sixteenth African client of France (third in 1973), but on the other hand it is the second in order of the countries most aided by that country, after Senegal, and France accounts for 75 per cent of aid going to Madagascar.

A Regime in Search of a Revolutionary Organization

The political system of Madagascar as it has developed over the past ten years has one particular characteristic that is important in view of the goals that the regime has set itself: it does not have a revolutionary organization on which the authority of the regime can rest. The army, the Front and the *fokonolona* were all meant to fill this role, but none of them has truly become a tractable instrument of power. The regime is often condemned for this reason; it has none the less contrived to survive.

(1) The End of the Army's Political Monopoly

The armed forces occupied a position of sole power from February to June 1975, but no longer have more than a formal and reduced role to play. They remain one of the 'pillars of the revolution' with the High Council of the Revolution, the peasants and the workers, young intellectuals, and the women (see the charter). However, they do not control any political organ. The only institution where they are represented is the Military Committee for Development. This is composed of 30 members of the people's army and 20 members of the gendarmerie. Its role is purely consultative. The HCR, for its part, was originally composed entirely of military people, but since 1976 it has had a civilian majority. It includes the principal leaders of the political parties that participate in the Front, and many members of previous governments of the DRM.[21]

On his accession to power, Didier Ratsiraka addressed himself to the task of replacing a military legitimacy with one that was both democratic and revolutionary.[22] More concretely, he drew the lessons of the years 1972−75 and reduced the influence of an army of whose allegiance he was far from sure and attempted to transform it into an efficacious instrument of his policies and of his protection.[23]

One of the first reforms of the new regime was precisely to reorganize the army.[24] The classical division of the armed forces into land, sea and air was abolished and instead four large groups were created: the army of development, the gendarmerie, the naval and air forces, and the army of intervention. The most notable results of this new mode of partition were, first, to contain the land army, the 'fief of the military oligarchy', within a simple structure that would train cadres and organize production. Second, the main core of the army's coercive power was reserved to a minority, the army of intervention, that was kept well in hand by the political leadership through control of nominations and the presence of technical assistants from the socialist countries.

The role of the 'People's Armed Forces' was also redefined. In conformity with their new status as 'people's soldiers' or as 'militants in uniform' the armed forces found themselves taking on more and more traditional activities of a social, cultural and economic kind. The latter were mostly in the realm of agricultural and industrial production.[25] These functions were fulfilled more or less fruitfully, at least as far as agriculture was concerned.

Whilst it no longer holds power, the army nonetheless occupies an important place in public life in Madagascar. First of all, its numbers are substantial (19,555 men against 4,700 in 1976, or 2.3 soldiers for every 1,000 inhabitants) and its part of the budget is large − over 30 per cent of GNP. Second, it constitutes an undeniable political force. Wooed by the financial advantages that the regime offers it and neutralized by the divisions that it harbours within itself on a par with the civilian population, the army has so far remained faithful each time the government has been confronted by the insurrectionary movements that are endemic in the country.

Faced with a political class that is divided and unstable in terms of its internal alliances, the armed forces do, however, represent a potential force that could, for example, manifest itself if the present head of state should disappear from the scene.

(2) A Multi-Party Revolution

Madagascar is one of the rare revolutionary countries not to be ruled by a single or unified party, and moreover to have allowed a real multi-party system to emerge that has an effective influence on the way in which the political institutions work.

True, the 1975 constitution envisaged a 'National Front for the Defence of the Revolution' (*Front national pour la défense de la Révolution*), the role of which was to provide theoretical and practical guidance for the revolution and to give impulse to the state's activity (articles 8 and 9); and a monopoly of political activity, notably in the electoral realm, is reserved to its members. Set up with some difficulty in 1976,[26] the Front has contained − depending on the time in question − from five to seven political parties that represent all strands of the political chess-board except for the old dominant party, although the authorized parties include a good number of ex-members and former sympathizers of this last. In the elections of 1982−83, the Front comprised seven parties.[27] First, there is the AREMA (the Vanguard of the Madagascan Socialist Revolution) that was created by President Ratsiraka and acts as a 'catch-all' party, often being seen − as was the SDP before it − as the party of the *fanjakana* (administration and central power). Second, there is the pro-Soviet AKFM-KDRSM, led by Fr. Andriamanjato, and professing scientific socialism. This party traditionally recruits its membership − but with increasing difficulty − in the Merina bourgeoisie of the capital. Third, the MFM-MFT Proletarian Party has an influence in the working class and the universities, but also more recently in certain milieux within the bourgeoisie of Antananarivo. Fourth, the VONJY-ITM draws part of its support from the political class of the old regime and has little ideological colouring; it has a strong local base, particularly in the south-east. Fifth, there is the Monima Ka Miviembeo, led by the old nationalist leader Monja Jaona. Sixth, the VS-Monima is a splinter group from the Monima. The two groups are very close to each other, in terms of both their popular roots, mainly in the peasantry, and their penetration of intellectual milieux. They are equally critical of the revolutionary feebleness of the regime, but are divided on the question of the tactics to be adopted towards the government. And finally there is a small party of the Catholic left − the UDECMA-KMTP, based chiefly on the east coast.

As for the share of seats in the various assemblies (the People's National Assembly and the local bodies), the AREMA takes the lion's share;[28] but this domination conceals both the division of the President's party into at least two fractions, and the bitterness of the political fighting in which the parties of the Front engage.

In a manner that differs from the normal practice of revolutionary socialism, Madagascar has witnessed, in fact, on a number of occasions elections that can reasonably be described as *competitive*. Each party has covered the country, mobilizing its electorate, calling for candidates and emphasizing its doctrinal originality, whilst maintaining an allegiance in principle to the official ideology. In 1982 and 1983 local, legislative and − more remarkably − presidential elections were 'contested' in this way. On the second of these occasions the incumbent president, Didier Ratsiraka, and Monja Jaona confronted each other violently in public. It will be claimed that the means at the disposal of the parties are unequal and favour the AREMA, and that the sincerity of the votes cast is not always clear. But it has rightly been pointed out that there has been on these various occasions a good deal less conformity than in certain other elections such as, to take only the example of Madagascar, those of the First Republic, when elections were officially competitive.[29]

As things are at present in the political life of Madagascar, diversity within the Front is tending to win out over unity. Conceived at the beginning as transitory, multi-party pluralism is becoming accentuated at the expense of the unity that a revolutionary front would seem to require. The head of state has himself acknowledged this, regretting that a future 'reorganization of the Front as a single party is not on the agenda'.[30] This development, whose origins lie in ethnic antagonism and a long tradition of aggressive pluralism, puts Madagascar in a special situation among states that have opted for a revolutionary socialism. The absence of a single-structure organization and the rivalries in which the political parties of the Front indulge have been interpreted as a sign of weakness in the regime. But on the contrary, this is in fact one of President Ratsiraka's principal sources of strength, if not the only one, expert as he is in using these divisions in order to perpetuate his rule.

(3) A Rebellious Fokonolona

The structure of the new state is unitary, but also decentralized. It rests on 'the socialist democratic community, the *fokonolona*', as the first article of the constitution puts it. With this reference to the *fokonolona* − the name of the ancient Madagascan collective organization − the socialist Republic adds a hallowed aura to one of the most interesting reforms in the recent history of Madagascar − a reform that was launched in 1973.

It will be recalled that the reform of the *fokonolona* in 1973 was the result of a difficult compromise.[31] It cannot be analysed simply as a reorganization of the regional administrative structure, nor as a fresh experiment in community development. What was involved was a challenge to a whole economic system and a whole pattern of power, with a view to establishing, first of all in the rural areas, control over development by the people. Its creators, first and foremost among them Colonel Ratsimandrava, commander of the gendarmerie and Minister of the Interior at the time, were not much concerned with ideological references. What they were proposing, none the less, was an experiment that was profoundly populist in its inspiration and very close − probably quite unconsciously − to the themes developed by Russian populism in the nineteenth century.[32] The restructuring that was undertaken involved a veritable act of faith in the peasantry and the communal institutions of the village, and in the capacity of the peasants to run their own affairs freely.

It rests on the conviction that the birth of a new world – characterized by control over development by the people – is to be achieved by the people's taking immediate and effective charge of the matters that affect their daily lives, starting with the production and marketing of agricultural goods. This transfer of responsibility should, through its own momentum and on condition that the autonomy of the peasant collective – the *fokonolona* – was respected, lead progressively to the total take-over of the nation's centres of decision-making. Grounded in autonomous development and self-administration, the *fokonolona* system should bring about the withering away of the state, whose central power incarnated the heritage of colonialism.

So conceived, *fokonolona* becomes, through the economic functions that it involves, the best way of bringing down capitalism without thereby opting for any one of the available models of socialism. The *fokonolona* option would absorb the strains and demands of a national renovation that saw itself as proceeding along the lines of a mode of development simultaneously modern and original. By the voluntary mobilization of human energy that it implies, *fokonolona* is perceived as the artisan of national independence.

These ideas were translated into practice by the abolition of the system of provinces and communes and the creation of novel structures designed to embody the power of the people and to diffuse it upwards to the national level. The decrees of 24 March 1973[33] envisaged an ascending pyramid of power comprising four layers of collectives, each one emanating directly from the one below, and the whole edifice resting on the *fokonolona* community. The reference to the *fokonolona* is a political revival of the past, but it also has institutional consequences. By an original process of administrative acculturation, the structure that has been set up reproduces, or at least claims to reproduce, the ancestral form of government. The system of administration and government thus created gives priority to the community over the state (the principle of the free constitution of the *fokonolona*, freedom of administrative and economic management, the subordination of the administration and public services to the collective) and establishes a system of direct local democracy.

The change from one republic to another did not affect the external aspect of the administrative apparatus created in 1973. The territorial structures were retained and the establishment of the four layers was completed and extended to the urban ex-communes.[34] None the less, the *fokonolona* form of organization underwent a transformation that imposed serious restrictions on the historic mission of these communities and on their prerogatives. President Ratsiraka, like most of the leaders of the left, in fact has serious criticisms to make of the institution. They question the revolutionary capacity of the peasantry and do not believe that it can serve as the true motor of the revolution. The autonomy and the free initiative of the peasant communities seem to them to be incapable of challenging socio-economic relations. *Fokonolona* is no longer considered to be the homogeneous collective that would resolve social contradictions by itself; it is seen, like any social group, as a terrain for the class struggle. The position of the new regime is in line with the Marxist canon. It is also nourished by the frankly disappointing results of the first few months of *fokonolona's* application, and particularly by the continuing relations of dominance that the reform was supposed to sweep away. Although it was accused of favouring centrifugal and conservative forces, *fokonolona* could not be rejected or ignored because of the respect that it evoked for the traditional values of the Madagascan nation. The term and the structures were preserved in 1975,[35] but the institution itself lost its character as a peasant community of a more or less spontaneous kind to become a simple 'decentralized collective' stripped of all anti-state or even non-state connotations. The autonomy that it once displayed was boxed in by a series of mechanisms and principles that erased all anarchistic traces. The liberty that the peasant had enjoyed to create collectives or to control their size disappeared. Democratic centralism was applied to *fokonolona* and elections were in principle reserved to candidates of the Front. From being the principal actor of the revolution, *fokonolona* became rather a structure to receive it. Madagascar acknowledged the institution's 'fullness of revolutionary power' but at least in a transitional phase 'socialist *fokonolona*' was to be restricted to a subordinate role as a relay and auxiliary of the revolution, whose guardians are to be found in higher places.

More concretely, the decentralized collectives were supposed to continue to constitute the framework of power; but this could not be the case without a minimum of shared commitment. In practice, they turned out to be, in fact, battlegrounds on which politicians and local power-holders confronted one another. As a general rule, they do not attract the commitment of the people either. Indeed, they are perceived as one more manifestation of *fanjakana* and thus to be treated, as far as the peasants are concerned, with a healthy mistrust. The new institutions have therefore for the most part become an inert structure, functioning according to the classic pattern of direct administration. However, the situation is at times different: in certain cases populations can be seen to be abiding by the letter of slogans that have been dinned into them over many years to the effect that the masses are the masters of their destiny and that power is theirs. These examples are often disorganized and do not necessarily respect the rules laid down in the texts or the revolutionary directives. Many cases arise of spontaneous, direct democracy, before which the elected local authorities have to give way or become their spokesmen. Pockets of power thus arise, responsible for meeting daily requirements, running their own affairs with the means at their disposal.

But these anarchical cases are limited to a minority of *fokonolona*, and do not seem to be of a kind that might threaten directly a state that is capable of controlling the higher echelons of the administrative and political hierarchy.[36]

Socialization of the Economy and Madagascar's Pragmatism

'Dynamite the old structures' − such are the words of the charter of the socialist Revolution and the slogan for the task that the leaders of the DRM have given themselves with a view to constructing socialist society. Since 1975 change has been extensive and, to use an expression often employed in Madagascar, has had its course set for 'all points of the compass'.

The reforms undertaken in the name of revolutionary socialism have involved, one after the other, all possible domains: the school and university systems, the army and national service, taxation, justice, the public administration, local government, the code covering investments, planning, public enterprises and co-operatives. Among these reforms some are particularly worth noting here because of the importance that the political leadership attaches to them. They are thus especially indicative of the true orientation that the regime has adopted. They are the reforms that concern the public running of economic development.

In the main, the strategy for development adopted since 1975 follows the analyses and proposals that have been made in relation to the new economic order. The satisfaction of the essential consumer needs of the population and the elimination of the country's dependence on foreign aid, without which there could be no true development ('aid must be considered only as a supplement, and never as a complement', according to the charter), requires 'a drastic transformation and restructuring that must begin at the inside of each state'. Given the ubiquity of foreign interest groups this transformation resolves itself first and foremost into a socialization of the means of production. As the charter puts it: 'The socialized sector must be given the means that it lacks, so that it can be born, grow and develop harmoniously, and so that it can become the true motor of political and economic life.' According to the planners, co-operatives and state-owned enterprises should account for 56.63 per cent of value added by the year 2000 (against 22 per cent in 1980).[37]

From this point of view the economy of Madagascar has been nationalized to a considerable extent and has experienced numerous structural changes. But the process has not affected all sectors to the same degree, and for some years now the rhythm has been slower and less pressing.

(1) In spite of having ambitious aims, involving the putting into practice of an *agrarian reform* and of numerous measures published in the official journal, the socialist revolution has in fact hardly touched the agricultural world.[38] The action of the leadership has affected essentially unused land. By a law of 20 June 1974, in a few years over 100,000 hectares of land belonging mostly to colonial proprietors was recuperated and, in a novel move, some nationalization of agricultural land took place. These measures concerning property in land were limited in their overall scope, but it should not be forgotten that vast stretches of land are totally unused, especially in the south and west of the island, where a policy of migration has been attempted since 1974, although without great success.

The 'co-operativization of agriculture' had no better fortune. It was the main plank of the agrarian reform and was supposed both to bring about a radical and irrevocable change in the existing social relations that were semi-feudal or colonial in numerous regions, and to increase a production of food that was too low to avoid recourse having to be made to hefty imports.[39] New co-operative structures were therefore suggested. These were conceived as taking place in two stages, and the co-operative system has a dual aspect that reflects the contradictory preoccupations of the leadership: on the one hand to collectivize agriculture and on the other to take into consideration a socio-economic context and a peasant mentality that hardly favoured a sudden and thoroughgoing reform.

In 1977, a first series of legislation was published very close, even in its vocabulary and style, to equivalent measures in certain socialist countries of Asia – for example North Korea or Mongolia.[40] It set up a co-operative system that took a radical view of the collectivization of the agricultural economy.[41]

This form of co-operative agriculture is considered by its creators as 'the most modern'. But it is also probably of a kind that will condemn any socialist experiment in a rural world where there will be strong resistance both from local power-holders and from landlords, many of whom belonged also to the political and administrative apparatus, and from peasants attached to traditional forms of agriculture. It was no doubt through an awareness of these risks, and through the experience of foreign models that did not come up to form and each time had to be reversed, that the leadership considerably relaxed the co-operative system by setting up in 1978 a third type of co-operative on a much more liberal pattern.[42]

At all events these co-operatives are few in number. They have been set up principally on land taken in hand by the state because it was abandoned. And when the co-operatives were established (some 50 in 1979) they were generally seen by the peasantry as an arm of the governing party – the AREMA – and as a means for benefiting from state subsidies.[43]

(2) On the other hand *the policy of public ownership in the fields of industry and commerce* has progressed, since June 1975, at a pace that contrasts with the abstention in principle that the First Republic exercised, and this despite the wide extent of foreign interests. In 1972 only 5.1 per cent of the total turnover of the 575 largest firms (those employing over five people) was in Madagascan hands, and both the key industries and the tertiary sector escaped the control of the state and remained dominated by foreign capital. In a few months entire sectors of industry, trade, raw materials, and banking passed under the control of the state. Today the state controls 100 per cent of banking, insurance, water and electricity, 85 per cent of exports, 70 per cent of imports and foreign trade, and 40 per cent of industry. Increasing in tempo in 1975, state control acquired different forms. Nationalization, which had only once been adopted, in 1974, for the French water and electricity company of Madagascar, now became systematic. The four commercial banks were nationalized, as were all insurance companies, cinematographic distribution, the principal export–import companies, the oil companies, and various firms in the textile and sugar industries.[44]

Other examples of public control took the classic form of majority participation in enterprise capital (merchant marine companies, textile and sugar firms that were not nationalized). The mixed economy, condemned in the context of a capitalist regime, was rehabilitated in the case of the Madagascan revolution because, according to the Charter of the Revolution, 'the state represents the true interests of the people' and is no longer an institution buckling the bourgeoisie to imperialism.

The rapid swelling of the public sector and the determination to transform social relationships led the leadership to reorganize the way in which public enterprises were run and to set up new structures. This was the objective of the 'Socialist Enterprise Charter', published for the first anniversary of the DRM and redrafted on 1 May 1978.[45] The reform had ambitious aims since it was a matter not only of making enterprises more efficient but also of changing social relationships and the status of the worker. Among the chief provisions of the Charter should be noted the restructuring of the field of public enterprises by grouping them into integrated economic sectors, the whole culminating in a Policy Council that had oversight over central planning and the marketing activities of economic units. It is at this level, where decentralization of management and the priority of national goals have to be reconciled, that power over the policy and running of enterprises lies. The enterprises, whose freedom of management is protected from state intervention, are in principle (although with certain exceptions)[46] organized on identical lines, whatever their previous legal status was (mixed public and private firms, public firms, public corporations etc.); this is the model of the 'socialist enterprise'.[47] Besides a reorganization of the decision-making centres and organs, it offers the workers possibilities of participation, but without any restriction on the direct or indirect power of the state's representatives.[48] This is further evidence of the leadership's refusal, mentioned above, to permit any reference to self-management to appear in legislation.

In the new distribution of economic roles, the *private sector* has an ambiguous place. The law assigns it an essential place in the economy — but a provisional one, although on this last point the leadership has taken changing and conflicting attitudes at different times. According to the official doctrine of the DRM's first years, private enterprises were supposed to disappear in time, the only ones still to be tolerated being those operating in areas that require heavy financing, a technology or technical assistance that private companies could offer, or even simply, and ambiguously, because they 'make possible the correct carrying out of certain activities'.

In contrast with the transitional period, there is no longer an exhaustive and restrictive list of economic activities reserved to the state. Since 1980, and in certain cases since 1978, the leadership has tried to dispel this uncertainty, which hardly encourages investment. The respective roles of the state and of private investors are now stipulated in terms favourable to the latter.[49] Private, including foreign, capital is no longer given only a secondary place in economic development. It can, first of all, participate in a 'socialist enterprise' in the vital sectors as a partner, although a minority one, of the state 'in studies of state investments'. Outside the strategic sectors, according to the head of state, 'private investors are free to invest' subject to restrictions imposed by the present situation (such as an obligation not to steer investment in directions that would involve massive imports of inputs and of raw materials). This new attitude has taken concrete form in a number of measures aimed at stimulating a real mobilization of the private sector to promote development: a slackening of price controls, simplification of the administrative procedures for industrial exports, and more recently, the adoption of a new investment code.[50]

Equally indicative of this tendency is the questioning of certain structures and mechanisms of economic administration that at the time when they were created were presented as essential to the success of the Madagascan revolution. A particularly topical example is the liberalization of rice marketing. In 1983 the government went back on a reform that ten years earlier had been aimed at eliminating the system of trade in rice. Now it has drawn the lessons of repeated failures and of the almost total inefficacy of public control of the rice market, and has withdrawn the monopoly of the state companies – a monopoly that had in fact been reconfirmed a few months earlier.[51]

These recent developments can be interpreted as being no more than a simple tactical turn required by the particularly delicate situation that Madagascar at present confronts, given that growing economic difficulties in the years to 1982 could only be resolved by massive recourse to international aid, from Western countries as well as from the more demanding IMF.[52]

It could also be judged, however, that Madagascar is moving towards a fundamental shift in its political orientation. The abandoning of a developmental strategy that gives priority to socialization is evidence of this, although it remains true that the vital sectors are now controlled by the state and that there is no intention of denationalizing them. There are other indications, such as the clear realignment of Madagascar with the Western world, starting with the United States and France, and the fact that the President's statements are becoming more sensitive to spiritual values and are at times even marked by a degree of religious sentiment.

At all events, whatever the ultimate objectives of the regime (and there appear to be divisions on this point) and whatever the intentions of the head of state, these adjustments represent the triumph of pragmatism over a voluntarism that held sway in 1975 and the triumph of economic facts over political considerations, but also over social reality. The regime seems to have taken note of the feeble receptiveness of the popular mind and of Madagascan society to the principles of Marxism-Leninism and to their manifestations.

The fragile equilibrium that has been achieved seems to be severely threatened by the difficulties that confront a leadership that is now on the defensive, and an isolated head of state – difficulties stemming from a seriously deteriorating economic situation[53] and a growing insecurity, and their effects fall most heavily on the public servants, artisans, and small traders – that is, the people who most contributed to the fall of the First Republic and who alone could bring popular support to the regime. They are difficulties that stem also from a rising tide of opposition that is not only now open, but has managed to rise above ethnic and ideological cleavages to present a common front.[54] The avowed hostility of the united churches,[55] criticizing the Marxist commitment of the regime and the deterioration in public and social life, marked by a degree of corruption never before equalled in Madagascar, has been joined by attacks from the political formations of the Left that are disappointed by the ideological inconsistency of the President of the Republic. More recently it has been the turn of the bourgeoisie to feel disquiet at an economic liberalization that is likely to work against its interests, lacking as it does financial means strong enough to counter the competition of foreign capital.

The build-up of challenges to which the leadership has to respond is likely to tax to the utmost the capacity of the Madagascan political system to maintain order in its house. This system will be able to survive only if it changes its form. Recent developments would suggest that the process has already begun.

NOTES

Jean du Bois de Gaudusson is Professor of Public Law and Political Science at the University of Bordeaux I, and Director of the *Centre d'étude d'Afrique noire.*

1. P. Chaigneau, *Madagascar, un Etat à orientation socialiste* (Paris: Nanterre, State Doctoral Thesis, 6 vols., 1984); and 'Un mode d'orientation socialiste à la périphérie du système; le cas singulier de Madagascar', in *Revue Pouvoirs* (Paris) No. 21 (May 1982), pp. 109–16.
2. J. Larteguy, 'La guerre secrète du 3e océan', in *Paris-Match*, 13 Nov. 1981, p. 154.
3. Cf. R. Archer, *Madagascar depuis 1972; la marche d'une révolution* (Paris: L'Harmattan, 1976), postface by S. Andriamirado.
4. On the First Republic see Charles Cadoux, *La République malgache* (Paris: Berger-Levrault, 1969); and P. Pascal,
5. In 1965 there were 1780 French personnel in Madagascar.
6. The most serious consequence of these disputes was the disgrace and then the arrest in 1971 of A. Resampa, General-Secretary to the SDP. He appeared to be the most likely successor to President Tsiranana.
7. The rate of impoverishment of the rural world in the period 1960–70 was in the order of 30 per cent. See P. Hugon, 'Conjoncture et politique économique à Madagascar depuis l'indépendance', in *Annuaire des pays de l'océan Indien* (Presses universitaires d'Aix-Marseille), Vol. I (1976), pp. 325–44.
8. On this period see Charles Cadoux, 'La deuxième République malgache; vers l'édification d'un Etat de type nouveau' in *Annuaire des pays de l'océan Indien*, Vol. II (1977), pp. 35–50.
9. Programmatic speech of 27 July 1972. J.O. RM, 2 Sept. 1972.
10. These are the sectors that are regarded as of strategic importance for independent development. The list there drawn up includes: banks, energy, insurance, mines, foreign trade and transport, pharmaceuticals and the cinema. In most cases the state was content to participate, but in others it took direct responsibility for a sector by setting up a state company (a new formula in Madagascar), described as a company of national interest for the promotion of the economy. In this way were set up SONACO for foreign trade, SINPA for the marketing of agricultural produce, SINTP for public works and SINEE for water and electricity.
11. Amongst these an important role is often attributed to the 'Club of the 48'. This is a network of representatives of the major families of Antananarivo and of the upper Madagascan bourgeoisie that seems to function as an efficient and discreet channel of communication and pressure. President Ratsiraka's elder brother is a member of it.
12. This 'general political plan', published on 12 April 1975, contains ten points: continuity of foreign policy based on 'positive neutralism'; popular control of development; co-operation with the private sector; deconcentration and decentralization coupled with the maintenance of an 'adapted' *fokonolona*; a just distribution of incomes and means of production; education in Madagascan and French pending the 'nationalization of a common language'; agrarian reform; reorganization of the armed forces; preparation of a new constitutional framework.
13. *Afrique-Asie*, No. 151, Dec. 1977, p. 32.
14. With a marked preference for the North Korean Kim II Sung and the ideas of *juche*, to which a conference was devoted in Antananarivo in 1975.

15. See J. du Bois de Gaudusson, 'La nouvelle constitution malgache du 31 Decembre 1975' in *Revue juridique et politique, indépendance et coopération*, No. 3 (July 1976), pp. 261–385; Charles Cadoux, 'La deuxième République malgache', pp. 50–77.

16. Articles 14, 15 and 16 of the constitution.

17. The HCR is styled in article 55 the 'Guardian of the Madagascan Socialist Revolution' and is given the general task of assisting the President of the Republic in his mission of maintaining the revolutionary line and ensuring that other bodies, in particular the government, adhere to it.

18. In April 1976 a 'General Office of Investigation and Documentation' was unofficially created (the DGID); it was directed by a brother-in-law of the President.

19. Madagascar therefore withdrew from the existing common African Madagascan and Mauritian organization (the OCAM).

20. At present relations between Madagascar and France are back to normal. The only bone of contention is the 'scattered islands' (les Glorieuses, Europa, Juan de Nova and Banas de India). These are under French sovereignty but are claimed by Madagascar.

21. Since the foundation of the Second Republic three prime ministers have held office: Colonel Rakotomalala, Justin Rakotoniaina and Colonel D. Rakotoarijaona.

22. Since 5 December 1983, by having himself appointed Admiral, Didier Ratsiraka has been the highest-ranking military officer.

23. Obsessed by fear of plots, Didier Ratsiraka has organized a strengthened bodyguard. His safety is protected by a praetorian guard officered by North Koreans. The North Koreans have also financed and built near the capital what Antananarivans call the presidential 'bunker' – an ensemble of residential quarters and barracks that is surrounded by the greatest secrecy.

24. The armed forces were reorganized in November 1975; for these reforms see P. Chaigneau, op. cit. pp. 677–98.

25. It falls to two organizations in particular to perform this role. The National Military Office for Strategic Industries (OMNIS) was created in 1975 and has been reorganized many times since. This public body is charged, under the direct authority of the head of state, with framing national policy for strategic and military industries, with prospecting for strategic and military industries, together with oil, uranium, and natural gas, and with acting as a holding company for industrial enterprises considered strategic. A Military Operation for Agricultural Reproduction (OPRIMA) was set up in 1979 and was charged with reclaiming new acreage for rice and for boosting production of coffee, peanuts and vanilla, and with the transport of agricultural produce.

26. On the Front's constitution, see J. L. Calvet, 'Chronique politique et constitutionelle' in *Annuaire des pays de l'océan Indien* (Aix-Marseille: Presses universitaires, 1978) under 'Madagascar'.

27. For a recent study, see P. Chaigneau, 'Le système de partis à Madagascar' in *Penant*, Nos. 781/2. Aug.–Dec. 1983, pp. 306–45.

28. In the elections to the executive committees of the *fokontany* on 27 February 1983 the AREMA won 63,092 seats; the AKFM 7,200; the VONJY-ITM 6,179; the MFM 5,670; the Monima-K 1,070; the UDECMA 174; and the VS/Monima 112. In the legislative elections of 28 August 1983 the AREMA won 64.83 per cent of the vote and 117 seats; the AKFM 8.79 per cent and nine seats; the VONJY-ITM 10.6 per cent of the vote and six seats; the MFM 11.1 per cent and three seats; the Monima-K 3.71 per cent and two seats.

29. See Charles Cadoux, 'Les élections générales de 1982–1983 à Madagascar: des élections pour quoi faire?' in *Année africaine 1983* (Paris: Pedone, 1985), pp. 67–85.

30. *Madagascar Matin*, 18 April 1984.

31. On the different sources of inspiration, see S. Andriamirado, 'Heurts et malheurs des *fokonolona*' in *Autogestion et socialisme*, No. 39, September 1977, p. 51 *et seq.*; also R. Archer, op. cit. pp. 139–47.

32. See J. du Bois de Gaudusson, 'Propos sur les aspects idéologiques et institutionnels des récentes réformes des *fokonolona*; le *fokonolona* en question' in *Annuaire des pays de l'océan Indien* (Aix-Marseille: Presses universitaire, 1978) Vol. V pp. 17–36.

33. For a detailed account of these decrees see J. du Bois de Gaudusson *L'administration malgache* (Paris: Berger-Levrault, 1976) pp. 32 *et seq.*

34. There are 11,380 *fokontany*, 1,250 *firaisampokontany*, 110 *fivondronampokontany*, and six *faritany*. From 1975 the expression *fokontany*, which emphasized the territorial aspect, was substituted for the expression *fokonolona* to designate the different administrative units.

35. The principles of the reform are contained in the constitution and are developed in the decree of 27 December 1976, which has been frequently modified and added to.

36. Nonetheless one should note the difficulties that the central power sometimes has in controlling certain *faritany* (provinces) whose elected authorities show a contentious sense of autonomy and a determination to exercise all the powers they have been given and more, assuming they can escape central control.

37. The direction of development is defined by a series of plans that are in principle of a command nature: see the Fundamental Options for Socialist Planning and the First Plan 1978–80 (both published by the national press in Antananarivo in December 1977).

38. The reorganization of the administration in the rural areas (see above) and the nationalization of the marketing of rice and its derivatives (see below) had been effected before in 1973.

39. These imports amounted to 62.3 million dollars in 1982; in 1980 the total amount of exported agricultural products was 191 million dollars.

40. Decree No. 77-038 and 77-039 of 29 June 1977 constituting respectively the Socialist Co-operative Movement (J.O., 16 July) and the Socialist Producer Co-operatives (J.O., 16 July); decree 77-139 of 29 June 1977 approving the standard statutes and the agreement procedures for socialist co-operatives in artisan production. The co-operative movement involved also activities concerned with the distribution and collection of foodstuffs.

41. The agricultural producer co-operative is defined as an 'economic entity uniting producing peasants that have been freed from capitalist and feudal relations of production according to the principle of free consent so as to hold their means of production in common, to manage their activities in a democratic and planned manner and to divide the product of their labour according to the principle: "From each according to his abilities, to each according to his work"' (Art. 1 of the Charter of Socialist Producer Co-operatives). It can take two forms, depending on its degree of collectivization. In those of 'type 1' the co-operative owns the means of production. In those of 'type 2' the 'worker peasants' retain ownership of their land and of their means of production but they contribute them voluntarily to a collective production effort. The distribution of incomes is determined by the amount of work done, which is fixed according to its quality and quantity, and also by the amount of land held, which is handsomely rewarded.

    In both cases, work is done by teams and under-teams according to an annual production plan that must be approved by higher authorities. Peasants are obliged to put in a certain number of days' work on the collective, but they have a right to an individual plot of land.

42. By the decree of 28 July 1978 the co-operative of 'type 3' is defined as the free and voluntary co-operation of small and middle peasants in order to 'stimulate the socialist transformation of mutual aid; to achieve better equipment and to acquire chemical provisions; to benefit from more effective technical expertise; to group, stock and market their produce in an advantageous manner; and to improve the common lands put at their disposal by the state' (Art. 2 of the model statute). Each member of the co-operative remains proprietor of his land and of his tools of production 'that he can put at the service of the co-operatives if they require it' (Art. 4). As for income, each member keeps the produce of his piece of land, after payment for days of work exchanged and deductions for all common expenses.

43. See M. Camacho, 'Structures coopératives et transformations sociales', in *Terres malgaches*, No. 17 (Oct. 1977), p. 31. See also D. Desjeux, *La question agraire à Madagascar* (Paris: L'Harmattan, 1979).

44. For details of this policy and in general for Madagascar's developmental strategy, see J. du Bois de Gaudusson, 'Madagascar: des entreprises publiques aux entreprises socialistes' in *Les entreprises publiques en Afrique* (Paris: Pedone, 1979, for the Bibliothèque du Centre d'étude d'Afrique noire de Bordeaux), pp. 223–233.

45. Ibid., pp. 234–64; Mme Cavagnol-Noeliarilanto, *La notion d'entreprise socialiste à Madagascar*, thèse de 3e. cycle, Aix-Marseille III, 1981; Ramarolanto-Ratiaray, 'L'entreprise socialiste à Madagascar' in *Revue internationale de droit comparé* (Paris) July–Sept. 1984, pp. 541–90.

46. This is particularly the case of nationalized enterprises set up in the oil sector in order to enforce the state's powers as set out in the oil code of 6 June 1980.

47. The charter defines a socialist enterprise as 'an economic entity that is the property of the nation, and that operates in the interests of the working people and in activities that determine the development of the country or have a strategic character in the process of consolidating national independence and the construction of socialism. The socialist enterprise is an instrument for improving the condition of the workers by the function that it performs, the guarantee of work that it provides, and the well-being that it distributes' (Art. 2).

48. The Socialist Enterprise Charter provides for elected representatives of the work-force in the Management Committee (two to four representatives out of 17 to 21 members) and in the Policy council (two out of nine members); the workers also have their own organs that appoint the representatives to the various committees and councils; socialist enterprises also have the task of running certain social activities.

49. See for example the quite unequivocal statements since 1978 of M. Rakotovao-Razakaboana, Minister of Finance and the Plan until 1982, and since then member of the HCR, and those of President Ratsiraka himself (for example, on 17 January 1983).

50. This code, adopted by the National Assembly on 11 June 1985, is clearly liberal in its inspiration, even if it states that the objective is still to apply the charter of the socialist revolution. As its preamble says, 'The present economic situation, given the new developmental priorities that we have adopted and also the international environment arising from world crises, has prompted the formulation of this new Code, which seeks: to make more clear and more precise the role that private investment might play in the Madagascan socialist revolution; to establish the principle of equal treatment between agents; to set up an automatic system for benefiting from the advantages of the code once the required criteria have been respected; to streamline the procedures for drawing up applications and for taking decisions so as to give a fresh impulse to investment; to give enterprises new means for participating in the development and *malgachisation* of the economy.' 'Over and above the above-mentioned aims and principles this Investment Code lays the groundwork for the quality that is required of any entrepreneur, whose obligation is to foster the development of the country.'

51. Rice is the staple food of ten million Madagascans who consume more of it than the Chinese (400 grammes of paddy per person per day). But production is stagnant: about two million tonnes of paddy since 1970, whilst the annual harvest diminishes (239,000 tonnes in 1980, 108,000 in 1983). The deficit of marketed production rose from 75,000 tonnes in 1972 to 350,000 in 1982).

52. Madagascar joined the IMF on 23 September 1963 and was the first country of the EADI to use the Special Drawing Rights (9.4 million SDRs in 1977). After its policy of 'indebtedness at any price' Madagascar found itself unable to repay those debts and had to sign – not without internal political upheavals – an agreement with the IMF on 27 June 1981. This agreement was followed by several others that were dependent on Madagascar's being prepared to take austerity measures, including the privatization of the trading system. In mid-May 1985, Madagascar's debts to the IMF reached 14.3 million SDRs on a quota of 66 million: see P. Hugon, 'La crise financière en Afrique subsaharienne et l'insertion du FMI', in *Cahiers du CERNEA* (Paris: Universitaire de Paris X – Nanterre, 1985); P. Jacquemot, 'Le FMI et l'Afrique subsaharienne', in *Le Mois en Afrique*, Aug.–Sept. 1983, pp. 107–20, and on Madagascar in particular pp. 114–5.

53. All indicators show a sharp economic recession. The GNP and consumption levels in 1983 (in current francs) were lower than their 1975 level; in the decade of the 1970s the GNP fell by two per cent a year; the level of internal savings fell from 11.3 per cent (1974) to 3.2 per cent (1982); investment fell from 25.4 per cent to 11.8 per cent (1983). The investment policy launched in 1978 has led to a large external debt. The outstanding debt went from 315.6 million SDRs in 1978 to 1459.9 million in 1982, that is, from 17.7 per cent to 51.8 per cent of the GNP, representing 55 per cent of exports in 1983 and 86 per cent in 1984. The public debt actually spent reached $1,565 million in 1982 ($347 in 1979). National inflation and a deterioration in the infrastructures of transport and the main public services (distribution of food, health, etc.) should be added to these figures.

54. Such was the case particularly during the long strike at the University (October 1980 – June 1981).

55. The first official and formal questioning of the Madagascan socialist revolution goes back to the first national synod of the Catholic church in October 1975. A Council of Christian Churches of Madagascar was set up in 1980, grouping the four chief Christian denominations; it published a number of pastoral letters concerning events that had not been reported in the media. At its first congress in August 1981 – the political significance of which did not escape the authorities – the churches affirmed their determination to take a stand against a situation that they claimed to be catastrophic, and to demand that the nation 'take itself in hand'.

The Morphology of Radical Military Rule in Africa

Samuel Decalo

Since the collapse of the Portuguese colonial empire and the rise on its ashes of successor nationalist governments, the number of radical regimes in Africa has remained fairly constant. Encompassing roughly one-fifth of the continent, the occasional withdrawal from this camp (for example, Guinea) has been counterbalanced by the new convert (Burkina Faso). Side-stepping for the moment issues of definition and criteria — they would embroil us prematurely in an examination of the myth–reality syndrome of African political life — this group of militant countries is essentially composed of military regimes catapulted to power by coup d'état (Benin, Congo, Burkina Faso, Somalia, Libya, Ethiopia and Madagascar) and those that surfaced in the aftermath of prolonged wars of liberation against colonial rule (Angola, Mozambique, Algeria, Zimbabwe). This analytical distinction, based as it is on the origins and composition of the elite in power, is not wholly satisfactory, and a more complex analytical rearrangement of the states involved could better serve to highlight differences and similarities. However that may be, the second group of states (with or without the addition of Guinea-Bissau) is usually viewed as *sui generis* in the light of value transformations and social dislocations attending prolonged guerrilla wars of liberation, and is in any case outside the frame of reference of this article.

With the exception of Libya[1] and Ethiopia, where a segment of the armed forces rebelled against and demolished neo-feudal *anciens régimes*, the radical military administrations under analysis are second- or third-generation cliques of officers that seized power after unstable antecedent sequences of alternating civilian or military rule of various political hues. Each upheaval was a reaction to specific local circumstances. In each instance a host of considerations, parochial as well as altruistic, played a role in impelling a segment of the army to seize power and (later) to declare itself for the radical path of development. Despite their diverse origins and differing initial motivations, there are significant points of similarity among the military-headed Afro-Marxist states, their policies and internal power dynamics, and the forces that shape their evolution and constrain their objective attainments in office.

The new military juntas are largely youthful in composition, and are both better trained and better educated than previous military regimes.[2] They have forcibly dislodged their establishmentarian or apolitical (as the case may be) superiors in the military hierarchy,[3] anchored themselves in Marxist class dogma (very loosely or selectively interpreted), and established officially populist but in reality authoritarian systems of varying degrees of social oppressiveness. In the process they have, often reluctantly, forged uneasy and unstable links with like-minded urban social-class cohorts and elements of the intelligentsia, discrediting and supplanting much of the political elite of yester-year, and formally eradicating traditional authority and hierarchies. The precise policies they have pursued in office have differed from country to country, despite certain similarities and a broad *pro forma* commitment to ultimate goals that are often objectively not particularly controversial, even though couched in strident Marxist jargon. With few exceptions, the actualization of the socio-economic transformation allegedly being attempted is greatly con-strained by existential realities, both domestic and global, and by pragmatic considerations, just as these factors have in the past limited the scope of action for all antecedent administrations, civil or military, militant or conservative.

Despite considerable internal tension and the occasional upheaval — and in Ethiopia civil war and invasion; in Somalia military defeat — these regimes have succeeded in stabilizing themselves to a remarkable extent, including those in societies hitherto regarded as particularly volatile (Benin, Congo, Madagascar). Viewing themselves as symbolizing the wave of the future, rejecting the sterile infighting and crass corruption of the civilian past (although they themselves suffer heavily from both), and willing to use force to remain in power, the Afro-Marxist states have acquired a certain aura of permanence on the continent. Espousing policies anathema to segments of the propertied, traditional and bourgeois classes (and in due time falling foul of the left as well), governing societies rent with a multiplicity of cleavages without the direct assistance of patrimonial or traditional allies, and caught in the vice of acute scarcity of resources and escalating demands from society, their longevity in office is indeed striking.

Without exception these military juntas view themselves as *permanent* fixtures of political leadership in their own societies.[4] Notwithstanding a measure of political institutionalization and constitutional experimentation, often on corporatist lines and using Leninist organizational models, they have no intention of either vacating office, truly sharing power with civilian for-mations, or liberalizing the political process by allowing for the introduction of competitive politics — options in any case foreclosed by the single-party Marxist state that they erect. Their presence at the centre of the political vortex has unleashed social forces that have indelibly marked the nature of the array of domestic political power and the scope of socio-economic options, even if the concrete attainments of Afro-Marxism may be in most cases rather modest and mixed. Any analysis of the developmental alternative offered by these regimes, and the forces that shape and constrain radical military rule in Africa, requires a broad overview of the origins and causes of these regimes.

The Birth of the Military Marxist State in Africa

The emergence of the Afro-Marxist state under military auspices was in general a convoluted process hardly presaged by the initial coup that catapulted the military cliques to power. Indeed, a very sharp distinction must be made in most cases between the causes of the military *take-over* and the reasons for the subsequent adoption of Marxism as the ideological anchor of the revolution. *The two are in the majority of cases motivationally distinct*: the first is permeated by parochial considerations, while the second is very much an *ex post facto* outgrowth of weariness with previous developmental formulas and the military's quest for 'grand' solutions.

The African military Marxist state was most definitely *not* the culmination of a process of polarization of the internal contradictions of largely transitional societies, punctuated by escalating class struggle.[5] Nor was it even – except in a minimal and indirect manner – the logical outgrowth of an evolutionary radicalization of urban elements (trade unionists, students, teachers, unemployed lumpenproletariat) that set the stage for a popular take-over by militant cliques in the armed forces, dedicated to the 'transfer' of state power to the 'oppressed classes' and to a radical shift of development priorities, emphases and policies.[6] And, needless to say, the coup, subsequently to be enshrined as 'the revolution', had nothing to do in its origins with the traditional African farmer, the backbone of society – the sporadic *jacquerie* in Ethiopia and Madagascar notwithstanding.

Certainly, *incipient* class-consciousness of sorts had developed in some urban sectors of these societies; but objectively – to the degree that comparative assessments are feasible in the absence of much empirical evidence – much less so than in some of their larger or more economically developed neighbours. Revolutionary slogans, unsophisticated Marxist rhetoric, and even in a few instances minuscule Marxist groups or proto-parties, had surfaced previously in some of the countries under analysis. Following the 1963 coup in Dahomey there was even a 'soviet' set up by the striking trade unionists in Cotonou, although it was promptly disbanded by the army. And in Congo, one of Africa's most urbanized and demographically youthful states, tumultuous even under colonial rule, a revolutionary ethos had developed just prior to the overthrow of the reactionary Fulbert Youlou in 1963.

Yet much of this radical militancy, accompanied or not by what may be termed revolutionary anticipation or strivings, was, apart from Congo and possibly Ethiopia, very limited and intermittent, more in the nature of sloganeering or conspiratorial gamesmanship, an outgrowth of nationalist and anti-colonialist frustrations over bread-and-butter issues, and usually imbued with very parochial or non-revolutionary considerations, including ethnic and regional ones.[7] Congo apart, in every single instance the ultimate declaration in favour of a Marxist or developmentally radical path came without the semblance of an existing cohesive revolutionary movement, and without the assistance of or pressure from a viable Marxist party. Moreover, where such nuclei did exist (or where they sprang up in response to the 'revolution'), they invariably fell foul of the military elite, and were kept at arms' length and denied a firm role in the new order established under military aegis. Indeed, in every instance, the true left (and not just the Maoist fringe) remained just as much shackled as other, more ideologically suspect civilian factions, in a position of subservience to the military hierarchy.

The revolutionary coup that swept aside the preceding civil or military administration – conservative (Dahomey, Upper Volta, Somalia) or reactionary

(Ethiopia, Congo, Madagascar) – did not immediately usher in the African Marxist state, since the original inspiration and motivations were not Marxist or even socialist. The military clique that ousted Dahomey's Presidential Council in 1972, for example, was not particularly radical, let alone Marxist, at the time of the upheaval. Although the purge of the senior military hierarchy catapulted into centre-stage a group of youthful, third-generation, politically unknown junior officers (some of whom were to become the architects of the future People's Republic), the coup at its inception was but the latest move in a debilitating game of civil–military musical chairs that had gained Dahomey notoriety and distinction.[8] Some of the key officers, including the head of the junta, Major Kérékou, had hardly been exposed to Marxism,[9] although they were later to build up impressive Marxist credentials. As one Beninois close to the regime only half-humorously put it, 'They only started reading their Marx after the coup had succeeded'.[10] And to this day, just as in other African Marxist regimes, conservative, pro-Western, even crassly capitalist officers have been retained in high office – so long as their *personal* loyalty is beyond doubt.

Although following the 1972 coup (later declared a revolution) the military pledged a host of reforms and voiced an array of populist and nationalist complaints about Dahomey's abject state of servility and neo-dependence *vis-à-vis* the metropolitan power, the initial ideological pronouncements in Cotonou categorically *rejected* the 'external lessons' of either 'socialism, communism or capitalism';[11] it was only on the second anniversary of the 1972 revolution, after a committee had been set up to examine developmental and ideological alternatives, that a firm commitment was made to Marxism.[12]

Nor was the Marxist or radical path immediately opted for after the overthrow of the civilian élites in Ethiopia, or Somalia, and many members of the military juntas that supplanted them were not known to be particularly radical or ideologically-inclined. In Ethiopia the overthrow of the emperor was a revolutionary act, of course; but the radical land reforms and socialization of agriculture preceded by a full year the adoption of Marxism as the guiding light. Indeed, the Dergue originally had neither ideology nor any specific programmes in mind, and it was nearly three years before Marxism was discovered to be the appropriate path of development for Ethiopia.[13] In each instance a consolidation phase followed, during which the precise direction of the revolution was hammered out in either a peaceful (Benin, Somalia) or turbulent (Ethiopia, Madagascar) tug-of-war with other social strata and factions.

The upheaval in Ouagadougou may be one exception to this rule. Thomas Sankara's radical and populist predispositions had been well publicized before his coup, and some were promptly translated into policy after the take-over. As one observer noted, Sankara had undoubtedly read not only his Marx, but also Lenin, Mao, Giap and Guevara;[14] yet even here, neither a grand blueprint for action nor a compact ideological statement of radicality accompanied the coup, suggesting 'he had no clear idea of how to confront Upper Volta's chronic poverty'.[15] Idiosyncratic factors played a role in triggering Sankara's take-over (he had been arrested and released three times in the previous two months), and as elsewhere the civilian left was slowly shut out of power in the new regime.

Even Marien Ngouabi, who seized power from the beleaguered socialist regime of Alphonse Massemba-Debat in 1969, promptly to declare a People's Republic (thereby becoming the doyen of the African military Marxist state), could hardly have been categorized at the time as a genuine true believer. The primary triggering causes of Ngouabi's take-over were hardly ideological, having very parochial and personalist overtones.[16] And once the regime was established in power, within the context of an extremely volatile Brazzaville teeming with unruly and nihilistic formations of youth and unemployed labour voicing revolutionary demands and manipulated as stepping-stones to power by ambitious power-seekers, the further structural and ideological radicalization of Congo, implicit in the declaration of a People's Republic, may well be viewed as being as much a pragmatic (and opportunistic) act as an affirmation of sincere convictions.

A detailed empirical analysis of the aetiology of the radical military state reveals numerous such anomalies and paradoxes. These in turn have powerful explanatory value in suggesting reasons for inconsistencies between rhetoric and reality, myth and practice, in the contemporary policies of the new military élites. Thus, there may have been isolated pockets or cells of revolutionary sentiment in some of these countries (Ethiopia, Madagascar, Congo), or a somewhat less tangible predisposition for radical experimentation in others (Benin, Upper Volta, Somalia); moreover, the juntas that 'percolated' into power may have contained a sprinkling of junior officers with known radical inclinations: nevertheless, the military upheavals that were in due course to usher in the new order were to a significant extent triggered by a variety of non-ideological considerations, and were often not primarily Marxist at their inception.

A close empirical examination of the personal and collective motivations behind the seizures of power, and of the subsequent faltering ideological gyrations, underlines the fact that in many cases the declaration of the radical path was, *to some extent at least*, a pragmatic, *ex post facto* attempt at ideological differentiation from the antecedent administration, by a young military junta of primarily reformist bent, against a backdrop of weariness and disenchantment with the meagre fruits of a decade or more of independence. In a somewhat similar vein, Jowitt has suggested that the rise of 'unestablished elites ... lacking the authoritative credentials of high social and political status' may lead to the adoption of 'new political and ideological designations' that provide the regime with political differentiation from antecedent ones, as well as identifying 'internal bonds and external boundaries'.[17]

This eventual radicalization 'from above' by military cliques, not initially particularly radical but seeking urban social allies, unshackled the Marxist option from the existing stigma uniformly applied to it since the colonial era. It expressed the nationalist dream of yesterday, albeit in different garb, and offered new hope of a better future, made possible through the use of hitherto untried methods. It appealed especially to youth, by offering this statistically dominant group a higher purpose in life, indeed, a deeply satisfying and meaningful global role, in exchange for their previous subservient and drab status in regimes demanding political quietism and conformity. By legitimating the radical alternative in societies hitherto largely shielded from it, and by forging links with formerly 'forbidden'[18] progressive allies, the new military rulers gained valuable initial support from those dynamic social elements that were excluded from the former array of power and influence, although in so doing they were sowing the seeds of future confrontation.

The scramble on to the ideological bandwagon by groups previously functionally disenfranchised, or by ambitious self-seekers, or both, inevitably further radicalized both rhetoric and revolutionary expectations. This produced violent anarchist undercurrents, especially in Congo, Ethiopia and Madagascar, but elsewhere too. It also released a major middle-class backlash (in Ethiopia, Benin, Congo, Burkina Faso) by those threatened by the rearrangement of power in society. These twin reactions, often visible simultaneously, punctuated the initial consolidation of the radical military regime, at times taxing it to the utmost and forcing it to reveal its iron fist. The reactions were much less severe in Somalia, where many of the regime's goals threatened fewer people and, to some extent, in Burkina Faso, where Sankara's charismatic popularity allowed him to ride out the reaction from both left and right in 1984–85.

In Benin, however, the mass exodus of the middle class of teachers, civil servants, skilled administrators and commercial elements crippled entire sectors of the administration, including the educational system, nationalized in 1974/75. By the time the gates were belatedly shut, through the imposition of exit visas and the confiscation of the property of those departing illegally,[19] fully one-half of the country's qualified teaching personnel and senior administrators had left the country. Some were to lend their support from abroad to counter-revolutionary plots against what one source called 'a caricature of Marxism'.[20]

The radicalization of the revolution in Cotonou rapidly polarized the military into ideological factions. Despite the initial purge of the senior officer corps and subsequent purges that saw fully half of the officer corps displaced, the army remained divided on a multiplicity of planes, reflecting the fundamental cleavages of society itself as well as personal rivalries. The politicization of the military transferred it to the centre-stage of political and ideological conflict, throwing together strange bedfellows and stimulating curious competitions, camouflaged in the guise of a struggle over socialist rectitude. While unduly harsh, more than a kernel of truth rests in *West Africa*'s observation that 99 per cent of Cotonou's rhetoric is irrelevant since it merely 'expresses generational rivalries in more flattering ideological terms'.[21]

In the social tumult accompanying the declaration of a People's Republic, the more militant army officers were slowly eclipsed (Beheton, Bodjogoumé, and even Azonhihou, prime ideologue of the Beninois revolution), and in one instance (Aikpé) liquidated. Still reeling from the haemorrhage of skilled personnel, from the vicious union strikes that followed Aikpé's elimination, and from the 1977 mercenary assault, the Kérékou regime remains to this day suspect, challenged, under strong ideological pressure, by a variety of Marxist civilian formations clamouring for a greater role and stricter ideological orthodoxy.

This ebb and flow in the military's popularity after the initial seizure of power is visible in all the states under review. It is an axiom that coups have 'enormous divisive potentials ... [creating] hostilities, anxieties and suspicions',[22] just as an ideological upheaval is a 'highly conflictual process' as 'society is restructured around new value premises'.[23] In Burkina Faso, after emerging as one of the most popular coup-leaders on the continent, Sankara rapidly antagonized 'a large part of the political and trade union forces that allowed him to come to power'.[24] Although the coup unlocked the gates to power to the radical left (hitherto sometimes very much ignored, sometimes hounded), within months Sankara's efforts to bring about the coalescence of all progressive elements behind the revolution were in a shambles.

Rejected by the orthodox left (the UPRC) that refused to join the cabinet, and clashing with the other Marxist groups in the country (LIPAD, ULC) that had developed usurpationist inclinations in their manoeuvrings for a better position in the new order, Sankara also alienated much of the union movement. This movement, very aware of its role in bringing all previous regimes to their knees, was fundamentally more concerned with bread-and-butter issues. The austerity regimen and the sharp cuts in fringe benefits, decreed in an effort to drag Burkina Faso out of its economic morass, rapidly swung the unions into an opposition stance. The arrest of their leaders and other punitive measures, including restrictions on their right to strike against the 'progressive' state, completed the process of alienation.

Barely a year after the coup, the hand-picked NCR, prime organ of the revolution, was derisively dismissed as riddled with 'anarchists, putschists and other fishers in troubled waters',[25] with Sankara bitterly complaining that 'the main enemies are not right-wing reactionaries but left-wing reactionaries'.[26] The officer corps, purged of its senior hierarchy after the coup, was twice again to be hand-sifted. After the October 1984 dischargings due to 'unsocialist' behaviour by military cadres in administrative posts (including theft, rape and fraud), no more than 50 per cent of the original pre-1983 corps remained intact, and further conspiracies were still to emerge from the 'purified' corps.

In Brazzaville, despite Ngouabi's prompt declaration of a People's Republic and other radical policy-shifts that catered to the vehemently expressed revolutionary demands of youth and other militant elements, the most dangerous challenges to his authority still came from the left. Constant reactionary plots and attempted coups, many bearing ethnic overtones, emphasized that the revolution could well turn out to be transitory. Yet it was the unruly and role-expansionist paramilitary JMNR youth formations (ultimately crushed by force), and the dangerous putsch attempt by the ambitious 'Maoist' Lieutenant Ange Diawara (Propaganda Commissar of the Army), that taxed Ngouabi most.

Moreover, Congolese politics had historically been characterized by sharp ethnic cleavages that had formed the building blocks of power. The Marxist upheaval did little to change this. If anything, the ideological polarization, superimposed on existing ethnic rivalries, and the civil—military tug-of-war vastly complicated efforts to form a coalition of support for the new order. Even moderate Marxists, aware of the external constraints limiting further radicalization of the People's Republic, bridled at the *northern* and *military* credentials of the leader of the revolution. As one source put it, '*Who* the leader of the Congolese Revolution is matters as much as *what* his specific policies are. Socialism under a *petit-nordiste* is simply not socialism to us.'[27]

As purge followed purge, the flimsiness of Ngouabi's true power base became transparently clear. Both police and gendarmerie had to be disbanded and later restructured under Ngouabi loyalists. The vanguard party (PCT), originally hand-picked and screened for militancy and socialist rectitude, was found to be packed with 'incorrigible anti-Marxists', 'tribal reactionaries' and 'deviationists' following the 'infantile leftism' of Diawara.[28]

Both the central committee and the political bureau of the party were twice thoroughly decimated in the purges, in one instance to five and three members respectively. Most party cells atrophied or were closed down, as total membership fell in 1972 to barely 160![29] And throughout these purges, rationalized as a gigantic struggle over socialist rectitude, reminiscent of those in Stalin's Soviet Union, Ngouabi's prime allies were the pro-French bon vivant Captain Alphonse Raoul and the conservative materialist-minded Colonel Joachim Yhombi-Opango,[30] together with his own praetorian guard, the para-commando battalion.

Similar tensions developed in Madagascar, Ethiopia, and to a lesser extent Somalia, between the newly converted military Marxists and both radical and conservative civilian strata. In Ethiopia the Dergue did not declare itself to be Marxist until 1976, its earlier radical measures (requiring little ideological justification) anchored in a vaguely defined 'Ethiopian socialism'. The eventual massive transformation of Ethiopian society under the Dergue's leadership notwithstanding, the regime is regarded as a *reactionary* 'fascist' dictatorship by students, trade unionists and intellectuals alike, whose ranks have been systematically brutalized and severely depleted by arrests, purges, liquidations and the Red Terror. The Ethiopian revolution's military base and its continuing Shoan–Amharic political leadership[31] have denied the regime both legitimacy and support, just as its bloody confrontations with virtually all the country's social strata have robbed the revolution of vitality and unity.

In an identical manner in both Somalia and Madagascar, scientific socialism was stumbled upon, discovered belatedly as a mobilizational and developmental tool by military cliques neither particularly ideological nor especially radical. Indeed, in Somalia Marxism was, in its *origins*, but 'a lexical weapon in the struggle for hegemony between the army and police':[32] and, as Laitin further observes, 'a non-socialist but vigorous development-conscious military in control of the Somali government would have acted much the same way' as the 'Marxist' regime in office.[33]

In Madagascar the architect of the Marxist-Leninist revolution was a bourgeois technocrat,[34] Captain Ratsiraka, with no previous ideological convictions. His early Marxist pronouncements painfully underlined the recent and as yet incomplete nature of his metamorphosis. The regime's sharp gyrations in office, its incredible doctrinal eclecticism, frequent purges of both

left and right, and an unwillingness to commit itself firmly in any direction: all
of this made 'sincerity and depth of the ideological engagement of the leadership ... doubted both by non-socialist foreign observers and the doctrinally
pure scientific socialist intellectuals at home'.[35] Although Ratsiraka's
commitment to Marxism-Leninism was codified in the *Red Book* of October
1975 and seemingly reaffirmed in a host of declarations and policies, his
overwhelmingly *nationalistic* and *pragmatic* preoccupations ensured the
exclusion of the 'Marxist' Malagasy Republic from Soviet lists of African
states on the road to scientific socialism.

With obvious parallels to the experience of revolutionary regimes elsewhere,
although without denying the Marxist convictions of some, the frequently very
calculated and pragmatic *ex post facto* embracing of Marxism and Marxist-
Leninist ideology by what were originally relatively moderate military cliques
with limited social reforms in mind goes a long way towards explaining some
of the internal contradictions of the present-day African military Marxist state.
A number of specific features can be pointed to: the nearly uniform sharp
cleavage between strident ideological rhetoric and much more moderate concrete policies; the gyrating, zigzag ideological course of the revolution; the
never-ending alternating purges of all segments of society, left and right alike;
the inordinate stress on personal loyalty to the leader of the revolution above
all other considerations, including ideological rectitude; the avid preoccupation
with structural or paper reorganizations (or both) and epistemological trivia,[36]
leading to the creation of all the outward trappings of a communist state while
leaving intact much of the essence of reality;[37] the Alice-in-Wonderland blend
of myth and reality in the African Marxist state, leading scholars to insist
on the better explanatory value of semiological analysis as opposed to programmatic content;[38] and, last but not least, the striking disjunctions between
the new, 'socialist' morality constantly expounded to farmers and workers,
and the crassly exploitative, acquisitive and elitist comportment of the leaders
of the revolution themselves.[39]

Numerous factors play a role in producing these glaring inconsistencies.
The cruel clash of ambitious reformist zeal with resilient socio-economic
realities cannot but produce anomalies and contradictions. The fundamental
difficulty of effecting rapid, meaningful and lasting socio-economic change
in some of the world's least viable countries is a major developmental con-
straint that cannot be ignored or overemphasized. Moreover, most African
states remain exceedingly weak administratively and organizationally: their
penetrative capabilities are limited,[40] the aura of omnipotence surrounding
the African military Marxist state notwithstanding. The fact that the military
juntas attempting these social transformations are not ideologically monolithic,
and are beset by internal schisms and rivalries and hemmed in by civilian
predators on their power, further complicates the task.

Ultimately, however, these and other considerations merely add the flesh
of detail and depth to the bones of the analysis. Fundamental to any analysis
of the present-day military Marxist state in Africa is the fact that the social
base of the revolution was *bourgeois* and *military*. Rhetoric and ideological
rationalization aside, the class interests of the leaders of these regimes *remain*

bourgeois and military. The *initial* impetus for the military take-over was primarily *reformist* and broadly *nationalist* and *anti-colonialist*. With time, the goals of society may have become more ambitious, yet in no instance has serious interest been evinced in the internationalist aspect of the Marxism that military leaders embrace, nor is the universality of the doctrine secure from pragmatic tinkering. The *motivations* for the 'revolutionary coup' were hardly revolutionary, or for that matter purely altruistic: in every instance, they have been strongly permeated with *personalist, regionalist*, and *ethnic* or *corporate* considerations, and these, *mutatis mutandis*, underlie many of the intra-military tensions and splits that continue to plague the military regime. Even in the most 'populist' (Burkina Faso), not to speak of the most elitist (Ethiopia), and in spite of the existence of various civil–military governing amalgams, ideological commitment to the primacy of a Marxist-Leninist vanguard party has not changed by one iota the fundamental fact that power stems from the barrel of the gun, that is, the military.[41]

It follows axiomatically that the Marxism formally espoused by the military leaders of the revolution − bearing in mind their recent pragmatic conversion (Sankara apart) and their bourgeois class interests − would of necessity be self-taught, ideologically immature and crude, and riddled with inconsistencies, resulting in deviations unacceptable to the orthodox left. Pragmatically applied in specific contexts, it is often more an *affirmation* of strivings for ideal goals, or national aspirations, than a concrete blueprint for action, and it is intermittently used as a legitimating cloak to bludgeon into line recalcitrant elements of left or right that, deploying similar ideological syllogisms, are directly or indirectly attempting to usurp power from the military. The internal contradictions of the African military Marxist state are thus concerned as much with the social origins, class interests and initial motivations of the sponsors of the revolution as with domestic and external socio-economic limitations and constraints.

The Practice of Military Marxism in Africa

There is little homogeneity in either the ideology or the practice of African military Marxism. The ideology is defined and interpreted differentially, and if there is a consensus on core themes or assumptions, the concrete policies that stem from these are nevertheless highly eclectic and pragmatic. In essence, what is involved is the selective adoption and flexible application of certain tenets of Marxist theory set against a broad ideological commitment to Marxism-Leninism. Although allied internationally to the Eastern bloc that supports it financially (albeit selectively and quite frugally), African military Marxism is in essence an indigenous mutation, and conceptually it may be seen as the radical pole on the continuum of 'African socialism'.

Tempered by pragmatic, parochial and system-unique considerations, constrained by existential domestic or international realities, narrowly circum-scribed by the imperatives of continuing dependency relationships with the metropolitan powers, the global market economy, producer prices and sources of international risk capital, and watered down with the passage of time, the *practice* of African Marxism – disencumbered of esoteric adornments – appears at times as a relatively uncontroversial blend of *étatism* and cultural nationalism, albeit couched in Marxist jargon. The continued financial support granted to such regimes by the metropolitan power (primarily France), and to a lesser extent international consortiums, attests to a similar assessment of the relatively innocuous and unthreatening nature of the revolutionary path in Africa. Moreover, although the shift to the left has resulted in the adoption of new international postures and the forging of new alliances, the low level of financial aid from the Eastern bloc reflects a parallel scepticism on its part of both the value and the ideological dedication of the expanded Marxist camp in Africa.

The above qualifications notwithstanding, the dialectical result does constitute a distinct pole on the continuum of development alternatives facing Africa and is likely to attract new converts. This is despite the fact that, rhetoric (and Ethiopia) apart, the radical Marxist state differs from the non-doctrinaire, moderate African socialist state more in terms of *style* and *degree* (that is, of *étatism*, cultural nationalism, etc.) than in any substantive or programmatic innovations.[42] Because of the highly pragmatic manner in which Marxist theory is sifted for value within the African context, and the totally irreverent manner in which most African military Marxist leaders barely pay lip-service to fundamental tenets of orthodoxy (the role of religion, proletarian internationalism, the revolutionary role of the working class, for example), Soviet and Western Marxist theoreticians have had very ambivalent feelings about these new hybrids. While recognizing the evolutionary nature and potentials of such regimes as regards scientific socialism[43] (headed by alliances of 'bourgeois revolutionary elements'), the fundamental flaw of the African military Marxist state, from the orthodox perspective, has been precisely pinpointed and lamented. Namely, that Marxism is treated by radical leaders 'not as an historically inevitable social and economic formation but only as the most effective method of eliminating age-old backwardness and bondage to the imperialist metropolitan countries'.[44] In other words, African military Marxism is a means to an end. Consequently it is hardly sacrosanct, or immune to deviationist interpretations, nor is it anchored in the Marxist international vision. The world-wide evaporation of the sway of Soviet ideological orthodoxy has encouraged the emergence of eclectic mutations such as the African Marxist variants.

The central themes commonly stressed by radical military regimes in Africa revolve around the issues of *centralization* of power, *anti-colonialist étatism* and *cultural nationalism*. The 'mix' varies from state to state, at times quite significantly. In general, considerably more attention has been paid to the first, if only because it axiomatically defines the distribution of power in the state. Within the new, centralized hierarchy, including all ancillary structures, is lodged the supremacy of a vanguard Leninist party of militants, in which the military, after suitable constitutional and epistemological adjustments, becomes but one corporate component, albeit the central one.

Étatism is expressed in the stress on the centralization of control over the means of production in state hands, agriculture usually being excepted.

Through nationalization of expatriate or multinational holdings, or both, and the parallel erection of an expanding public sector, the 'motor' of the economic revolution is created. By siphoning profits from the former private sector into new, socially productive areas (such as infrastructure-building, technical education, and the opening up of geographically isolated areas), further industrialization is attained, with the state commanding the 'heights' of the economy and giving it direction and purpose. Although all military Marxist states in Africa have taken this direction, results have been mixed.

By contrast, cultural nationalism has often been placed on the back burner after the first flush of the revolution. Aiming at the purge from the national consciousness of vestiges of the old colonial order, in order to 'cleanse the countryside of all social, economic and cultural fetters, which keep it in a backward state', according to Sankara,[45] it usually contains strong puritanical streaks. Cultural nationalism was a very important component in the articulated goals and subsequent policies of Siad Barre in Somalia, and was given substance in Benin, Congo, Ethiopia and Madagascar as well. In Burkina Faso, whose change of name from 'Upper Volta' was triggered by 'the need to decolonize everything',[46] 'bourgeois' music and nightclubs were banned, French nationals were decreed to require entry documents (as did Burkinabé going to France), and the French ambassador lost his primacy as doyen of the resident diplomatic corps.[47] Yet the Burkinabé revolution is still very much in its infancy, and similar nationalistic policies have withered away over time in many other of these states, as indeed elsewhere in the continent.

Both the new ideological dedication of the post-revolutionary state and the military's attempt to legitimate its centralization of all power in the society lead to the eventual institutionalization of an elitist party of militants. Yet the very concept of a Leninist party, representative of the working class, supreme organ in the state and organizational weapon of the revolution, runs counter to the military's jealous monopolization of the decision-making process. *Without exception no military junta has been willing truly to share power with civilian formations, even those directly beholden to it, notwithstanding rhetoric to the contrary.* Power has always remained solidly in military hands – even in the relatively 'civilianized' regime of Madagascar – with the newly established revolutionary structures possessing only nominal powers and retained in a purely ancillary capacity.

Thus the fundamental contradiction between, on the one hand, the populist and Marxist organizational principles extolled by the military and, on the other, the reality of power in the military Marxist state in Africa produces both ideological inconsistencies and civil–military friction. Opposition to the military's monopoly of power, merging with the ultra-left's rejection of the pragmatic and bourgeois courses of the revolution, has produced many of the civil–military clashes noted above. This tug-of-war, coupled with intra-left doctrinal and personal rivalries, has prevented the solidification of the left behind Sankara in Burkina Faso, and postponed its coalescence in Ethiopia and Madagascar into the 1980s. Even where civilian groups have been forcibly compressed under a single ideological umbrella under tight military control

(Benin, Congo), conspiratorial caucus activity and jockeying for primacy have not been eliminated.

Other ancillary structures have likewise resisted centralization under military auspices. The social backbone of the revolution has always been youth and organized labour. Yet after the overthrow of the *ancien régime* the former often develops into an unruly anarchic element, attracted to fiery leaders calling for a further radicalization of society. Ngouabi's difficulties with the JMNR have already been noted; these have been duplicated in Benin, Ethiopia, Madagascar and Somalia, where youth has often acted as a highly independent force, quelled and controlled only with great difficulty.

Organized labour, on the other hand, has tended to become ideologically polarized in a more complex manner. Resisting efforts to harness it in a subservient capacity, swayed by parochial issues, and split into militant and conservative wings, organized labour has often been swung into stances of confrontation, hardly making it the proletarian bulwark of the revolution. Restless under its military-appointed leadership, labour has supported platforms of both the counter-revolution (Congo, Benin, Burkina Faso) and the ultra-left (Congo, Benin, Ethiopia, Madagascar). The recent experience of Sankara in Burkina Faso is especially instructive. Since the coup d'état, which was greeted with great satisfaction by organized labour, Sankara's main travails have been with the trade unionists. Outflanked on the left by syndicalist direct action (the 'overthrow' of the mayor of Ouagadougou, the manager of Voltelec, etc.), Sankara was at the same time challenged from the right by 'illegal' strikes, demands for the lifting of austerity cuts and, in January 1985, the petition against the erosion under his aegis of 'democratic and trade union freedoms' in Burkina Faso.[48]

Such tensions within the new vanguard structures tend to be endemic in these societies. The façade of revolutionary unity projected by the regime is highly misleading, even when structures are hand-sifted for ideological rectitude or personal loyalty, or both. Because of the constant civilian pressures for the recognition of the Leninist principle of the supremacy of the party over state organs, including the army, the organizational base and autonomy of the Marxist-Leninist party set up under military auspices (often reluctantly) have been deliberately kept low. Even in Ethiopia, where the regime of Mengistu Mariam went to great lengths to foster grass-roots *kebeles* (which in 1978 unleashed the Red Terror), the structures were tightly controlled from the centre. The Congolese Labour Party (set up in 1969), the Benin People's Revolutionary Party (1974), the Somali Socialist Revolutionary Party (1976), and the Ethiopian Union of Marxist-Leninist Organizations (1977), are all weak, *nominally ancillary* structures, with Madagascar's AREMA only slightly less so.

Just as the military loses much mobilizational ability by keeping revolutionary structures under a tight rein, the revolution's vitality is further sapped by the superficiality of the revolutionary ardour of much of the movement's membership. For many civilians (and, for that matter, military officers), party affiliation, membership and office are not necessarily a function of political conviction. For many, indeed, joining the party is a very pragmatic act, motivated by the new social 'prerequisites' and skills now in vogue for professional survival and advancement: command of the jargon of class struggle, and membership of militant groups. As *West Africa* succinctly put it with reference to the devouring pace of the Congolese revolution, 'to survive at such a time you had to know the revolutionary jargon, at the very least'.[49]

It was hardly to be expected that unity within the new revolutionary structures would result from the ideological metamorphosis of a multiplicity of previously existing coteries of ethnic, regional and personal power-pyramids. Since considerations of socialist rectitude often constituted little more than the socially accepted cloak for personal advancement, conflict in some African military Marxist states may be conceptualized as non-programmatic, a 'political [conflict] between the ins and outs, each interpreting the ideology to suit its own needs'.[50]

If the centralization of all power in the hands of the military, operating through a tightly controlled party of militants, has been a tumultuous experience that still taxes the juntas in some states, efforts to centralize the means of production and shake off neo-dependency relationships have been even more problematic. Here too, there is a harsh clash between, on the one hand, the objective reality of what is at best only feasible or what has been attempted and sometimes attained and, on the other hand, the wildly unrealistic expectations of the benefits to be had from the adoption of the Marxist model of development. For, as Young so eloquently puts it, 'the dream of the command socialist economy is far removed from the reality of the desperately impoverished crisis-management state',[51] especially in the light of the African state's limited penetrative, administrative and coercive capabilities.[52] Indeed, while a number of healthy economic advances have been scored by the military Marxist state in Africa (including a more evenly balanced regional allocation of resources), by 1981 several were reeling from the fiscal drain of parasitic public sectors, and had to adopt humiliatingly retrogressive policies of privatizing enterprises previously nationalized with great public fanfare.

Although the six states under consideration differ markedly from one another, apart from Congo they all possess weak unviable agrarian economies. Dependent on foreign sources for infusions of risk capital, development funds and technical aid, their economies have been artificially stabilized by budgetary subventions from the metropolitan powers, with which they remain inextricably linked in a myriad of ways through a host of bilateral agreements.

In each instance the state sector was quite modest prior to the revolution. Their economies were dominated by expatriate consortiums, and even petty trade and industry were in foreign hands. Social pressures for services and employment had produced progressively bloated, underemployed and preponderantly urban public payrolls, consuming up to 85 per cent (Benin) of the national budget, thereby stultifying efforts at indigenous capital-formation and disengagement from the apron-strings of the metropolitan power.

The rise of the radical African state provided the ideological justification and rationalization for nationalizing foreign capital and rapidly expanding the public sector, options that had been increasingly put forward under the nationalist banner in the preceding era. The socialization of the means of production proceeded by and large cautiously and with many inconsistencies. Thus, for example, in Benin, Somalia, Madagascar and especially Congo, many of the *least* viable enterprises were nationalized, while the most profitable − those capable of becoming the 'motor' of the revolution − were left untouched in expatriate hands.

With the exception of Ethiopia, a country that embarked on a programme of genuine land reform for reasons unique to itself, no African military Marxist regime has seriously pushed for either collectivization or fundamental agrarian reform, although rhetoric in favour of this has not been absent in many cases. An awareness of the *administrative* nightmare of the task, and of the likely resistance to it by traditional society, in addition to the urban and trade unionist bias of much of the ruling stratum, shielded African peasantries from radical socialist experimentation such as was attempted in Guinea, Tanzania, Mali and, more recently, Ethiopia. Instead, decentralized structures have been erected in the countryside to harness the peasantry to the revolution; progressive elements (for example, youth), appointed as rural 'animators', have usurped the authority of the chiefs; the co-operative movement has been given a powerful boost; and regional agro-industry has been opted for as the optimal method of transforming the rural areas.[53]

The limited goals of the revolution in the countryside notwithstanding, the results have still been mixed. Not all the envisaged funding was ultimately forthcoming, so that even modest goals had to be severely scaled down; many projects that actually left the drawing-boards did so because of overt favouritism, frequently based on ethnic or regional considerations. When agrarian output and productivity did increase, it could usually be traced directly to variables totally extraneous to the leadership in office or its ideology and policies. Normally, however, the prospects for a major breakthrough under the new order were frustrated by the apathy of traditional farmers: uninspired by the exhortations of desk-bound 'animators', whose attention was riveted to the prospects of promotion in the capital, they were in addition barely supported by either fiscal appropriations or administrative follow-up by central ministries. Indeed, referring to Congo, at the time the continent's only People's Republic, the most respected reference work on Africa noted that 'Socialism has made no difference to either the vast masses of people, living on subsistence agriculture in the country and largely unaware of the political leaders in the capital, or to the country's economy, which remains largely under the control of French interests'.[54]

The nationalization and expansion of the modern industrial and commercial sector was, in any case, the central preoccupation of most regimes, and it is in this domain that most effort was expended. Since no regime was willing truly to frighten off private capital[55] or to alienate the metropolitan power, whose interests were directly threatened by such a policy, the pace of nationalization was slow, and it was the small expatriate private company or local branches of foreign financial institutions that were initially taken over. The large expatriate consortiums that controlled the most profitable segments of the national economy were in general left untouched, since jeopardizing their royalty payments (axiomatic in the case of nationalization) was viewed as directly threatening the stability of the regime itself.

Yet the very declaration in favour of Marxism-Leninism dried up sources of international risk capital[56] and triggered an outflow of existing funds. In Burkina Faso, where over 60 per cent of the country's sparse revenues stem from customs duties, imports promptly declined by a half after Sankara's coup, as entrepreneurs liquidated stock and cancelled orders pending clarification of the substantive implications of the 'revolution'. The slump in the Malagasy economy following Ratsiraka's declaration in favour of scientific socialism was likewise sharp, and the left–right ideological gyrations of Antananainvo, including trade overtures to South Africa, were all attempts to escape the negative repercussions of the chosen option. And in both Congo and Benin, veritable ideological somersaults and complex rationalizations were necessary on the part of their Ministers of Finance, in addition to formal and internationally binding state guarantees by Paris, in order to persuade new venture capital − so assiduously courted despite the anti-capitalist diatribes emanating from Cotonou and Brazzaville − that the sanctity of private capital could be taken for granted.

The objective dimension of the nationalizations must also be noted. For, although expatriate interests may have thoroughly dominated the pre-revolutionary economies in the backwaters of Ouagadougou, Mogadishu and Cotonou, it was often the very frailty of the national economy that magnified the role of foreign capital. In Dahomey, for example, as early as 1973 Kérékou inveighed against the 'exploitative' expatriates who were 'the main cause' of the country's problems.[57] A year later came the first nationalizations, culminating in the eventual centralization in state hands of much of the economy. Yet, breaking the expatriate 'stranglehold' involved, in the case of Benin, the expropriation of assets valued at barely $8 million. This sum represented only 20 per cent of all financial aid granted to Benin by France during 1970−74, and *less* than actual aid in the pipeline that was promptly blocked, subject to clarification of compensation arrangements. Indeed, the sum was objectively so minute that ultimately France virtually subsidized the cost of Benin's nationalizations, just as later she picked up the tab for the dispatch to Cotonou of Marxist schoolteachers.

In Congo, a bout of nationalizations had preceded the rise of Ngouabi in 1969 and his declaration of a People's Republic. These left the most profitable sectors of the economy (oil, potassium) in expatriate hands, out of fear that a possible international pull-out might wreck the economy. Vociferous pressures on Massemba-Debat to complete the process of nationalization − viewed as the panacea for rampant unemployment − plagued the regime until its dying days. In 1967 Massemba-Debat complained bitterly against 'infantile-leftist' demands since 'there is *nothing* to nationalize in the country'.[58] After his overthrow the public sector was further expanded, but the Hollé mines were nationalized only *after* they had become unviable (flooded and about to be abandoned), and the oil sector remained in foreign hands into 1980: all of this was done on terms significantly more favourable than those offered to expatriate consortiums elsewhere by *conservative* governments that had no need to offer additional inducements to placate fears of eventual confiscation.[59] As *West Africa* wrily pointed out in its obituary on Ngouabi, 'this revolutionary intellectual in a state of constant debate with his party militants'[60] established 'the appearance of a socialist order led by the PCT, but left the running of the economy to French expatriate capital and proprietors'.[61]

While pragmatic considerations may have limited the practical import of the nationalizations in some African Marxist states, they did little to restrain the rapid expansion of the state sector that uniformly followed the adoption of Marxism-Leninism. Through nationalizations and infusions of new public funds, both domestic and foreign, an intricate, voracious and highly wasteful para-state sector was born. Not only did it not become the 'driving motor' of the revolution, as socialist theory would have it, but it began to threaten directly the economic survival of the radical option.[62] By 1981–82, the financial drag of the socialist sector was so heavy that some segments had to be abandoned and others privatized, as the radical African state from Somalia to Madagascar was in retreat, forced reluctantly into a bout of 'right-wing revisionism' that required accommodation to hard realities. A similar disillusionment with the practical result of a decade or two of socialist experimentation elsewhere, culminating in its termination in Guinea and admission of failure in Tanzania (in 1984–85), may signify the end of an era of overoptimistic expectations of radical socio-economic change in Africa.

The tendency of African states to use the civil service as a means of alleviating chronic unemployment[63] meshed with the demands of youth and labour for new revolutionary structures and more control over the national economy. A direct result of this was a vastly expanded para-state sector and burgeoning civil service: in Benin, for example, there was an increase of 30 per cent in the civil service and the erection of 46 new state companies in addition to the original pre-revolutionary 13 – all despite a formal freeze on hiring and policies of austerity. The new para-state bodies required costly managerial appointments and resulted in considerable duplication of administrative and running costs (spent on a car-pool, a messenger service, stationery, etc.) for enterprises often economically marginal at best.

A bloated public sector, running up a state deficit and barely accountable fiscally, developed in all the states under review, supporting the pessimistic observation of scholars that para-state enterprises in Africa attain no economic goals.[64] Discouraging growth in the private sector, their sustenance consumed an ever larger segment of the state's resources. Productivity plummeted, mismanagement and corruption seeped in, and political sinecures multiplied (including the appointment of political commissars to ensure 'proper' on-the-spot political indoctrination). The absence of even rudimentary fiscal accountability in some countries,[65] coupled with salary increases and generous fringe benefits in money-losing enterprises (such as the thirteenth-month bonus cheque in Congo), resulted in nothing less than the plunder of state coffers by civilians and military alike. Indeed, within *months* of the Burkinabé revolution, the first batch of military and police officers were already on trial for looting the resources of the state over which they had been placed as custodians.

Nowhere else has this process been more visible than in Congo. With nationalization, enterprises previously in relatively healthy financial shape succumbed to effects of a permutation of mismanagement, overstaffing, padded payrolls and embezzlement. The nationalized sugar industry (SIA-Congo) is a perfect case in point. It was transformed in the early 1970s from a profitable enterprise into one of chronic deficits following a decline of 3,000 million francs CFA in annual profits.[66] Other state companies required progressively larger subsidies to avert the fiscal collapse of economic sectors originally deemed viable. Ngouabi himself was to characterize the chaotic situation in the public sector as 'organized bungling';[67] but his solution to the problem — appointing officers from his trusted para-commando battalion to key supervisory positions in the economy — only *expanded* the pool of those partaking of the plunder and those drawing an administrative salary from the state. Within weeks, the first of those hapless enough to be caught in their misdeeds were being sent back to barrack duties, the army itself having become 'a sink of corruption'[68] and the state utterly incapable of doing anything about the rampant speculation.

With the expected revenues from the 'motor of the revolution' not forthcoming — indeed, with that 'motor' constantly stalling and requiring so much stoking as to preclude the financing of *new* development projects — many of the revolution's intermediate goals have had to be sacrificed.[69] Nor has the international financial community been very charitable in its assessment of the syndrome of contrast between rhetoric and reality in African Marxism-Leninism, and marked fluctuations in global commodity prices have played further havoc with fiscal and cash-flow projections. In the absence of adequate finances, administrative skills, motivated cadres and dedicated day-to-day leadership, the *substantive* (as opposed to structural) economic advances of the African military Marxist state have been modest. In Burkina Faso, less than 20 per cent of the junta's goals for the first year were attained; in Benin and Congo barely 65 per cent of the twice scaled-down development plans were implemented; in Madagascar a radical shift (and not the first) back to the liberal market economy approach was necessary in 1984 in order to avert a massive economic shambles;[70] and in Ethiopia civil strife and external war camouflaged the very real economic collapse that occurred independently of both.

Thus, the major *economic* constraints on the radical African state, just as its political ones, are largely internal to its own dynamics. Young's observation, that 'the overdeveloped state itself proved to be an engine of dependency, not of socialism, much less of development',[71] is fundamental to any analysis of the economic performance of the African Marxist regime. The roots of the problem are three:

   (a) the alienation of still avidly courted and much-needed foreign capital, by rhetoric that stresses its evil and prophesies its immediate demise;
   (b) the centralization of the means of production in the hands of public hierarchies, motivated not by considerations of either profitability (that is, capitalism) or the higher social good (that is, socialism), but rather by narrow sectarian interests and the exigencies of power;
   (c) the normal constraints imposed by the global economy on mini-states producing a small range of primary commodities.

The fact that several African military Marxist states have set themselves tasks involving the total transformation of society (including its basic values) does not truly change the basic assessment very much. For fundamentally little did truly change with the adoption of Marxism-Leninism in Ouagadougou, Cotonou, Antanananivo, Brazzaville or Mogadishu. No new 'socialist man' or morality was born; no real Marxist party sits at the helm of the nation. No new international realities were established, nor were old ones significantly altered: the accretion to the Marxist camp of new African allies may have marginally shifted East−West tabulations, but not the reality of either the world economy or the international balance of power. Some individuals in Ethiopia, Benin or Burkina Faso may well echo, with different degrees of sincerity, Ngouabi's glorification of domestic scientific socialism as an 'experiment which will be set down in the history of political parties of the world',[72] yet the fact still remains that in all practical respects the birth of the military Marxist state in Africa was of little import.

Scarcity and dependency relationships are still the order of the day, inexorably restricting choice and action, triggering frustration and widening the gap between rhetoric and reality. Cleavages, friction and political actions now manifest themselves in ideological garb: the underlying roots in regional, ethnic and religious rivalries (in Ethiopia) or caste divisions (in Somalia) have been 'replaced' by a tug-of-war between the proletariat and 'infantile-leftists' or 'tribal reactionaries'. Yet strife and competition for scarce resources remain an integral part of the political picture. Mismanagement, corruption and the absence of fiscal accountability continue to sap scarce state resources much as they did previously. The perpetrators may now be youthful political commissars, dashing but avaricious junior officers and fiery but equally venal ideologues of the Glorious Revolution, but the motivations are the all-too-familiar human ones.

All this, of course, is not to suggest that nothing of substance has happened since the radical take-over, or that the radical state of today is no different from its conservative predecessor. Rather, what is being underlined is the resilience of fundamental socio-economic relationships, human motivations and basic values, that do not disappear merely by virtue of structural and epistemological changes, legislative decrees or ideological proclamations. Preoccupation with the *accoutrements* of a Marxist system does not create such a system, no matter how flexibly defined or sympathetically assessed. It may well be a necessary anticipatory or preparatory phase, especially in Third World countries, and it certainly is psychologically satisfying, since it imparts immediately the 'flavour' of revolutionary change. Indeed, the very adoption of Marxism-Leninism may be regarded to some extent as a *psychological* reaction, as 'an instance of political rage produced by political impotence'[73] by ultra-nationalistic military leaders straining to leave their imprint on history.

However, over-preoccupation with the trivial or superficial − all too visible in some radical military regimes in Africa − may be the result of the inability or unwillingness to forge much beyond the realm of strident rhetoric, symbolic structural reorganization and only modest concrete change. Often confused with really meaningful change,[74] structural reorganizations do little to change reality: they merely modify the *structures* that interact with reality, without affecting the substance itself.

Nevertheless, military Marxism could well be the wave of the future in much of the continent, and certainly in the less developed countries. As political hierarchies collapse and new military juntas seek differentiation from antecedent regimes; and as youth and urban labour come of political age, reject the seemingly rudderless leadership of the post-colonial state, and seek 'grand designs' for an uncertain but uniformly gloomy future, the anti-colonial, internationalist, pre-determinist appeal of Marxism cannot but grow.

At the very least, African military Marxism caters to fundamental psychological strivings of intellectuals, students, unionists and Africa's increasingly large, vocal and restless disenfranchised urban lumpenproletariats. It offers them, *inter alia*: (1) a vision of a developmentally better future such as no other ideology even suggests; (2) the unity of purpose, drive and euphoria missing from society since the heyday of independence, that can be provided only by ideological fervour and the strict discipline of sacramental values; (3) a definitive role and higher purpose in the evolution of society along the pre-determined Marxist path; (4) the elevation of political conflict from the ethnic level to that of the class, focusing attention upon less parochial issues, even if earlier concerns still colour social interaction; and (5) a satisfying manner of expressing strongly felt but hitherto suppressed *anti-colonial resentments* without straying too far from accepted norms or the 'acceptable' Prospero–Caliban relationship with the metropolitan power.

That the concrete achievements of Afro-Marxism may continue to be quite modest is a small price to pay if the ideology provides these benefits to society, especially since it is perceived as the 'historically correct' one in any case. Moreover – and this is often forgotten – it is African Marxism's failure *in comparison with its stipulated expected benefits* that tends to evoke negative assessments, but *not necessarily* its mediocre performance in contrast to *equally mediocre* prior 'capitalist' administrations *in the same country*. That neither set of alternatives seems to work well in these states underlines the difficulties and the slowness of fundamental change in transitional societies. The social goals posited by military Marxist regimes in Africa are clearly impossible of attainment in the foreseeable future, irrespective of the guiding ideology. The actual performance of African Marxist military elites suggests little more than that there can be no saints – civilian or military, radical or conservative – in conditions of acute scarcity and sharp competition for survival.

NOTES

1. The Libyan experience will not be included in this study. The country's oil-wealth grants it policy options foreclosed to even the most developed of the other states (namely, Congo), sharply setting it apart for purposes of comparative analysis.
2. The two tend to go hand in hand. Post-independence office training programmes have higher academic requirements than earlier ones (frequently crash programmes under the pressure of Africanization), where lengthy service as NCOs in colonial armies was a suitable substitute for formal education or training.

3. 'A soldier without political education is a virtual criminal', according to Captain Sankara: see *West Africa*, 29 February 1984.
4. There is a parallel trend in many non-radical military regimes on the continent today to regard themselves as quasi-permanent.
5. In Burkina Faso (formerly Upper Volta) the doctrinaire, pro-Albanian PCRV Communist Party refused to join the post-coup Sankara cabinet (as did similar splinter groups in both Benin and Ethiopia), arguing that 'a military coup cannot serve as a substitute for genuine popular revolution': *West Africa*, 12 Dec. 1983.
6. In the case of the Burkinabé 'revolution', even the government publication, *Carrefour africain*, acknowledged that at the time there had been 'no widespread political unrest, only weariness': cited in *Africa Research Bulletin – Political Series*, Sept. 1983.
7. See the excellent article by Richard Jeffries, 'Political Radicalism in Africa: The Second Independence', *African Affairs*, July 1978.
8. See Samuel Decalo, 'Regionalism, Politics and the Military in Dahomey', *Journal of Developing Areas*, April 1973; 'The Politics of Instability in Dahomey', *Geneva–Afrique*, Vol. 7, No. 2 (1968); and 'The Army in a Praetorian State: Dahomey', in Samuel Decalo, *Coups and Army Rule in Africa* (New Haven: Yale University Press, 1976).
9. Interviews in Cotonou and Porto Novo, July–August 1971.
10. Interview in Cotonou, July 1973.
11. *Africa Research Bulletin – Political Series*, July 1973.
12. See Colin Legum (ed.), *Africa Contemporary Record, 1972–73* (London: Rex Collings, 1973), p. B581.
13. See, for example, Marina and David Ottaway, *Afrocommunism* (New York: Africana Publishing House, 1981), p. 133.
14. Roger Jouffrey, 'Thomas Sankara et la révolution voltaïque', *Afrique contemporaine*, No. 130 (April–June 1984), p. 46.
15. *West Africa*, 12 Sept. 1983.
16. See Samuel Decalo, 'Revolutionary Rhetoric and Army Cliques in Congo/Brazzaville', in Decalo, *Coups and Army Rule in Africa*.
17. Kenneth Jowitt, 'Scientific Socialist Regimes in Africa: Political Differentiation, Avoidance, and Unawareness', in Carl G. Rosberg and Thomas M. Callaghy (eds.), *Socialism in Subsaharan Africa* (Berkeley, CA: University of California Institute of International Studies, 1979), p. 140.
18. *West Africa*, 13 Aug. 1984.
19. *West Africa*, 4 Aug. 1975, 15 Sept. 1975.
20. Cited in Colin Legum (ed.), *Africa Contemporary Record, 1975–76* (London: Rex Collings, 1976), p. B672. The 1977 mercenary assault on Cotonou was the most visible attempt at a counter-revolution but there were other plots.
21. *West Africa*, 27 Jan. 1977.
22. David Rapoport, 'The Praetorian Army: Insecurity, Venality and Impotence', in Roman Kolkowicz and Andrzej Korbonski (eds.), *Soldiers, Peasants and Bureaucrats* (London: George Allen & Unwin, 1982), p. 257.
23. Thomas Callaghy, 'The Difficulties of Implementing Socialist Strategies of Development in Africa: The First Wave', in Rosberg and Callaghy, *Socialism in Subsaharan Africa*, p. 112.
24. *Le Monde*, 23 April 1985.
25. *West Africa*, 1 Oct. 1984.
26. *Le Monde*, 23 Feb. 1985.
27. Interview in Kinshasa, June 1972.
28. *Le Monde*, 30 Oct. 1973.
29. *Le Monde*, 18 Dec. 1971.
30. Yhombi-Opango briefly succeeded Ngouabi after the latter's murder. He had been the *bête noire* of Brazzaville youth, which constantly castigated him for his 'false revolutionary attitude' and 'capitalist' lifestyle: see *Jeune Afrique*, 11 March 1972, and *African Research Bulletin – Political Series*, Dec. 1971.
31. Mengistu Mariam himself is of mixed Amharic origins, and numerous members of the Derg are also of Amharic origin: see Marina and David Ottaway, *Ethiopia: Empire in Revolution* (New York: Africana Publishing Co., 1978); and above, p. 38, note 29.

32. Crawford Young, *Ideology and Development in Africa* (New Haven: Yale University Press, 1982), p. 63.
33. David Laitin, 'Somalia's Military Government and Scientific Socialism', in Rosberg and Callaghy, *Socialism in Subsaharan Africa*, p. 198.
34. Philippe Leymarie, 'Madagascar: comment repartir?', *Revue française d'études politiques africaines*, No. 16 (Aug. 1975), p. 15.
35. Young, *Ideology and Development*, p. 50. These reservations were cogently expressed by Sennen Andriamirado: see Young, p. 60, citing from Robert Archer, *Madagascar depuis 1972* (Paris: Editions de l'Harmattan, 1976), p. 181.
36. Such as edicts on the proper way to commence, address and conclude official correspondence in a revolutionary state.
37. In a penetrating and suggestive analysis of Congolese youth, Erny noted the degree to which wish-fulfilment and reality had become blurred where youth 'had developed a culture of the word, in which spoken words seemed all-powerful ... [and] the management of words ... was regarded as the key to the social drama in which they were all involved': see P. Erny, 'Parole et travail chez les jeunes d'Afrique Centrale', *Projet*, Sept.–Oct. 1966.
38. David Laitin, in Rosberg and Callaghy, *Socialism in Subsaharan Africa*.
39. Arriving at mass meetings with peasants aimed at extolling the role of labour, self-sacrifice and socialist modesty, while chauffeur-driven in Mercedes-Benz cars (Benin); the plunder of state resources once in office (see below), etc.
40. Callaghy, in Rosberg and Callaghy, *Socialism in Subsaharan Africa*, p. 116.
41. A similar observation was recently made with respect to the 'civilianized' Beninois regime: see *West Africa*, 13 May 1985.
42. The contrary views of the Ottaways, that 'the differences between African socialist and Marxist-Leninist countries are more pronounced and significant than the similarities', cannot be taken seriously. Their work on Afro-Communism purposely excluded from analysis the Peoples' Republics, and indeed *all* the radical military regimes except Ethiopia, on the grounds (not analysed) that their ideological commitment is 'suspect': see Marina and David Ottaway, *Afrocommunism*, p. 202.
43. Madagascar is usually pointedly excluded.
44. P. I. Manchkha, 'Communists, Revolutionary Democrats and the Non-Capitalist Path of Development in African Countries', *Current Digest of the Soviet Press*, Vol. 27, No. 51 (21 Jan. 1976), as quoted by Jowitt, in Rosberg and Callaghy, *Socialism in Subsaharan Africa*, p. 150.
45. *West Africa*, 2 April 1984.
46. *West Africa*, 20 August 1984. This was *not* the case in Benin, where the former name, Dahomey, was really rejected because of its affiliation to one of the regional–ethnic groups in the country.
47. See, *inter alia*, *West Africa*, 24 Oct. 1983, 19 Dec. 1983; also *Jeune Afrique*, 13 Feb. 1985.
48. Freedoms deemed appropriate by Sankara 'in neo-colonial administrations', but not in the context of a popular republic: see *West Africa*, 18 March 1985.
49. 'Brazzaville: Ten Years of the Revolution – Part Two', *West Africa*, 20 Aug. 1973.
50. David and Marina Ottaway, *Afrocommunism*, p. 201.
51. Young, *Ideology and Development*, p. 30.
52. Callaghy, in Rosberg and Callaghy, *Socialism in Subsaharan Africa*, p. 116.
53. In the most recent instance, in Burkina Faso, each of the country's 25 provinces was projected to have a factory processing some local agricultural product, together with a bakery (even in the absence of local wheat), a cinema and a livestock project: see *West Africa*, 27 September 1984.
54. Colin Legum (ed.), *Africa Contemporary Record, 1970–71* (London: Rex Collings, 1971), p. B305.
55. An inordinate amount of time and epistemological juggling has been devoted by Marxist leaders to 'explain' why their radical rhetoric need not threaten private capital seeking investment prospects in the radical state. A curious offshoot of this anomaly was that in 1971–72, at a time of overt diplomatic coolness between the US and Congo when American citizens and scholars could not obtain visas to Congo, US capitalists were more than welcome and visas were even waived: interview at the Congolese Mission to the United Nations,

May 1981. See also Gilbert Comte, 'Le socialisme de la parole', *Le Monde hebdomadaire*, 26 March 1979.

56. Barely a trickle had been interested in any case in the potentialities of Benin, Upper Volta, Somalia and Madagascar, and even Congo had had difficulties, under the conservative régime of Youlou, in attracting funds into the country.
57. *West Africa*, 1 Jan. 1973.
58. *Afrique nouvelle*, 26 April 1967.
59. Colin Legum (ed.), *Africa Contemporary Record, 1969–70* (London: Rex Collings, 1970), p. B419.
60. 'Brazzaville: Ten Years of Revolution – Part Two', *West Africa*, 20 Aug. 1973.
61. *West Africa*, 28 March 1977.
62. See, *inter alia*, Donald L. Sparks, 'African Parastatals: Public Enemy or Economic Saviour?' (paper presented to the 1982 African Studies Association Meeting). See also E. J. Wilson, 'Contested Terrain: A Comparative and Theoretical Reassessment of State-owned Enterprise in Africa', *Journal of Commonwealth and Comparative Politics*, Vol. 22, No. 1 (March 1984).
63. Selenk Ozgediz, 'Managing the Public Service in Developing Countries', *World Bank Staff Working Papers, No. 577* (Washington, DC, 1983); Leroy P. Jones, *Public Enterprise in Less Developed Countries* (Cambridge: Cambridge University Press, 1983); and T. Killick, 'The Role of the Public Sector in the Industrialization of Africa', *Industry and Development*, No. 7 (1983), pp. 57–88.
64. Tony Killick, *The Performance of Public Enterprise* (London: Heinemann, 1981), and his 'The Role of the Public Sector in the Industrialization of Africa' (Vienna: UNIDO, 1981).
65. See, *inter alia*, Lapido Adamelkun, 'Accountability and Control in African Public Bureaucracies', *International Review of Administrative Sciences*, Vol. 40, No. 4 (1974).
66. For a brief account see *Le Monde*, 30 April 1975.
67. *West Africa*, 9 April 1973; see also Legum, *Africa Contemporary Record, 1975–76*, p. B472.
68. *West Africa*, 15 Aug. 1970, 2 April 1973.
69. In Benin the budgetary self-sufficiency of the Kérékou regime gave way in 1985 to dependence on French subsidies as the para-state sector's fiscal needs proved impossible to meet: see *West Africa*, 18 March 1985, 8 April 1985.
70. *Le Monde*, 23 Feb. 1985.
71. Young, *Ideology and Development*, p. 42. The observation, made with reference to the Congolese experience, is quite valid for all the states under consideration here.
72. *Le Moniteur africain du commerce et de l'industrie*, 10 Aug. 1972.
73. Jowitt, in Rosberg and Callaghy, *Socialism in Subsaharan Africa*, p. 148.
74. Decalo, 'Ideological Rhetoric and Scientific Socialism in Two Peoples' Republics: Benin and Congo/Brazzaville', in Rosberg and Callaghy, *Socialism in Subsaharan Africa*, p. 264.

The Political Orientation Speech (*Discours d'orientation politique*), delivered by Captain Thomas Sankara in Ouagadougou, Upper Volta, on 2 October 1983

PEOPLE OF UPPER VOLTA!
COMRADE MEN AND WOMEN, MILITANTS OF THE REVOLUTION!

In the course of this year of 1983 our country has experienced moments of a particular intensity that have left an indelible mark in the minds of many of our fellow-citizens.

During this period the struggle of the People* of Upper Volta has seen moments of advance, but setbacks too.

Our People has been tested in heroic battles, to achieve final victory on the night of 4 August 1983 — a night that has now gone down in history. Soon the irreversible forward march of the Revolution in our country will have passed its second month.

For two months the fighting People of Upper Volta has arrayed itself as one man behind the National Council of the Revolution [NCR] to build a new, free, independent and prosperous society in Upper Volta; a new society delivered from social injustice, and from the centuries-old domination and exploitation of international imperialism.

Now that this brief distance has been run I invite you, with me, to cast a look back, so as to draw the lessons needed to enable us to determine correctly the revolutionary tasks that are arising now and will arise in the near future.

By giving ourselves a clear vision of the march of events, we shall strengthen ourselves further in our struggle against imperialism and against reactionary forces.

In sum: where did we come from? And where are we going? These are the questions of the moment that call for a clear and resolute answer, free of any doubts, if we intend to march steadfastly on towards ever greater and ever more resounding victories.

THE AUGUST REVOLUTION REPRESENTS THE GOAL OF THE STRUGGLE OF THE PEOPLE OF UPPER VOLTA

The triumph of the August Revolution is not only the result of the revolutionary stroke delivered to the reactionary Holy Alliance on 17 May 1983. It is the crowning moment of the struggle of the Volta People against its internal enemies.

---

*The use of capital and lower-case letters in this translation follows the punctuation of the original text.

It is a victory over international imperialism and its allies within the nation. It is a victory over retrograde, shady and obscurantist forces.

It is a victory over all the enemies of the People who have hatched plots and intrigues against it.

The August Revolution is the final stage of the popular insurrection launched after the imperialist plot of 17 May 1983 that aimed at stemming the mounting tide of democratic and revolutionary forces in this country.

That insurrection was symbolized not only by the courageous and heroic stance of the Commandos of the Town of Po who ferociously resisted the pro-imperialist and anti-popular power of the Doctor-Commander Jean-Baptiste OUEDRAOGO and of Colonal SOME Yoryan.

But it also formed part of the popular and democratic forces which, in alliance with the soldiers and the Patriotic Officers, managed to organize an exemplary resistance.

The insurrection of 4 August 1983, the victory of the Revolution and the coming to power of the National Council of the Revolution are therefore without question the consecration and the logical end of the struggles of the Volta people against neo-colonial domination and exploitation, against the subjugation of our country, [and] for the independence, freedom, dignity and progress of our People. Simplistic and superficial analyses, restricted to the reproduction of ready-made schemes, can do nothing to change the reality of the facts.

The August Revolution has, in its triumph, established itself as heir to the popular uprising of 3 January 1966 and as its continuation: the sequel, and the development to a qualitatively higher stage of all the great popular struggles that have occurred one after another these last years and that have all demonstrated the systematic refusal of the Volta People, and in particular its working class and the toilers, to let themselves be governed as they had been before. The clearest and most significant landmarks of these great popular struggles are represented by the dates of December 1975, May 1979, October and November 1980, April 1982 and May 1983.

It is an established fact that the Great Movement of Popular resistance that followed immediately on the reactionary and pro-imperialist provocation of 17 May 1983 created favourable conditions for what occurred on 4 August 1983. As it happens, the imperialist plot of 17 May had the effect of precipitating on a wide scale a regrouping of democratic and revolutionary forces and organizations that mobilized themselves during that period by taking initiatives and embarking on bold enterprises of a kind that until then had never been known.

Meanwhile the holy alliance of reactionary forces around the moribund regime was suffering from its inability to stem the tide of revolutionary forces that were mounting an ever more open assault on the anti-popular and anti-democratic regime.

The mass demonstrations of 20, 21 and 22 May had a wide national echo above all because of their great political significance and because of the fact that they were living proof that a whole people, and in particular its youth, was giving its open support to revolutionary ideals defended by those who had been treacherously stricken down by the forces of reaction. They have had a great practical effect because they expressed the determination of a whole people and all of its youth who stood up to confront realistically the forces of domination and of imperialist exploitation. It was the clearest possible demonstration of the truth which proclaims that when the People stands up, imperialism and the social forces allied with it tremble.

History and the process through which the popular masses arrive at a political consciousness follow a dialectical path that escapes the logic of reaction. That is why the events of the month of May 1983 made a handsome contribution to speeding up the process of political clarification in our country, reaching such a pitch that the popular masses in their entirety made an important qualitative leap in their understanding of the situation.

The events of May 17 contributed greatly towards opening the eyes of the Volta People, and imperialism with its system of oppression and exploitation was revealed at a stroke in all its brutality and cruelty.

There are days that hold in themselves lessons of a richness that cannot be compared with that of a whole decade.

In the course of these days the People learns with unheard-of speed and with such a depth of understanding that a thousand days of study are nothing by comparison.

The events of the month of May 1983 have allowed the Volta People to know its enemies better.

So from now on in Upper Volta everyone knows:

WHO IS WHO!

WHO IS WITH WHOM AND AGAINST WHOM!

WHO IS DOING WHAT AND WHY!

This kind of situation that constitutes the prelude to great upheavals has helped strip naked the frustrations of class contradictions in Volta society.

The August Revolution has come, therefore, as a solution of social contradictions that could no longer be stifled by compromise solutions. The enthusiastic rallying of the great popular masses to the August Revolution is a living expression of the immense hope that the Volta People places on the coming of the NCR, so that at last the satisfaction of their deepest aspirations for democracy, for liberty, for independence, for true progress, and for the restoration of the dignity and the grandeur of our country, that 23 years of neo-colonial regime have palpably flouted, can be realized.

THE HERITAGE OF TWENTY-THREE YEARS OF NEO-COLONIALISM

The Coming of the NCR of 4 August 1983 and the establishment of a revolutionary power in Upper Volta since that date, have opened a glorious page in the annals of our People and our country.

However, the heritage that 23 years of exploitation and imperialist domination have left us is heavy and baleful.

Our task of constructing a new society, a society freed from all the ills that keep our country in a situation of poverty and economic and cultural backwardness, will be difficult and arduous.

In the 1960s, when French colonialism, hemmed in on all sides, discomfited at Dien-Bien-Phu, bogged down in enormous difficulties in Algeria, was constrained to draw the lessons from these defeats and to accord our country national sovereignty and territorial integrity; this was welcomed positively by our People, who did not stand idly by but developed the appropriate forms of struggle. This *fuite en avant* on the part of French colonial imperialism constituted for our People a victory over the forces of oppression and foreign exploitation. From the point of view of the popular masses this was a democratic reform, whilst from the point of view of imperialism it represented a sea-change in the forms of domination and exploitation to which our People was subjected.

This sea-change, however, has resulted in a realignment of classes and social strata and in the assertion of new classes.

In alliance with the reactionary forces of traditional society the intellectual petty-bourgeoisie of the time, with total contempt for the masses at the base of society that had acted as a springboard for its accession to power, embarked on the organization of the political and economic foundations of new forms of domination and of imperialist exploitation.

Fear that the struggle of the popular masses might become more radical and end in a truly revolutionary solution lies at the bottom of imperialism's chosen strategy, which consists in keeping a continuing grip on our country and in perpetuating the exploitation of our people through the agency of third parties within the nation.

Volta nationals were to take up the baton of foreign domination. and exploitation. The whole organization of neo-colonial society was to be reduced to a simple operation of substitution of one form of domination for another.

In their essence, neo-colonial society and colonial society do not differ in any way from each other.

And so for a colonial administration we have seen a neo-colonial administration substituted that is identical in every way with the first. For the colonial army is substituted a neo-colonial army with the same attributes, the same functions and the same role of guardian of the interests of imperialism and of those of its allies within the nation.

For the colonial school system is substituted a neo-colonial school system that has the same goals of alienating the children of our country and of reproducing a society that is essentially at the service of imperialist interests and secondarily at the service of imperialism's lackeys and local allies.

Volta nationals have embarked, with the support and benediction of imperialism, on the organization of a systematic pillaging of our country.

Out of the crumbs that fall to them out of this pillage they transform themselves little by little into a truly parasitical bourgeoisie unable any longer to restrain its voracious appetite.

Moved only by their own selfish interests they will now no longer refrain from the most dishonest methods, engaging in corruption on a grand scale, embezzling public funds and goods, trafficking in influence and property speculation, practising favouritism and nepotism.

It is this that explains all the material and financial riches that they have managed to accumulate by climbing on the backs of the working People. And not content with living on the fabulous dividends that they draw from the shameless exploitation of their ill-gotten goods they get up to all manner of tricks in order to acquire political responsibilities that will allow them to use the apparatus of the state to further their exploiting and their skulduggery.

No year goes by without their giving themselves fat foreign holidays. Their children desert the schools of the country for a prestigious education in other countries. At the slightest little illness all the state's resources are mobilized in order to guarantee them expensive treatment in luxurious foreign hospitals.

All this goes on under the eyes of a Volta People that is hard-working, courageous and honest, but which is sunk in the most wretched poverty. For the rich minority the Upper Volta is a Paradise; but for the majority constituted by the People it is a barely tolerable inferno.

Within this great majority those that earn wages and salaries, despite the fact that they are assured of a regular income, suffer from constraints and snares imposed by the consumer society of capitalism, they see the whole of their income spent even before they get it. And the vicious circle continues without end, without any prospect of a break.

In their respective trade unions wage and salary earners engage in struggles to demand an improvement in their living conditions. The vigour of these struggles sometimes forces the neo-colonial power-holders to throw out some ballast. But what they give with one hand they take away with the other. So that a ten-per-cent increase in wages is announced with a great fanfare, but is immediately followed by taxation measures that cancel out the beneficial effects that are expected from the pay-rise. After five, six or seven months workers always end up realizing that the stakes have been raised and mobilize for a further fight. Seven months is more than the reactionaries who are in power need in order to draw breath and work out other ruses. In this endless fight, the worker always ends up the loser.

Within this great majority there are the 'Wretched of the Earth', the peasants who are daily expropriated, robbed, set upon, flouted and humiliated and who none the less are amongst those whose work creates wealth. It is by their productive effort that the country's economy, despite its fragility, maintains itself. It is on their toil that all those Upper Volta nationals for whom the country is an Eldorado grow fat.

And yet it is they who suffer most from the lack of construction investment and of a transport infrastructure, from a lack of a properly structured and staffed health service.

It is these peasants, creators of the nation's wealth, who suffer the most from the lack of schools and educational equipment for their children. It is their children that will swell the ranks of the unemployed after a lightning period on the benches of schools that are badly adapted to the reality of the country.

It is among them that illiteracy is at its highest (98 per cent). It is, again, they who need to know more in order that their productive toil can produce a better return, and yet who profit the least from investments in health, education and technology.

The peasant youth, who have the same mental reactions as youth as a whole (is more sensitive, that is, to social injustice and is more favourably inclined towards progress), has taken, in a spirit of revolt, to deserting the countryside, depriving it of its most dynamic elements.

The first reflex pushes these young people into the large urban centres of Ouagadougou and Bobo-Dioulasso. There they hope to find more rewarding work and to benefit from the advantages of progress. Shortage of work drives them to idleness and to the vices that follow from it. At length they will find their salvation, if they do not end in gaol, in leaving the country and going abroad where humiliation and the most shameless exploitation await them. But does Upper Volta society offer them any other choice?

Such, putting it in the most succinct way, is the situation of our country 23 years after neo-colonialization: paradise for some and an inferno for the others.

After 23 years of domination and imperialist exploitation, our country remains a backward agrarian one where the rural sector, that employs over 90 per cent of the active population, represents only 45 per cent of gross national product and provides 95 per cent of the total exports of the country.

More simply, it must be said that whereas in other countries farmers who constitute less than five per cent of the population manage not only to feed themselves properly and to guarantee the needs of the entire nation, but also export immense quantities of their agricultural produce, in our country over 90 per cent of the population, in spite of a desperate struggle, know only shortage and famine and are obliged to turn, with the rest of the population, to importing agricultural produce or to international aid. In addition, the imbalance between exports and imports accentuates the dependence of the country on foreign countries. The resulting trade deficit grows perceptibly year by year and imports are covered by exports only to the tune of 25 per cent.

To put it clearly we buy abroad more than we sell, and an economy that works on that basis ruins itself little by little and heads for catastrophe.

Private investments coming from abroad are not only insufficient, but interest payments on them drain the country's economy and so they make no contribution to its powers of accumulation. It is estimated that 1,700 million francs CFA in hard currency left the country during the period 1973–79 as interest on investments from abroad, whilst new investments total only 1.3 thousand million francs CFA per year on average. A large part of the wealth thus created with the help of foreign investment drains away abroad rather than being reinvested as so to increase the productive capacity of the country.

The lack of strength in productive investments leads the state in Upper Volta to play a fundamental role in the nation's economy so as to make the effort necessary to complement private investment.

The situation is a difficult one since we know that payments into the state budget are mostly taxation receipts, which represent 85 per cent of the total budget income and are made up for the most part of taxes on imports and income tax.

The money accruing to the state goes on financing, apart from the national investment effort, the state's expenses, 70 per cent of which are spent on paying the salaries of public servants and on making sure that the public administration works. What can then be left for social and cultural investments?

In the educational sphere, our country is among the most backward, with only 16.4 per cent of children in school and illiteracy running at 92 per cent on average. That is, of 100 Volta people, barely eight seem to be able to read and write in any language at all.

In health terms the disease and death rates are the highest in the sub-region because of the proliferation of transmitted diseases and nutritional deficiencies.

How are we to avoid such a catastrophic situation given that we have only one bed for 1,200 people and one doctor for 48,000?

These few statistics alone are enough to illustrate the heritage of 23 years of neo-colonialism, 23 years of a policy of total national abandon.

This most deplorable situation cannot leave indifferent any Voltese who loves and honours his country.

Our People, courageous and hard-working, has never been able to put up with such a situation. And since it has understood that it is not a matter of fate but of the organization of society on unjust foundations for the profit of only a minority, it has always worked out various forms of struggle in a search for ways and means of bringing the old order of things to an end.

That is why it enthusiastically welcomed the coming of the National Council of the Revolution and the August Revolution that is the crowning of its efforts and of the sacrifices that it has undergone for the sake of toppling the old order and establishing a new order capable of restoring the People of Volta to their proper stature and of giving our country a creditable place among free, prosperous and respected nations.

The parasitic classes that had always reaped a profit from colonial and neo-colonial Upper Volta are and will be hostile to the changes brought about by the revolutionary processes that got under way on 4 August 1983. The reason is that they are still attached by an umbilical cord to international imperialism. They are still fervent champions of the privileges that are theirs by virtue of their allegiance to imperialism.

Whatever is said or done, they will remain true to themselves and will go on thinking up plots and intrigues in order to regain their 'lost kingdom'. No re-conversion of mentality or attitude is to be expected of these nostalgic people. They do not understand and are not sensitive to any other language than that of fighting, the fight of the revolutionary classes against the exploiter and the oppressors of peoples. Our Revolution will be for them the most authoritarian thing possible; it will be an act whereby the people will impose its will by all possible means at its disposal and if necessary by force of arms.

These enemies of the people, who are they? They were revealed to the eyes of the people during the events of 17 May in all their hatred of the forces of the revolution.

These enemies of the people have been identified by the people in the forge of revolutionary action. They are:

(1) The bourgeoisie of Volta, that can be broken down, according to the function that they each fulfil, into a state bourgeoisie, a comprador business bourgeoisie and middle bourgeoisie.

The state bourgeoisie: It is this group that is known by the term politico-bureaucratic bourgeoisie. It is a bourgeoisie that a situation of political monopoly has enriched in an illicit and corrupt fashion; it uses the state apparatus just as the industrial capitalist uses the means of production in order to accumulate surplus value drawn from the labour power of the workers.

This part of the bourgeoisie will never of its own accord give up its old advantages and stand passively by as revolutionary changes unfold.

The business bourgeoisie: This section by its very activities is attached to imperialism through many links. The elimination of imperialist domination means for it the death of the goose that lays the golden eggs.

That is why it will oppose the current revolution with all its might. It is in this category that are to be found, for example, venal merchants who try to beggar the people by withdrawing goods from circulation for purposes of speculation and economic sabotage.

The middle bourgeoisie: This section of the Volta bourgeoisie, although it has links with imperialism, is its rival for control of the market. But since it is economically weak it is squeezed out by imperialism. It therefore has a grudge against imperialism but it also is frightened of the people, and this fear might lead it to face up to imperialism.

However, because imperialism's domination of our country prevents it from playing its true role as a national bourgeoisie, certain of its elements, in certain conditions, could be favourable to the revolution, which puts them objectively in the camp of the people. However, a revolutionary mistrust must be maintained between these elements that join the revolution and the People. For it is under this cover that opportunists of all kinds flock to the revolution.

(2) Reactionary forces whose strength derives from the traditional feudal structures of our society. These forces, in most cases, managed to put up a firm resistance to French colonialist imperialism. But since our country achieved national sovereignty they have aligned themselves with the reactionary bourgeoisie to oppress the Volta People. These forces have held the peasant masses in the situation of a reservoir from which they draw support for electoral contests.

In order to maintain their interests, which they have in common with imperialism but which differ from those of the people, these reactionary forces most often have recourse to the decadent values of our traditional culture that are still alive in the rural areas. In so far as our Revolution intends to democratize social relations in the countryside, to make the peasantry aware of its responsibilities, and to make available to it more education and more knowledge for its own economic and cultural emancipation, these retrograde forces will be opposed to it.

Such are the enemies of the people in this revolution, enemies that the

People itself identified during the events of the month of May. These are the individuals who made up most of the band of isolated marchers who, protected by a military cordon, demonstrated their class support for the already moribund regime that stemmed from the reactionary and pro-imperialist coup d'état. Beyond these classes and social strata just listed the rest of the population constitutes the People of Volta.

A People that finds imperialist domination and exploitation abominable and has not ceased to show it in daily concrete struggles against different neo-colonial regimes.

This People in our revolution comprises:

(1) The working class of Volta, young and not numerous, but that has managed to show through continual battles with the employers that it is a truly revolutionary class. In this revolution, it is a class that has nothing to lose and everything to gain. It has no means of production to lose, it has no bit of landed property to defend within the framework of the old neo-colonial society. On the contrary, it is convinced that the Revolution is on its side, because it will come through it enlarged and fortified.

(2) The petty bourgeoisie, made up of a vast social stratum that is very unstable and very often vacillates between the cause of the masses and that of imperialism.

In its great majority it always ends by siding with the popular masses. It includes very diverse elements, among them:
— small tradespeople;
— petty bourgeois intellectuals (public officials, students, school pupils, employees of the private sector, etc.).

(3) The peasantry of Volta, for the most part composed of small peasants attached to small plots of land owing to the gradual disintegration of collective property since the introduction of the capitalist mode of production in our country. Mercantile relationships eat away ever more at communal links, and replace them with private property in the means of production. In the new situation that is thus created by the penetration of capitalism into our country-side, the peasant of Volta, bound to small-scale production, incarnates bourgeois relations of production.

So, in view of all these considerations, the peasantry of Volta forms an integral part of the petty bourgeoisie.

By its past and its present situation it is the social stratum that has had to pay the greatest tribute to imperialist domination and exploitation.

The backward economic and cultural situation of our countryside has for a long time kept the peasantry apart from the great currents of progress and modernization, leaving it content to play the role of reservoir for the reactionary political parties.

Nevertheless, it has an interest in the revolution and is, from the point of view of numbers, its principal force.

(4) The lumpenproletariat: it is this category of *déclassé* elements that, because of their workless situation, are predisposed to be at the beck and call of reactionary and counter-revolutionary forces in order to meet their foul needs. In so far as the revolution can convert them by giving them useful activity they can become its fervent partisans.

THE CHARACTER AND SCOPE OF THE AUGUST REVOLUTION

The world's revolutions never resemble one another. Each revolution has an originality that distinguishes it from others. Our revolution, the August Revolution, is no exception. It takes account of the particularities of our country, of its degree of development and of its subjection to the world capitalist imperialist system.

Our Revolution is a Revolution that is taking place in a backward agricultural country where traditions and the ideology of a feudal type of society weigh enormously heavily on the popular masses.

It is a Revolution in a country that, because of the domination and exploitation that imperialism exercises over our people, has moved from a colonial situation to one of neo-colonialism.

It is a Revolution that is being made in a country characterized by the absence of an organized working class conscious of its historic mission, and therefore having no tradition of revolutionary struggle. It is a revolution that is being made in a small continental country at a time when, on the international level, the revolutionary movement is crumbling day by day without any hope of seeing the constitution of a homogeneous bloc capable of driving forward and maintaining in practical terms new-born revolutionary movements.

This set of historical, geographical and sociological circumstances gives our Revolution a particular stamp.

The August Revolution is a Revolution that has a dual character: it is a Democratic and Popular Revolution. It has as its primary tasks the liquidation of imperialist domination and exploitation, the purging of the countryside of all social, economic and cultural shackles that keep it in a state of backwardness. This is the origin of its *democratic character*.

It draws its *popular character* from the fact that the popular masses of Volta have a full stake in this revolution and in consequence are mobilized around democratic and revolutionary slogans that really express their true interests, in opposition to those of the reactionary classes allied with imperialism.

The popular character of the August Revolution resides also in the fact that in place of the old machinery of state a new machinery is being built that will be able to guarantee the democratic exercise of power by the people and for the people.

This Revolution of ours, having these characteristics, is an anti-imperialist Revolution, yet is being conducted within the framework of a bourgeois economy and social structure. By analysing the social classes of Volta society we have supported the idea that the Volta's bourgeoisie is not a single homogeneous reactionary and anti-revolutionary mass. In fact, what is characteristic of the bourgeoisie of underdeveloped countries in a capitalist framework is their congenital incapacity to revolutionize society as did the bourgeoisie of European countries in the 1790s − that is, when the bourgeoisie was still a rising class.

Such are the characteristics and the limitations of this Revolution that began in Upper Volta on 4 August 1983. Having a clear perception and an exact definition of its content forearms us against the dangers of deviation and of the excesses that might inhibit the victorious march of the Revolution.

All those who have taken their stand behind the August Revolution should be imbued with the guiding line that has just been outlined so as to be able to take up their role as conscious revolutionaries and, as true intrepid and indefatigable propagandists, spread it amongst the masses.

It is not enough to call yourself a revolutionary, you must be imbued with the deep significance of the revolution and be its fervent champion. That is the best way of defending it against the attacks and distortions that counter-revolutionaries will not hesitate to launch against it. To know how to link revolutionary theory with revolutionary practice will be the decisive criterion making it possible to distinguish consistent revolutionaries from all those who flock to the revolution from motives that are foreign to the revolutionary cause.

POPULAR SOVEREIGNTY IN THE EXERCISE OF REVOLUTIONARY POWER

One of the distinctive traits of the August Revolution that gives it its popular character is, as was pointed out, that it is the movement of the immense majority in the interests of the great majority.

It is a Revolution made by the popular masses of Volta themselves with their slogans and their aspirations. The object of the revolution is for the People to take power. That is why the first decree of the Revolution, after the Proclamation of August 4, was the appeal addressed to the People to create Committees for the Defence of the Revolution (CDRs). The National Council of the Revolution is convinced that this Revolution is truly popular, and will be bound to proceed to the destruction of the machinery of the neo-colonial State and to organize a new machinery capable of guaranteeing popular sovereignty. The question of knowing how this people's power will be exercised and how it will be organized is an essential question for the future of our Revolution.

The history of our country up to today has been dominated essentially by the exploiting and conservative classes that have exercised their anti-democratic and anti-popular dictatorship by their grip on political power, the economy, the ideology, culture, the administration and justice.

The Revolution has as its first objective to wrest power from the hands of Volta's bourgeoisie allied to imperialism and to give it to the alliance of popular forces that constitute the People.

This means that the People must counter the anti-democratic and anti-popular dictatorship of the reactionary alliance of the social classes favourable to imperialism with its own democratic and popular power.

This democratic and popular power will be the foundation, the solid base of revolutionary power in Upper Volta. It will have as a primary task the total reconversion of the whole machinery of the State with its laws, its administration, its tribunals, its police and its army that were shaped for serving and defending the selfish interests of reactionary classes and social strata. Its task will be to organize the fight against counter-revolutionary attempts to reconquer the 'Paradise Lost', so as to crush completely the resistance of reactionaries who hanker after the past. And it is there that the role of the CDRs becomes so necessary: to support the popular masses in the assault on reactionary and counter-revolutionary citadels.

FOR A PROPER UNDERSTANDING OF THE NATURE, THE ROLE, AND THE FUNCTIONING OF THE COMMITTEES FOR THE DEFENCE OF THE REVOLUTION

The construction of the democratic and people's State that is the ultimate objective of the August Revolution will take more than one day to complete. It is an uphill task that will demand enormous sacrifices of us. The democratic nature of the Revolution imposes on us a decentralization and a deconcentration of administrative power so that administration can be brought nearer to the People, and so that public business can be a matter of interest to each and every one. In this immense, long-term task we have undertaken to reshape the administrative map of the country in order to achieve greater efficiency.

We have begun to renew the Office of Administrative Services in a more revolutionary form.

At the same time, we have set aside officials and military personnel who for a variety of reasons are unable to keep in step with this Revolution. There is still much for us to do and we are aware of this.

The National Council of the Revolution, which in the revolutionary process that was unleashed on 4 August 1983 is the power that provides the elaboration, leadership and supervision of the life of the nation on the political, economic and social levels, has to have local branches in the various sectors of the nation's life. And that is where lies the deep significance of the creation of the CRDs, the representatives of the revolutionary power in the villages, urban districts and places of work.

The CDRs constitute the authentic organization of the People in its exercise of revolutionary power. They are the instrument that the People has forged in order to make itself the true master of its fate and thereby to extend its control into all sections of society.

The arms of the People, the power of the People, the wealth of the People — it is the People that wields these and it does so through the CDRs.

The roles that they play are great and diverse. Their first charge is to organize the People of Volta as a whole for engaging in the revolutionary struggle. Organized in this way in the CDRs the People acquires not only the right to take an interest in the problems of its own development, but also participates in the making and execution of decisions.

The Revolution, as a just theory for destroying the old order and building in its place a society of a new type, should be led only by those who have an interest in it.

The CDRs are, then, the assault troops that will attack any centres of resistance. They are the builders of revolutionary Upper Volta. They are the active ingredient that must take the revolution to every Province, to all our villages, all public and private services, all homes and all milieux. In order to do this the militant revolutionaries within the CDRs must compete in enthusiasm in addressing the following primary tasks:

(1) Direct action by members of the CDRs. To revolutionary militants falls the task of the political education of their comrades. The CDRs must be schools of political instruction.

The CDRs are the appropriate framework for discussion by militants of the decisions of higher organs of the Revolution, the NCR and the government.

(2) Action directed towards the popular masses aims to lead them to support massively the NCR's objectives, by means of intrepid and unceasing agitation and propaganda. For the CDRs have to be able to counter the propaganda and lying calumnies of reaction with an appropriate revolutionary explanation and propaganda, on the principle that only the truth is revolutionary.

The CDRs must harken to the masses so as to be aware of their state of mind and their needs, so as to inform the NRC of these in good time and make appropriate concrete proposals.

They are called upon to examine questions that affect the furthering of the interests of the popular masses, supporting initiatives taken by them.

Direct contact with the popular masses, by periodically organizing open assemblies to discuss questions of mass interest, is an imperative necessity for the CDRs if they wish to further the correct application of the NCR's objectives. Thus, through propaganda, the decisions of the NCR will be explained to the masses. Measures designed to improve their standard of living will also be explained in this way.

The CDRs must fight with the popular masses of the towns and of the countryside against their enemies and against the adversities of nature, for the transformation of their material existence and their morale.

(3) The CDRs must work in a rational manner, thus illustrating one of the characteristics of our Revolution: thoroughness. Consequently, they must formulate plans of action that are coherent and ambitious, and that must be binding on all their members.

Since 4 August, a date that henceforth is a historic one for our People, the Volta population has responded to the call of the NCR and developed initiatives for forming CDRs. So it is that the CDRs have sprung up in villages, in urban districts, and soon in workplaces, in public services, in factories, within the Army. All this is the result of spontaneous action by the masses. It is time to work on their internal structure on a clear basis, and on their organization at national level. To this task the National General Secretariat of the CDRs has been harnessed.

While we wait for clear and final results to emerge from the present task of reflection on the basis of accumulated experience, we shall be content to present in rough outline the general guiding principles of the way in which the CDRs function.

The first idea that was followed in setting up the CDRs was the democratization of power. The CDRs thus become the organs through which the People exercises the local power that stems from the central power held by the NCR.

The NCR constitutes, outside the sessions of the national congress, the sovereign power. It is the leading organ of this whole edifice, the guiding principle of which is democratic centralism.

Democratic centralism is based firstly on the subordination of lower organs to higher ones, with the highest of all being the NCR to which all organizations are subordinated. Secondly, this centralism remains democratic, since the electoral principle is in force at all levels and the autonomy of local organs is recognized for all questions that fall within their competence, although within the limits of, and with due respect to, the general directives issued by the superior organ.

ON REVOLUTIONARY MORALITY WITHIN THE CDRs

The Revolution is aimed at the transformation of society in all realms — economic, social and cultural. It aims to create a new man of Volta, with an exemplary morality and a social comportment that inspire the admiration and the confidence of the masses. Neo-colonial domination led our society into such a state of decay that it will take years to purify it.

However, the militants of the CDRs must forge a new consciousness and a new comportment with a view to setting a good example to the popular masses. Whilst making the Revolution, we must look to our own qualitative transformation. Without a qualitative transformation of those very people who are supposed to be the artisans of the Revolution, it is practically impossible to create a new society freed from corruption, robbery, mendacity and general individualism.

We must make the effort to ensure that our deeds match our words, and to watch our social comportment so as not to present a target for counter-revolutionaries who lie in wait for us.

If we keep in mind that the interest of the popular masses takes precedence over personal interests we shall not be led astray.

The activity of certain militants who entertain the counter-revolutionary dreams of amassing possessions and profits through the CDRs must be denounced and resisted. The practice of the vendetta must be eliminated.

The quicker these deficiencies can be combatted, the better it will be for the Revolution.

The revolutionary, from our point of view, is someone who can be modest whilst being extremely determined in the tasks that have been given him. He performs them without vanity and expects no recompense.

We have recently discovered that elements who have actively participated in the Revolution, and who expected that in order to do this they should have privileged salaries, honours and important jobs, have turned to undermining activities out of spite because they did not get what they wanted. This is proof that they have participated in the Revolution without ever understanding its real objectives. You do not make revolution in order simply to substitute yourself for the overthrown potentates of yesteryear. You do not participate in revolution from acquisitive motives fed by a desire for an advantageous position: 'Move, so that I can put myself there.' This kind of motivation is foreign to the ideals of the August Revolution, and those who display it reveal their deficiencies as petty bourgeois trimmers, when they are not a case of dangerous counter-revolutionary opportunism.

The image of the revolutionary that the NCR wants to inculcate in everyone's consciousness is that of a militant who shares the weal and woe of the masses, who has faith in them and respects them. He does not consider himself as a master to whom the masses owe obedience and submission. On the contrary, he puts himself to school with them, he listens attentively to them and heeds their advice. He renounces authoritarian methods worthy only of reactionary bureaucrats.

The revolution is to be distinguished from destructive anarchy. It demands discipline and an exemplary form of conduct.

Acts of vandalism and adventurist actions of all kinds weaken the revolution and repel innumerable masses, instead of strengthening it by the adhesion of great numbers of people.

That is why the CDRs must raise the level of their sense of responsibility towards the people and seek to inspire respect and admiration.

These failings usually reveal an ignorance of the character and objectives of the Revolution. And in order to arm ourselves against them we must immerse ourselves in a study of revolutionary theory. Theoretical study raises our understanding of things, enlightens our actions and guards us from many presumptuous attitudes.

We must henceforth assign particular importance to this aspect of the question and try to provide a good example that will encourage others to follow us.

FOR THE REVOLUTIONIZING OF ALL SECTORS OF VOLTA SOCIETY

All the political regimes that have succeeded one another so far have done their utmost to put in place a series of measures for running neo-colonial society better. The changes that these various regimes have instituted have amounted to installing new ruling teams in a continuation of neo-colonial power.

None of these regimes wished, or was able, to challenge the socio-economic bases of Volta society. That is why they failed.

The August Revolution does not aim just to set up another regime in Upper Volta. It marks a break with all the regimes that the country has so far known. It sets as its final objective a new Volta society within which the citizen of Volta, inspired by a revolutionary consciousness, will be the maker of his own well-being, a well-being that will match the effort that he has put into achieving it. To this end, the Revolution will be, whether conservative and reactionary forces like it or not, a total and profound upheaval that will spare no sphere, no sector of economic, social or cultural activity.

Revolutionizing all spheres and sectors of activity is the watchword corresponding to the present moment. Strong in the guiding line so fixed, each citizen, at whatever level, must undertake to revolutionize his sector of activity.

As at present, the philosophy of revolutionary transformation will affect the following sectors:

(1) The National Army;
(2) Policy Towards Women;
(3) Economic Construction.

(1) The National Army: Its Place in the Democratic and Popular Revolution

According to Upper Volta's defence doctrine a conscious people should not entrust the defence of its country to a group of men, however capable they are. Politically conscious people themselves assume the defence of their country. Therefore, our Armed Forces are but one detachment better specialized than the rest of the People for the tasks of internal and external security of the Upper Volta. In the same way, although the health of the population is the concern of the People and of each individual citizen of Volta, there exists, and will exist, a more specialized medical service able to devote more time to the question of public health.

The Revolution imposes three missions on the National Armed Forces:

(a) To be fit to combat any internal and external enemy and to participate in the military training of the rest of the People. This presupposes an improved operational capacity that turns each soldier into an efficient combatant, unlike the old army, that was nothing but a paid and uniformed mass.

(b) To take part in national production. In fact, the new soldier should live and suffer among the People to whom he belongs. Gone, the budget-devouring army! From now on, apart from learning how to use arms, it will work in the fields, it will raise herds of cattle, flocks of sheep and poultry. It will build schools and dispensaries and ensure their functioning, it will maintain roads and carry the mail, medical patients, and agricultural produce between the regions by air.

(c) To make a revolutionary militant of every soldier. Gone are the days when it could be claimed that the army was truly neutral and apolitical whilst it was being turned into a buttress of reaction and a guarantee of imperialist interests.

Gone are the days when our Armed Forces used to behave like a body of mercenaries in a conquered territory. Those times have gone forever. Armed with a political and ideological training, our soldiers, non-commissioned officers and officers engaged in the revolutionary process will cease to be licensed criminals and will become conscious revolutionaries, moving among the people like a fish in water.

Bearing arms in the service of the Revolution, the People's National Army will have no room for any soldier who despises, derides and brutalizes the People. A people's Army in the people's service, that is the new Army that we shall build in place of the neo-colonial Army, a real instrument of oppression in the hands of the reactionary bourgeoisie that used it in order to dominate the people.

Such an Army, from the point of view even of its internal organization and operational principles, will be fundamentally different from the old army.

So, instead of a blind obedience of soldiers to their chiefs, of subalterns to their superiors, there will develop a healthy discipline that, whilst remaining strict, will be based on the conscious commitment of men and troops. Contrary to the point of view of reactionary officers imbued with the colonial spirit, the politicization of the Army, its revolutionizing, does not mean the end of discipline.

Discipline in a politicized army will have a different content. It will be a revolutionary discipline. That is to say a discipline that draws its strength from the fact that the officer and the soldier, those with rank and those without, will be valued in terms of human dignity and will differ from each other only in their concrete tasks and their respective responsibilities.

Fortified by this kind of understanding of the relationships between men, military officers must respect their troops, love them and treat them equitably.

Here too the Committees in Defence of the Revolution have a fundamental role to play. Militants of the CDRs in the Army must be indefatigable pioneers of the building of the National People's Army of the Democratic and Popular State, the key tasks of which will be:

   (i) Internally, to defend the rights and the interests of the People, to maintain revolutionary order and to safeguard the democratic power of the people;

   (ii) Externally, to defend the integrity of the territory.

(2) The Women of Volta: Their Role in the Democratic People's Revolution

The weight of the ancient traditions of our society consigns women to the rank of a beast of burden. Women suffer doubly from all the plagues of neo-colonial society:

   — First of all they share the same tribulations as men;
   — Secondly, they suffer other afflictions at the hands of men.

Our Revolution concerns all oppressed people, all those that are exploited in present-day society. Therefore it concerns women, because the basis of their domination by men lies in the way in which the political and social life of society is organized. The Revolution, by changing the social order that oppresses women, creates the conditions for their true emancipation.

The women and men of our society are all victims of imperialist oppression and domination. That is why they wage the same struggle.

The Revolution and women's liberation go together. It is not an act of charity or an expression of humanism to talk of the emancipation of women. It is a fundamental necessity for the triumph of the Revolution. Women carry on their shoulders the other half of the heavens.

One of the primary tasks of the Revolution is to create a new mentality in the women of Volta that will allow them to assume the destiny of the country side by side with men. The same is true for the change that must be wrought in the attitudes of men towards women.

Up until now women have been excluded from the spheres of decision-making. The Revolution, in offering women responsibility, creates the conditions for freeing the fighting initiative of women.

The NCR in its revolutionary policy will work for the mobilization, the organization and the unity of all the living forces of the nation, and the women will not be left out of this.

Women will be associated with all the battles that we shall have to wage against the various shackles of neo-colonial society and for the building of a new society. They will be associated at all levels of policy-formulation, decision and execution, in the organization of the nation's life as a whole.

The ultimate goal of all this splendid enterprise is the construction of a free and prosperous society where woman will be the equal of man in all domains.

However, the question of women's liberation must be properly understood. It is not a mechanical equality between man and woman. Acquiring the usual habits of men – drinking, smoking, wearing trousers: none of that is the liberation of women.

Nor is it gaining diplomas that will make women equal to men or more emancipated.

The diploma is not a passport to emancipation.

True emancipation of women is giving them responsibility, of a kind that associates them with productive activities and the various battles that confront the People. The true emancipation of women is one that conjoins the respect and the considerate attention of men.

Emancipation, like liberty, is not handed out; it has to be won. And women themselves will have to defend their claims and mobilize for the realization of those claims.

The Democratic People's Revolution will create the conditions needed to allow Volta's women to realize themselves fully and completely. For how can you abolish a system of exploitation if the women, who constitute over a half of our society, remain exploited?

(3) An Independent, Self-Sufficient and Planned National Economy at the Service of a Democratic People's Society

The process of revolutionary change launched on 4 August put great democratic and popular reforms on the agenda.

Thus, the NCR realizes that the construction of an independent, self-sufficient and planned national economy means transforming the present society radically, a transformation that itself presupposes the following major reforms:
- agrarian reform;
- administrative reform;
- educational reform;
- reform of the structures of production and distribution in the modern sector.

(a) Agrarian Reform: The aims will be:
- to increase the productivity of labour by a better organization of the peasantry and the introduction in the rural areas of modern agricultural techniques;

— the development of a diversified agriculture together with regional specialization;
— the abolition of all the shackles of the traditional socio-economic structures that oppress the peasantry;
— finally, to make agriculture the spearhead for industrial development.
This can be done by restoring its true meaning to the slogan of self-sufficiency in food, a slogan worn out through being proclaimed without conviction. It will be first of all a bitter struggle against nature, and nature, incidentally, is no more hostile in our country than in other countries that have won marvellous victories on the agricultural level. The National Council of the Revolution has no illusions of grandeur about gigantic and sophisticated projects. On the contrary, numerous small achievements in our agricultural system will allow us to convert our territory into a vast holding, an infinite series of farms. It will also be a battle against the robbers of the people, speculators and agriculture capitalists of all kinds. Finally, it will be a matter of protecting our agriculture against imperialist domination — the pillaging of our resources and disloyal competition with our local produce by imports whose only merit is their packaging for a bourgeoisie besotted with snobbery. Fair prices and industrial goods for agriculture will guarantee the peasantry markets for their produce all year round.

(b) Administrative Reform: This has the aim of making effective the administration inherited from the colonial period.
To do this it will be necessary to rid it of all the ills that afflict it — a ponderous, pettifogging bureaucracy and its consequences — and to set in motion a complete revision of the structure of the public service. The reform must result in an administration that is less costly, more effective and more supple.

(c) Educational Reform: This aims at fostering a new orientation in education and culture.
It must lead to the transformation of the schools into an instrument at the service of the Revolution. Those who emerge from them with qualifications must not put themselves at the service of their own interests and those of the exploiting classes, but at the service of the popular masses.
The revolutionary education that will be given in the new schools must inculcate in each pupil an ideology, a Volta personality, that frees the individual from mere imitation. It will be one of the vocations of the schools in the democratic people's society to teach pupils and students to study in a critical and positive manner the experiences and ideas of other peoples. In order to put an end to illiteracy and obscurantism the accent must be put on mobilizing all energies so as to organize the masses, make them aware, and create in them a thirst for learning by showing them the disadvantages of ignorance.
Any policy of struggle against illiteracy is doomed to failure without the participation of those most interested by it. As for the culture of the democratic people's society, it must be three-sided: national, revolutionary and popular. Everything anti-national, anti-revolutionary, and anti-people must be banished.

On the contrary our own culture, that has celebrated dignity, nationalism, courage and the great human virtues, will be magnified.

The democratic people's Revolution will create favourable conditions for the birth of a new culture. Our artists will have their hands free to move bravely forward. They must seize the occasion offered them to raise our culture to the world level.

Let the writers put their pens at the service of the Revolution. Let the musicians sing not only of the glorious past of our people but also of its radiant and promising future.

The Revolution expects our artists to be able to describe reality, to portray it in a living way, to express it in harmonious notes whilst showing our People the correct way towards a better future. It expects them to put their creative genius at the service of a Voltese culture – national, revolutionary and popular.

They must be able to draw on what is good in the past, that is, in our traditions, and on what is positive in foreign cultures, so as to give our culture a new dimension.

The inexhaustible source for the creative inspiration of the masses lies in the popular masses themselves.

The main preoccupation of our artists should be to be able to live with the masses, to take part in the popular movement, to share the joys and sufferings of the People, to work and fight with it.

Before producing a piece of work the question should be asked: to what are we dedicating our creation? If we have the conviction that it is for the People that we are creating, then we should know clearly what the People is, what are its components, what are its profound aspirations.

(d) Reform of the Structures of Production and Distribution of our Economy:
Reforms in this area are aimed at progressively establishing effective control by the people of Volta over the circuits of production and distribution. For without a real mastery over these circuits it is practically impossible to build an independent economy at the service of the people.

People of Upper Volta!

Comrade Men and Women, Militants of the Revolution!

The needs of our People are immense. The satisfaction of these needs requires that revolutionary transformations be undertaken in every sphere.

In the sphere of *health and social security* in favour of the popular masses, the objectives that must be attained are:

- A health service available to everyone.
- The creation of a system of assistance and protection for mothers and children.
- A policy of immunization against transmitted diseases by increased vaccination campaigns.
- An effort to make the masses aware of the need to acquire good habits of hygiene.

None of these objectives can be attained without the popular masses themselves being consciously engaged in the battle for the health services from a revolutionary perspective.

In matters of *housing* – a crucial area – we must embark on a vigorous policy of putting a stop to speculation and to the exploitation of workers by the charging of excessive rents. Important measures must be taken in this area to:
- Fix fair rents.
- Embark on a rapid distribution of living quarters.
- Start building on a wide scale modern housing in sufficient quantity and accessible to the workers.

One of the chief concerns of the NCR is to unify the Upper Volta's different nationalities in a common struggle against the enemies of our Revolution. There are, in fact, a great many ethnic groups in our country that are distinguished from each other by their languages and their customs. It is all of these nationalities taken together that form the Volta nation. With its policy of divide and rule, imperialism did its utmost to sharpen the contradictions between them, so as to set one against another.

The policy of the NCR will aim to unite these various nationalities so that they can live in equality and have the same chances of success. To this end, special emphasis will be put on:
- The economic development of the different regions.
- Encouraging economic exchange between them.
- Combatting inter-ethnic prejudices and settling in a spirit of unity contentious issues that divide them.
- Chastising those who foster divisions.

In view of all the problems that confront our country, the Revolution appears as a challenge that we must surmount, inspired by a will to win, and with the real participation of the popular masses mobilized within the CDRs.

Before too long, when the sectoral programmes of development have been worked out, the whole territory of the Upper Volta will be one vast construction site where the co-operation of all Volta's population that is in good health and of an age to work will be required for the merciless combat that we shall wage in order to transform this country into one that is prosperous and radiant, a country where the People is sole master of the material and spiritual wealth of the nation.

Finally, we must situate the Volta Revolution in the world revolutionary process. Our Revolution is an integral part of the world movement for peace and democracy against imperialism and every kind of hegemonism.

That is why we shall strive to establish diplomatic relations with other countries without regard to their political and economic system, on the following basis:
- Reciprocal respect for independence, territorial integrity and national sovereignty.
- Mutual non-aggression.
- Non-intervention in internal affairs.
- Trade with all countries on an equal footing and on the basis of reciprocal advantage.

Our fighting solidarity and support will go out to movements of national liberation that are struggling for the independence of their country and the liberation of their peoples. This support is extended particularly to:

— The People of Namibia under the leadership of SWAPO.
— The People of the Sahara in its struggle to recover its national territory.
— The Palestinian People in defence of its national rights.

In our battle, the anti-imperialist African countries are our objective allies. Links with these countries are made necessary by the neo-colonial organizations and alliances that exist on our continent.

LONG LIVE THE DEMOCRATIC PEOPLE'S REVOLUTION!
LONG LIVE THE NATIONAL COUNCIL OF THE REVOLUTION!
FATHERLAND OR DEATH, WE SHALL OVERCOME!